P9-CSG-963

FAKES

ALSO BY DAVID SHIELDS

Jeff, One Lonely Guy
(with Jeff Ragsdale and Michael Logan)

The Inevitable: Contemporary Writers Confront Death
(as editor, with Bradford Morrow)

Reality Hunger: A Manifesto

The Thing About Life Is That One Day You'll Be Dead

Body Politic: The Great American Sports Machine

Enough About You: Adventures in Autobiography

"Baseball Is Just Baseball": The Understated Ichiro

Black Planet: Facing Race during an NBA Season

Remote: Reflections on Life in the Shadow of Celebrity

Handbook for Drowning: A Novel in Stories

Dead Languages: A Novel

Heroes: A Novel

ALSO BY MATTHEW VOLLMER

Future Missionaries of America

FAKES

An Anthology of Pseudo-Interviews,

Faux-Lectures, Quasi-Letters,

"Found" Texts, and

Other Fraudulent Artifacts

EDITED BY

DAVID SHIELDS

AND

MATTHEW VOLLMER

W. W. NORTON & COMPANY

NEW YORK · LONDON

BOCA RATON PUBLIC LIBRARY
BOCA RATON, FLORIDA

Copyright © 2012 by David Shields and Matthew Vollmer

All rights reserved
Printed in the United States of America
First Edition

For information about special discounts for bulk purchases, please contact
W. W. Norton Special Sales at specialsales@wwnorton.com or 800-233-4830

Manufacturing by Courier Westford
Book design by Ellen Cipriano
Production manager: Louise Mattarelliano

Library of Congress Cataloging-in-Publication Data

Fakes : an anthology of pseudo-interviews, faux-lectures,
quasi-letters, "found" texts, and other fraudulent artifacts / edited
by David Shields and Matthew Vollmer. — 1st ed.
p. cm.
Includes bibliographical references and index.
ISBN 978-0-393-34195-9 (pbk.)
1. American prose literature—21st century. 2. Creative nonfiction.
3. Counterfeits and counterfeiting in literature. 4. Found objects (Art)
I. Shields, David, 1956– II. Vollmer, Matthew.
PS659.2.F35 2012
818'.609—dc23
2012013070

W. W. Norton & Company, Inc.
500 Fifth Avenue, New York, N.Y. 10110
www.wwnorton.com

W. W. Norton & Company Ltd.
Castle House, 75/76 Wells Street, London W1T 3QT

1 2 3 4 5 6 7 8 9 0

CONTENTS

Introduction

Learning How to Fake It:

*A Brief (and Therefore Woefully Incomplete) Guide
to the Manufacture and Distribution of Fraudulent Artifacts*

A JUSTIFICATION

Future anthropologists may formulate a multitude of claims about what defines our present age (that we were more connected or more disconnected, more distracted or more attentive, more liberated or more bureaucratized), but one assessment seems certain: that we will be known as the first era to become enslaved by our information—and by the devices that deliver it. Though we might be quick to identify as our tyrants the monitors and mobile devices into whose screens we so worshipfully stare, other, more subtle mechanisms have claimed a far wider empire: those being the genres and linguistic forms that structure our information. Genres dictate the shape, sound, and appearance of our information; genres set parameters, define boundaries, establish limitations.

In short: genres tell our words—and therefore us—what to do.

Texts, tweets, status updates, blogs, itineraries, instructions, lectures, permit forms, advertisements, primers, catalogs, comment cards, letters of recommendation and complaint, end-of-year reports, accidentally forwarded e-mail, traffic updates, greeting cards, insurance claims, and message board comments: each one of these categories represents a distinct space in which a particular type of communication event takes place; each one dictates that the language residing within must behave in particular ways and pre-scripted patterns. Thus, language becomes codified, confined, and restricted. And because whatever happens to language happens to us, we, too, become restrained. We find ourselves held against our will, hostages to five-paragraph essays, medical forms, reports, and worksheets. Thwarted by instructions, story problems, and analyses, we are bound by credit card contracts, rental agreements, liens, loans, and wills. We sign on the dotted line without reading the fine print. We agree, in our impatience to click ever forward, to terms and conditions with which we may or may not agree.

But now imagine this: our oft-repressed language staging a rebellion. What would such an event look like? What if, in addition to relaying information, the language within one of these forms swerved, digressed, became elevated, and began to do something spectacular? What if the language within these forms enacted a giddy and imaginative revenge? What if, as we read through an index, catalog, disclaimer, or personal ad, we suddenly awoke to the story it was telling? Would not the thing—the artifact—come alive in a new and exciting way?

We—the authors of this manual, and the curators of the artifacts that follow—believe that it would. We believe in revival: that language can transform even the most lifeless of genres and therefore has the power to resurrect the soul, or whatever it is inside us that might otherwise wither, if not for the life-giving and life-sustaining energy of art. And so we ask you, whoever you might be, to join us in the reading, celebrating, and continued production of the joyous falsifications and fraudulent artifacts contained herein.

WHAT EXACTLY *IS* A "FRAUDULENT ARTIFACT"?

For our purposes, a fraudulent artifact is a text purporting to be a particular form of writing—a journal entry, a note, a yearbook letter, an e-mail, a transcript of a speech, a grocery list, a musical score, a screenplay—which also tells a story, stirs thought and emotion, inspires inquiry, initiates action, and/or calls into question that which is—or has purported to be—real. We use the word "purporting" because who is to say a text, even a fake one, is not what it *purports* to be? For example, is Daniel Orozco's "Officers Weep" not a series of police blotters? Yes it is. And yet: no it is not. Daniel Orozco, the author, is not a real policeman. Therefore, one could say that the "blotters" he's composed are not "real." And yet they appear to be. They persist in our imagination in ways that regular police blotters probably would not. They seem, as their obligatory notations morph into impassioned descriptions, like the best damn police blotters ever written.

Perhaps "fraudulent" is not an entirely suitable adjective. A fraudulent artifact takes a received form and infuses it with a story (possibly with characters, setting, surprising details, and a fast-beating heart in conflict with itself), and thus creates an object that is more "authentic" than the original upon which it was based—an object that becomes, in comparison to its original, archetypal. Perhaps we should have come up with a different name for these artifacts. Maybe we should have called them "classic" or "exemplary" or even "exquisite." In the end, though, we liked the idea of fraud. We like the idea of supporting artists for whom deception is the name of the game. There's a sort of honesty there, in the idea of "fraudulent artifact." A self-reflexivity. A confessional aspect that we find intriguing and real.

THE FIRST STEP: CHOOSE A FORM/GENRE

Each forgery—each fraudulent document—is different and, as such, will dictate its own terms, its own boundaries, limitations, margins, fonts, and layouts. It will be up to you—the forger—to know and learn the conventions of the form you choose. But first things first: begin by choosing a particular form or genre. Look to the following list for help.

• Grocery list	• Epistle	• Report
• Blog	• Phone text	• White paper
• E-mail	• Yearbook signatures	• Recommendation letter
• Poem	• Sympathy card	
• Post-It	• Web site	• Captain's log
• Complaint letter	• Instructions	• Phone call transcription
• Apology	• Police report	
• Love letter	• Prophecy	• Diary entry
• Breakup letter	• Editorial	• Prescription/ doctor's assessment
• Op-ed	• Product warning	
• Article	• Lesson book	• Readers Write section of magazine
• Advertisement	• Self-help	
• Political speech	• Recipe	• Epitaph
• Personal ad	• Devotional	• School journal
• Artwork tag	• Ancient text	• Receipt
• Label	• Writing on bathroom wall	• School essay
• Ingredient list		• Song lyrics
• Play	• Comedy roast	• Catalog
• Sermon	• Brochure	• Screenplay

• Billboard	• Obituary	• Postcard
• Print ad	• Wedding	• Fortune
• Internet banner	announcement	• Biography
• Spam	• Birth announcement	• Dream journal
• Online chat	• Will and testament	• Eviction notice
• YouTube comment	• Congratulatory card	• Ticket
• Inspirational poster	• Birthday card	• Album insert
• Facebook post (with	• Get well card	• Baby book
comments)	• License/ID/passport	• Memory book
• Twitter feed	• TV transcript	• Family genealogy
• Newsletter	• Voicemail transcript	• Medical history
• Transcript of	• Menu	• Fieldwork report
dictation	• Tabloid article	• Tattoo
• Encyclopedia entry	• Future news story	• Review
• PowerPoint	• Speech	• Fan page
• Informational video	• Board game rules	• "To do" list
• Eulogy	• Flyer	

IDENTIFY THE CONVENTIONS

An artifact, by definition, is an object—or in our case, a *text*—that has been constructed by a human being. As such, every artifact rises out of a series of decisions on the part of its maker. To choose one thing and not another in building an object is to hold fast to one idea of how it should be made (and how it should exist) while discarding others. If the "made thing" serves a purpose—if others recognize its necessity and decide to reproduce the object for themselves—some if not most of these original choices in the construction of the thing are sure to be replicated. In this way, over time, the artifact may change, but essential parts remain: a shelter, for instance, whether it be lean-to, pueblo, or chalet, may not have carpet or curtains or windows or chimneys, but it will surely have walls, an entrance, a roof. The made thing might be said to have a set of conventions—that is, qualities that set it apart as *that kind of thing*.

Thus, a reader comes to expect certain kinds of written artifacts to behave in particular ways. In order to create an authentic artifact, a fabricator must know the rules by which the artifact—again, in our case, a particular text—operates. A story problem may unfold in any number of ways, but it will no doubt present its reader with both a story and a problem. The prose of a newsletter might be said to frequently display a jaunty, freewheeling quality. Instructions may involve a series of terse commands. A letter will begin with a salutation. A diary will be written in first person, a contributor's note in third.

It is important to know and memorize the rules, not only because it will help you construct the sort of artifact you want to create, but because it will make the breaking of those rules that much more fun.

PAGE DESIGN AND LAYOUT: ALLIES IN SUCCESSFUL DECEPTION

No matter what kind of artifact you're creating, you will need to study the layout of that particular artifact and replicate it. To pass inspection, your artifact should not only behave like an artifact, it should also *look* like an artifact. You are, in essence, making an ID card to fool a bouncer who's seen every version of fake ID the world has to offer. Therefore, you'd better look proper. If you're writing an auction catalog, as Charles McLeod does in "National Treasures," then take a look at an actual auction catalog and format your document accordingly. If you're spoofing an Amazon review, as Chris Bachelder does in "My Beard, Reviewed," consider including the stars that accompany those reviews (even if you have to use asterisks). If you're writing a series of profiles of fictional colleagues, consider using actual photographs. If you want your artifact to resemble a series of e-mails—like Robin Hemley's "Reply All," for instance—include the "to," "from," time signature, and subject lines.

In other words: if you want to enter the building, know the dress code.

BENDING AND/OR BREAKING THE RULES

Breaking and/or bending the rules is an essential though often perilous part of the process of constructing a fraudulent artifact. Breaking the rules involves risk. Risk produces tension. Tension produces energy. Energy produces momentum. And you don't want your artifact wasting away on a shelf. You want it to go places.

If you study enough templates, you will begin to see places in the text where liberties have—or could have been—taken. Where boundaries have shifted. Where digressions are made. Know the limitations, then redraw them while your reader isn't looking. And don't be afraid to imitate what's come before. Lorrie Moore's "How to Become a Writer" relays a series of instructions (many of which are counterintuitive); Donald Barthelme's "The Explanation" obscures as much as it reveals; Joseph Salvatore's "Practice Problem" is a story problem that seems like maybe it's had one too many drinks, but in doing so has achieved a florid and vigorous eloquence.

VOICE: THE KEY TO CREATING A COMPELLING ARTIFACT

Your artifact must reveal something about its maker—that is, its *purported* maker. The maker is and isn't you. You are not its creator as much as you are merely a conduit through which language passes, a DJ mashing up a hundred songs for a single epic dance-off. As such, your artifact will need a voice. It should, when played or read—not only to be heard but to be listened to—make a particular and captivating sound.

What do we mean by voice? We mean that the sound made by the words on the page, whether spoken aloud or heard in the reader's head, must contribute to a coherent and idiosyncratic song. Whether you know it or not, you are creating, when you create an artifact, music. Music is the by-product of any great textual artifact—especially fraudulent ones.

Would you rather bang on a piano or follow a deliberate melody, however faint, however simple, however elementary? Have you read and memorized the masters? Could you copy the sounds they make, the sounds they have been known to make? One would hope so. Look behind you. Ask yourself: who has come before? Might you replicate the elevated diction of the King James Bible? The sibilances of Sylvia Plath? The austerity of Lao Tzu? Steal from the masters—then tweak what you've stolen. Because even though there's a reason this stuff's been around for awhile, there's also a reason it can't simply be imitated. New times call for new forms, new words, and new sounds. And if you won't make them, who will?

A FINAL NOTE

This guide is incomplete. You knew that from the beginning (supposing you bothered to read the subtitle of this introduction) but we figured it was worth mentioning again. Even so, we hope it is a start. We hope that you will continue to support the creation of counterfeit texts, elaborate forgeries, and fraudulent artifacts, and that they will continue to beguile and sustain you.

FAKES

1

Disclaimer

David Means

DISCLAIMER: NOTHING IN this story is true. All of the characters in this story are products of the writer's imagination. Any likeness of these characters and the situation described herein to those in real life is purely coincidental. In the unlikely circumstance that one or more of the characters in this story bear any resemblance to those living or dead, please be forewarned that it is so out of random chance (any other kind being excluded). Although the events in this story were drawn from real circumstances, this is in all ways a work of the imagination. Perhaps there might be characters like Julie Row in real life; if so, the author would like to express, if necessary before a court of law, that this work came to fruition in his imagination and all said resemblances to her are matters of chance. In the unlikelihood that there is a young woman living in the Stonewood Condominiums who rolls her hair up in the old plastic kind of curlers—prickly pink rolls with pink clamp shells—and wears a fine hairnet over them while she sleeps, if there is someone matching that description, the author would like to deny any a priori knowledge of the fact; even if said Julie Row lived by herself, had a tabby named Marvin, and was on the night of July 15, 1991, the night of her murder, alone and sad and feeling the soft night breeze work through the screen; even if said Julie Row had once been with a guy

named Rudy, and that Rudy had applied the hot, orange butt of his cigarette to the back of her wrist in a flaming moment (of panic and desire)—
his version of some kind of religious sacrament—the author will bear
no responsibility for similarities therein: thus if the said Julie Row,
lying back on the couch, her flat white stomach exposed, the knot of her
belly button—(an "outie")—picks the phone up to call her mother, Mrs.
Joanna Row of 415 Park Street, and says, "Mom it's Julie, how you
doing?" only to hear her mother's sharp Middle-Western voice say, "Do
I know someone by such a name?" and therefore flatly denying any
human connection with her daughter, who just stares long into the
phone receiver, holding it back, and then off at the blue flick of the television screen, and then outside at the flat asphalt parking lot where others such as her while away the last of a hot summer day—should,
through some pure coincidences, this conversation exist in real life, the
author would once again state: THIS WORK IS THE PRODUCT OF THE
AUTHOR'S IMAGINATION, even if Mrs. Joanna Row lay down on her
own divan after her phone was back in the cradle, her long, narrow face
tight with a bitterness certain readers in Alma, Michigan, might recognize, and cried tears (of remorse and anger), such tears being similar to
said person—in that case the author would, if necessary, bring to court
expert testimony as to the preponderance of such tears in small towns
(all over America). And if on July 15, 1991, said Julie Row, after listening to her mother's words, having turned to the television and then back
to those outside, spotted a guy named Bub leaning against his jacked-up
Toyota four-wheeler with the boom box going, who had a thing for
watching Julie in her white halter top when she hung by the pool, and
who once, while Rudy (her current main squeeze) was diving beneath
the glistening aqua-blue water, copped a quick feel from Julie, who
turned, blushed, and in the process became aware one might assume of
certain mortal certitudes broken in the course of hanging around with

a guy like Rudy, around men like Bub—after said character has looked out the window, stands responding to a soft knock on the door, and straightens the edges of her powder-blue terry shorts and pulls back on the hollow-centered door to reveal Bub himself; and should said character Bub, six-five, heavyweight, self-inflicted tattoos on his knuckles spelling BUB, with a small Fu Manchu—should said character actually exist in Alma, Michigan, with legal records corresponding to a man by that name tallying up several counts of aggravated assault, petty larceny, burglary, should someone by that name exist, and with said characteristics, the author would like to state, emphatically, that this unlikely resemblance between the product of his imagination and the world at large is PURELY AN ACT OF COINCIDENCE; and should it be brought to the court's attention that on the said night of July 15, 1991, a man with the description above was seen standing at the door of apartment 12 of the Stonewood complex, while the sprinkler system went on, spraying skyward a vast mist spanning all four units of the complex facing westward, drawing from the asphalt and the grass a musty odor, dank and rich, consuming those hanging around their cars, including Bub, with a sudden, short-lived memory flash of bygone summer days when the combination of dry earth and sudden rain brought out a dreamy primal memory of days when kids ran through barley fields, broke back cornstalks, and lay at times for no good reason facedown on sweet grass and listened to the earth move—a time when rain and dry earth shattered each other; days, this memory flash held, when there was an innocence to be spoken of—should said Bub have stood at the door under these conditions, the author would, again, like it to be clearly known that this work is purely a product of his imagination; although certain details have been drawn from REAL LIFE, ANY RESEMBLANCE TO PERSONS LIVING OR DEAD OR OTHERWISE IS PURELY COINCIDENTAL. AMEN.

2

George Saunders

Mrs. Ruth Faniglia
210 Lester Way
Rochester, NY 14623

Dear Mrs. Faniglia,

We were very sorry to receive your letter of 23
Feb., which accompanied the I CAN SPEAK!™ you
returned, much to our disappointment. We here
at KidLuv believe that the I CAN SPEAK!™ is an
innovative and essential educational tool that,
used with proper parental guidance, offers a
rare early-development opportunity for babies
and toddlers alike. And so I thought I would
take some of my personal time (I am on lunch)
and try to address the questions you raised in
your letter, which is here in front of me on my
(cluttered!) desk.

First, may I be so bold as to suggest that
some of your disappointment may stem from your
own, perhaps unreasonable, expectations? Because

in your letter, what you indicated, when I read it, was that you think and/or thought that somehow the product can read your baby's mind? Our product cannot read your baby's mind, Mrs. Faniglia. No one can read a baby's mind. At least not yet. Although we are probably working on it! What the I CAN SPEAK!™ can do, however, is recognize *familiar aural patterns* and respond to these patterns in a way that makes *baby seem older*. Say baby sees a peach. If you or Mr. Faniglia (I hope I do not presume) were to loudly say something like: "What a delicious peach!" the I CAN SPEAK!™, hearing this, through that hole, that little slotted hole near the neck, might respond by saying something like: "I LIKE PEACH." Or: "I WANT PEACH." Or, if you had chosen the ICS2000 (which you did not, you chose the ICS1900, which is fine, perfectly good for most babies) the I CAN SPEAK!™ might even respond by saying something like: "FRUIT, ISN'T THAT ONE OF THE MAJOR FOOD GROUPS?"

Which would be pretty good for a six-month-old, don't you think, which my Warranty Response shows is the age of your son Derek, Derek Faniglia?

But here I must reiterate: That would not in reality be Derek speaking. Derek would not in reality know that a peach is a fruit, or that fruit is a major food group. The I CAN SPEAK!™ knows it, however, and, from its position on Derek's face, gives the illusion that Derek knows it, by giving the illusion that Derek is speaking out of its twin moving SimuLips™. But that is it. That is all we claim.

Furthermore, in your letter, Mrs. Faniglia, you state that the I CAN SPEAK!™ "mask" (your terminology) takes on a "stressed-out look when talking that is not what a real baby's talking face appears like but is more like some nervous middle-aged woman." Well, maybe that is so, but with all due respect (and I say this with affection), you try it! You try making a latex face look and talk and move like the real face of an actual live baby! Inside are *over 5,000 separate circuits* and *390 moving parts*. And as far as looking like a middle-aged woman, we beg to differ. We do not feel that a middle-aged stressed-out woman has (1) no hair on head and (2) chubby cheeks and (3) fine downy facial hair. The ICS1900 unit is definitely the face of a baby, Mrs. Faniglia, we took over 2,500 photos of different babies and, using a computer, combined them to make this face on your unit, and on everybody else's unit, the face we call Male Composite 37 or, affectionately, "Little Roger." But what you possibly seem to be unhappy about is the fact that Little Roger's face is not Derek's face? To be frank, Mrs. Faniglia, many of you, our customers, have found it disconcerting that their baby looks different with the I CAN SPEAK!™ on, than with the I CAN SPEAK!™ off.

Which we find so surprising. Did you not, we often wonder, look at the cover of the box? The ICS1900 is very plainly shown, situated on a sort of rack, looking facewise like Little Roger, albeit Little Roger is a bit crumpled and has a forehead furrow of sorts.

Which is why we came up with the ICS2100. With the ICS2100, your baby *looks just like your baby*. And because we do not want anyone to be unhappy with us, we would like to make you the gift of a complimentary ICS2100 upgrade! We would like to come to your house on Lester Way and make a personalized plaster cast of Derek's real, actual face! And soon, via FedEx, here will come Derek's face in a box, and when you slip that ICS2100 over Derek's head and Velcro the Velcro, he will look nearly exactly like himself, plus we have another free surprise, which is that, while at your house, we will tape his actual voice and use it to make our phrases, the phrases, Derek will subsequently say. So not only will he look like himself, he will *sound like himself*, as he crawls around your home, appearing to speak!

Plus we will throw in several personalizing options.

Say you call Derek "Lovemeister." (I am using this example from my own personal home, as my wife Ann and I call our son Billy "Lovemeister," because he is so sweet.) With the ICS2100, you might choose to have Derek say—or appear to say—upon crawling into a room, "HERE COMES THE LOVEMEISTER!" or "STOP TALKING DIRTY, THE LOVE-MEISTER HAS ARRIVED!" How we do this is, laser beams coming out of the earlobes, which sense the doorframe! From its position on the head of Derek, the I CAN SPEAK!™ knows it has just entered a room! And also you will have over one hundred Discretionary Phrases to more highly personalize Derek. You might choose to have Derek say on his birthday, for example, "MOMMY AND DADDY, REMEMBER THAT TIME YOU CONCEIVED ME IN ARUBA?" (Although probably you did not in fact conceive Derek in Aruba. That we do not know. Our research is not that extensive.) Or say your dog comes up and gives Derek a lick? You might make Derek say (if your dog's name is Queenie, which our dog's name is Queenie): "QUEENIE, GIVE IT A REST!"

Which you know what? *Makes you love him more.* Because suddenly he is articulate. Suddenly he is not just sitting there going glub glub glub while examining a piece of his own feces on his own thumb, which is something we recently found our Billy doing. Sometimes we have felt that our childless friends think badly of us for having a kid who just goes glub glub glub in the corner while looking at feces on his thumb. But now when childless friends are over, what we have found, Ann and I, is that there is something great about having your kid say something witty and self-possessed years before he or she would actually in reality be able to say something witty or self-possessed. The bottom line is, it's just *fun*, when you and your childless friends are playing cards, and your baby suddenly blurts out (in his *very own probable future voice*): "IT IS VERY POSSIBLE THAT WE STILL DON'T FULLY UNDERSTAND THE IMPORT OF ALL OF EINSTEIN'S FINDINGS!"

Here I must admit that we have several times seen a sort of softening in the eyes of our resolute childless friends, as if they too would suddenly like to have a baby.

And as far as what you said, about Derek sort of flinching whenever that voice issues forth from him? When that speaker near his mouth sort of buzzes his lips? May I say this is not unusual? What I suggest? Try putting the ICS on Derek for a short time at first, maybe ten minutes a day, then gradually building up his Wearing Time. That is what we did. And it worked super. Now Billy wears his even while sleeping. In fact, if we forget to put it back on after his bath, he pitches a fit. Sort of begs for it! He starts to say, you know, "Mak! Mak!" (Which we think is his word for mask.) And when we put the mask on and Velcro the Velcro, he says—or it says rather, the ICS2100 says—"GUTEN MORGEN, PAPA!" because we have installed the German

Learning module. Or, for example, if his pants are not on yet, he'll say: "HOW ABOUT SLAPPING ON MY ROMPERS SO I CAN GET ON WITH MY DAY!" (I wrote that one, having done a little stand-up in my younger days.)

My point is, with the ICS2100, Billy is much, much cleverer than he ever was with the ICS1900. He has recently learned, for example, that if he dribbles a little milk out his mouth, down his chin, his SimuLips™ will issue a MOO sound. Which he really seems to get a kick out of! I'll be in the living room doing a little evening paperwork and from the kitchen I'll hear, you know, "MOO! MOO! MOO!" And I'll rush in, and there'll be this sort of lake of milk on the floor. And there'll be Billy, dribbling milk down his chin, until I yank the cup away, at which time he bellows: "DON'T FENCE ME IN!" (Ann's contribution—she was raised in Wyoming.)

Mrs. Faniglia, I, for one, do not believe that any baby wants to sit around all day going glub glub glub. My feeling is that a baby, sitting in its diaper, looking around at the world, thinks to itself, albeit in some crude nonverbal way: What the heck is wrong with me, why am I the only one saying glub glub glub while all these other folks are talking in whole complete sen-tences? And hence, possibly, lifelong psycho-logical damage may result. Now, am I saying that your Derek runs the risk of feeling bad about himself as a grown-up because as a baby he felt he didn't know how to talk very good? It is not for me to say, Mrs. Faniglia, I am only in Sales. But I will say I am certainly not taking any chances with Billy. My belief is that when Billy hears a competent, intelligent voice issuing from the area near his mouth, that makes him feel excellent about himself. And it makes me feel excellent about him. Not that I didn't feel excellent about him before. But now we can actually have a sort of conversation! And also—and most importantly—when that voice issues from his SimuLips™, he learns something invaluable, namely that, when he finally does begin speaking, he should *plan on speaking via using his mouth*.

Now, Mrs. Faniglia, you may be thinking: Hold on a sec, of course this guy loves his I CAN SPEAK!™, he probably got his for free. But no, Mrs. Faniglia, I got mine for two grand, just like you. We get no discounts, so much in demand is the I CAN SPEAK!™, and in addition, our management strongly encourages us—in fact you might say they even sort of *require* us—to purchase and use the I CAN SPEAK!™ at home, on our own kids. (Or even, in one case, the case of a Product Service Representative who has no kids, on his elderly senile mom! And although, yes, she looks sort of funny with that Little Roger face on her frail stooped frame, the family has really enjoyed hearing all the witty things she has to say, so much like her old self!) Not that I wouldn't use it otherwise. Believe me, I would. Since we upgraded to the ICS2100, things have been great, Billy says such wonderful things, while looking almost identical to himself, and is not nearly so, you know, boring as when we just had the ICS1900, which (frankly) says some rather predictable things, which I expect is partly why you were unhappy with it, Mrs. Faniglia, you seem like a very intelligent woman. When people come over now, sometimes we just gather around Billy and wait for his next howler, and just last weekend my supervisor, Mr. Ted Ames, stopped by (a super guy, he has really given me support, please let him know if you've found this letter at all helpful) and boy did we all crack up laughing, and did Mr. Ames ever start scribbling approving notes in his little green notebook, when Billy began rubbing his face very rapidly across the carpet, in order to make his ICS2100 shout: "FRICTION IS A COMMON AND USEFUL SOURCE OF HEAT!"

Mrs. Faniglia, it is nearing the end of my lunch, and I must wrap this up, but I hope I have been of service. On a personal note, I did not have the greatest of pasts when I came here, having been in a few scrapes and even rehab situations, but now, wow, the commissions roll in, and I have made a nice life for me and Ann and Billy. Not that the possible loss of my commission is the reason for my concern. Please do not think so. While it is true that, if you decline my upgrade offer and persist in your desire to return your ICS1900, my commission must be refunded, by me, to Mr. Ames, that is no big deal, I have certainly refunded commissions to Mr. Ames before, especially lately. I don't quite know what I'm doing wrong. But that is not your concern, Mrs. Faniglia. Your concern is Derek. My real reason for writing this letter, on my lunch break, is that, hard as we all work at KidLuv to provide innovative and essential development tools for families like yours, Mrs. Faniglia, it is always sort of a heartbreak when our products are misapprehended. Please do accept our offer of a free ICS2100 upgrade. We at KidLuv really love what kids are, Mrs. Faniglia, which is why we want them to become something better as soon as possible. Baby's early years are so precious, and must not be wasted, as we are finding out, as our Billy grows and grows, learning new skills every day.

Sincerely yours,
Rick Sminks
Product Service Representative
KidLuv Inc.

3

From *Some Instructions to My Wife Concerning the Upkeep of the House and Marriage, and to My Son and Daughter Concerning the Conduct of Their Childhood*

Stanley Crawford

Putting Things Away. Keep all things clean and keep them put away in their proper places, whereof you know, and take them out when needed and, when used, put them back into their places, whether they be cupboards, shelves, cabinets, boxes, sacks or bags, or the yellow or green trash containers under the sink; the ones made of plastic.

Friends Near and Far. When the women of the neighborhood wish to tell you of their sheets and bedding, turn a deaf ear, though it is permissible to listen if they live sufficient distances away, over a hundred miles away, for example, so that daily intercourse is not likely, and therefore it does not matter to me what they do, they and their husbands, between the sheets, and I will not have to lend either of them money, tools, seed, or grain, or advice, or help start their cars, repair their stovepipes, or move their freezers. For knowledge is power, my dear, and power diminishes in proportion to its ultimate destination or administration in time and place, in its terminus; far friends, as we know, are good friends, while with near friends one must live with deaf ears, although with friends both far and near it is perhaps best and wisest to be deaf while they are near and keen of ear when they are far, and both when they are in transit from the one state to the other.

Daily Appearances. Your seemingly interminable training will be complete when the appearance of each room of the house corresponds to its appearance for a set hour of the day, each day, for a set period of weeks, months, years—whatever. To make this clear, let us take an example. Supposing there is a cloud of dust in the living room—it is being swept, vacuumed, dusted, repaired—at four in the afternoon, then at every subsequent four in the afternoon there should appear a like or similar cloud of dust raised by a similar process, as generated by a like or similar person dressed in a like or similar manner employing approximately the same gestures to achieve the same end, a cloud of dust.

Running Lists. The keeping of a running list of household needs is, my dear, essential to the smooth operation of the entire house, and I cannot easily overemphasize the importance of it, however much I might try and try. For what could be more disastrous to the even temper of the household than to wake up one fine morning and discover snow piled halfway up to the roof and no sugar left in the kitchen—no butter in the refrigerator—no toilet paper in the bathroom? Thus a good rule is to make note of an item when it is two-thirds or three-fourths depleted, that is, when three out of four quarters of butter have been eaten, three out of four rolls of toilet paper used up, or six and two-thirds pounds of a ten-pound bag of sugar emptied. You may also find it useful to lay in a reserve of essential items for emergencies, as long as you make a note to replenish those that are used up during such emergencies as may have come to pass so that should emergencies recur there will always be emergency supplies from which to draw—for there is nothing worse than to discover in an emergency that the household is not only out of regular supplies but out of emergency supplies as well! The keeping of a list is not, however, as simple as it may first seem, for it is not enough to start at the top of the page and write out the items in the order in which they come to mind, that is, in an order in which their exhaustion draws near. Certainly one must start in this fashion, but this is not to say that you should finish here, with a randomly drawn-up list that corresponds to no order except that of chance. It is for this reason that I have posted in the pantry a floor plan of the supermarket at which we habitually shop, and with the most important items marked and labeled according to aisle and counter. Now of course I cannot guarantee the daily accuracy of this map—for unscrupulous supermarket operators are likely to scramble everything up overnight in order to confuse and bewilder their customers into buying their way out of the labyrinth—but I do take notes on the latest changes every time we shop so that I may then revise the map the moment we return home, as I think you have often noticed.

Thus I suggest that the mornings we set aside to go into town to shop you get up especially early in order to recast your first rough draft of a list into an order that corresponds to the path I have recommended you take through the supermarket, that is, starting from the right of the building, fresh produce, and threading your way through the aisles, up one and down the next, until you reach the left side of the building, the meat counter, and from thence pass directly to the checkout stalls. In this way the whole circuit can be completed in ten minutes or less and will not expose you to undue or prolonged temptations, while allowing me sufficient time to inspect the aisles and counters for changes or alterations of any sort.

Nor should you fail, upon returning home, to enter all items purchased, both separately and as totals, into the housekeeping account book I have provided for your exclusive use, and then to balance these totals against the cash contents of your purse and my wallet in relation to the original sums we first left the house in possession of or withdrew from the bank on the way. In this manner you can easily spot any miscalculations you may have missed earlier, notably overpricings, which may be brought to the attention of the supermarket manager the next visit into town, or any pure and simple losses, while accounting also by the same means for all coins or bills found on the sidewalks or in the parking lots or elsewhere, behind cushions or under chairs. In any case, whether we go shopping or not, it is a good idea to make certain twice daily, once in the morning, once in the evening, that such cash as we carry about with us is flowing through the course of the day without secret losses, which, if left undetected, could mount up to considerable sums over the years.

Inventory Lists. To know the contents of the house is also to know the contents of the Marriage, not only the large but the small as well, from major appliances and furniture down to handkerchiefs and doilies or even pins and needles, and it is for this reason that I have prepared an inventory list for your use in keeping up the house. Needless to say, you should carry it around with you at all times so that you can use it to verify the correct number and condition of our possessions and thus be able to discover almost at once when something is lost—disappears—is stolen—which is more likely to happen with the smaller objects of the household than with the larger. Nonetheless you will find it useful as you walk into the kitchen each day to ask, consulting your list, whether there are the right number of stoves, refrigerators, tables and chairs in the room and if not, why not, or, if they are all there as they should be, whether any of them is in need of repairs or maintenance or total replacement. In this way the condition of each object of the household can be ascertained by a glance at the list (without having to rummage through everything), and replacements can be ordered and purchased in advance, before the sheets rip or the towels fray or the shirts give out at the elbows, thus avoiding ill-timed failures, whether of garment or of appliance. And it is a task best carried out in the early morning hours of each day—as you may gather from observing me go over the yard and garden each morning with my inventory list in hand, noting down the condition of the trees, shrubs, fenceposts, walls, gates, livestock, garden rows, tools and supplies, car and truck, and whatever else might have been damaged by the passage of time or the weather or carried away in the darkness of the night.

Household Calendars. The function of the household calendar, that is, the various schedules I myself draw up for our joint use for the year in progress, is to assure that the days flow smoothly one after another in such a way as to spare either you or me, the joint partners of the Marriage, the sort of surprise or shock that can be occasioned by abrupt and unannounced changes. Health is a function of diet and regularity, and that is why I have made a point of marking down not only the hours at which I wish all meals to be served over the course of the year, but also a detailed menu for each meal, each day of the year—the menu and meal hours schedule I keep posted on the inside of the pantry door. You will note slight seasonal variations in both hour and menu content which are keyed—you might also notice—to slight variations in the hours I have set for going to bed and getting up in the morning, which are in turn reflected in the time and length of the afternoon nap. There are also minor variations tied to the phases of the moon. What is unpredictable here is the weather—yet I have attempted to make allowances, particularly for those days and weeks it is most likely to be extreme or abnormal. And the eating and sleeping schedules are also reflected in the dressing schedule to be found posted inside the clothes closet and on which I have indicated what articles of clothing I will wear for each day of the year, in turn mirrored in the seasonal bath and shower schedule, the whole indicating—if you read between the lines—those nights I have scheduled in advance for going out to be entertained or for other extraordinary activities, as listed on the schedule pasted to the inside of the glove-box door of the car. The utility of this system should by now be obvious to you, for should we find ourselves fully dressed up at five in the afternoon— having dutifully followed the bathing and dressing calendars—then it should be clear that this is a night to go out and that we should then proceed to do so, following as closely as possible the itinerary suggested inside the glove-box door, to Chinese or Italian restaurant, foreign or domestic comedy, chamber music or symphonic concert, and so on, whenever the facilities and activities in the neighboring towns permit, as usually they will.

The whole, of course, composes what I often refer to as our Marriage Almanac, on the composition of whose various calendars and schedules I spent at least three whole evenings each year, that is, the year preceding its actual issuance. For I have often observed that a Marriage will most often founder on the little matters of when and what to eat, what to wear and when to wash or clean it, when to go out and where to go and when to stay home, when to invite someone in and who it should be, and so on, and thus to follow the Almanac of our Marriage is to avoid making these decisions on the spur of the moment—since I have already made them months in advance, from an objective distance in time when I am neither hungry nor thirsty nor affected by the weather, hot or cold, nor can have any idea of what films or plays or concerts might be scheduled for the neighboring towns, and am thus best able to determine the shape and form, as it were, of the upcoming year, down to its most seemingly insignificant details. And further, by publishing my little Almanac—as I intend to do someday, in the distant future—and mailing copies to our friends, we will not only be able to inform them in advance of our schedule for each day of the year, thus sparing us unwanted or inconvenient visits, but provide as well a model of sorts upon which they may wish to reconstruct their own Marriages in order to reinforce and strengthen them.

The House. The house is the Marriage, and thus to maintain and keep in good repair the house, tidy and well cleaned, is to keep the Marriage too in good repair, tidy, well cleaned. The house, with its four walls, roof, floors, windows and doors, resembles the Marriage in other respects as well, so that if you focus your attention on the house you are focusing your attention on the Marriage as well. Many well-known proverbs come to mind here, all proven by time beyond memory, and I am content to let them stand as they are. In substance they state that it is the duty of the Wife to keep the interior of the house clean (as was said) as well as to offer food, drink, clothing, and bedding to those who enter its doors, that is, the invited, while it is the duty of the Husband, who I happen to be in this case, to keep the exterior surface of the house in good repair so that there will be no leaks, drafts, darkness where light is wanted, nor any intruders of any sort through any of the openings in the fabric which composes the outer walls. Yet if you fail to see me at these tasks, unremitting as they easily can be, guarding the ramparts, so to speak, oiling the locks on the doors, checking the tightness of the bars across the windows, scanning the horizon with my telescope—then do not suppose me gone. I am always around.

The Yard. As the house is the Marriage, so too can the yard or grounds or the land be seen to represent what came before the Marriage, and by that I mean the courtship, for a house can no more be built on thin air or on a cloud in the sky than can a Marriage begin without an introduction and a subsequent courtship. Thus as the house needs its lot or land to sit on, so does the Marriage need its courtship, its romance, or its affair to sit on also beforehand. And in the same way neither is the house nor the Marriage simply dropped from the sky onto the land without any preparation whatsoever, to fall wherever it may. Certain things must be investigated by the prospective Husband and Wife before building their house, which is also their Marriage. In the first place, the fiancés should study their lot or their land to make certain it is well drained and that its subsoil is such that it will be able to support the vast weight of the foundation and structure of their future house. Then they should decide where the house will be best situated in relation to scenic views or neighboring roads or highways, prevailing winds and breezes, and the course of the sun across the sky, supposing that they are wise in their choice of the site to begin with, and are well out of sight of neighboring houses, stores, factories, highways, and railway lines. Next they will have to arrange for the thickets of wild rose and plum and willow or whatever other wild vegetation there might happen to be growing to be bulldozed off into a corner and burned, for how else will they be able to build their house if the growth upon their property is rank and tangled? With their land cleared and naked of vegetation, they may order the digging of the trenches for the foundation and the pipes, and command that wires be brought down from the sky to deliver their electricity. They will watch the walls rising next—the walls which must be strong. Beams will be hoisted. The roof will be nailed on, tarred, graveled, and it must not leak. Then the plastering will begin inside the house to make the walls smooth and true, not only along the vertical but along the horizontal as well. The strong doors and tight windows go in, and the sleek drapery, and the rich carpets that are nailed down to the floors. A van arrives with the bridal furniture and appliances and the nuptial bedding. Finally the fiancés, now Bride and Groom, arrive with their honeymoon suitcases and trunks and move into their new house.

And as they lock the doors behind themselves and begin taking up residence in the house, so too do they begin taking up residence in the Marriage itself, which, like the house, has been built upon land stripped of all vegetation. Thus at first as the Bride and Groom look out the windows they will see not only desolation and loneliness on all sides—all the remains of their once flowering courtship. For as the house and thus the Marriage are built and moved into, so too is the land and thus the courtship laid waste to, the one growing out of and consuming the other and thus bringing about a momentary and ecological imbalance. But this is as it should be, for to prolong the courtship in the interests of preserving the flora and fauna of the land, so as not to disturb the mounds of red ants or cut back the poison ivy, is to postpone the building of the house and thus the Marriage in the mistaken belief that the courtship can last forever, in plain defiance of the laws of nature. Autumn and winter follow upon spring and summer, whereupon the once admired wild roses lose first their blossoms, then their leaves, then their hips— while the house stands upright, eternal, or relatively eternal—eternal enough, at any rate—and sheds the snow with its peaked roof and remains inside like spring and summer through the heating action of stoves and furnaces. And over the years the house asserts itself and comes to preside over the land upon which it stands, surrounding itself with well-trimmed lawns and well-planted flower beds in the place of the former growth which was wild and undisciplined. So too, then, should the Marriage work at replanting the devastated land of the courtship, not only with lawns and orchards, but with easily cared-for annuals and perennials as well, whose blooms are both predictable and regular throughout the various seasons of the year.

The Floor. Likewise the floor of the house can be considered the floor of the Marriage, that is, what the Husband and Wife stand on and walk on and what they rest the furniture on. As is well known, floors are both dirty and "clean" at the same time. Yet it can also be said that no floor is ever entirely clean so much that it is "not dirty" and "not very dirty." But it is an agreed-upon principle that the floors of the household are to be kept as clean as possible and that this is primarily your task and that you should furthermore guard against dirt being tracked into the house and therefore into the Marriage.

And should you perform your duties in this area in the proper manner, it follows that you will not have to worry about dirt being tracked out of the house, out (therefore) of the Marriage.

The Walls. The walls of the house represent the walls of the Marriage, and as one or two walls standing alone represent a ruin, so do four or more walls in multiples thereof represent the closing in upon, the rounding out of, the consummation of the copulatory embrace, though vertical rather than horizontal. The house then represents the sexual act frozen into architecture, and though doors will open and slam closed as children run in and out, and windows will be flung open in summer and latched closed in winter, and faucets be turned on and toilets flushed, and fires lit and be allowed to die out—we cannot ignore this fact. Therefore as you make your rounds throughout the house in the course of the day, cleaning the floors, walls, ceilings, and other interior surfaces (while I am at work outside rehanging shingles, touching up cracks in plaster, repainting the trim), it would be well to consider where you are. For as the interior of the house (and we also mean by "house" Marriage) is the female and what is outside the house is male, it follows that wherever I (who am the male) enter the house, which lies passive and horizontal and open unto my comings and goings, and as I wander among its furnishings (which we will call the organs), the overstuffed armchair, the pink sofa, the rich red carpets, and come upon you, surprising you and—but what more is there to add?

Electricity. The modern house with all its conveniences can no more function without electricity than can the modern Marriage function without its equivalent, and by that I mean the nervous energy which powers the Marriage. For the wiring of the house with its wires, outlets, and switches is also the wiring of the Marriage or the nerves of the Marriage through which electrical impulses are transmitted, causing light bulbs to glow, toasters to heat up, the motors of washing machines, blenders, and other appliances to turn, and so on. And as the electrical circuits should not be overloaded by turning on all the lights and appliances at once all over the house, so too should not the wiring of the Marriage be overloaded by putting too many demands on it at once if one is to avoid overheated lines and blown fuses. For the effect of the blown fuse is to plunge everything into darkness and make time stop. Yet this can sometimes happen accidentally, as when the Husband and the Wife are drawing power in large quantities from separate ends of the house unbeknownst to each other. In such cases either you or I but preferably both of us should immediately undertake to find candles and flashlights and go down into the basement and replace the fuse or reset the circuit breaker, and start all over again. But now and then the lights will go out unexpectedly in the middle of dinner, the result of a distant lightning bolt, for example, and there is nothing that either of us can do except sit quietly by the candles until the lights finally go back on. That is, there are two kinds of power failure with the Marriage, the one brought on from within, the other from without; the effect, however, is essentially identical.

The Refrigerator. The refrigerator in the kitchen stands as an island of cold in a sea of warmth within its various skins of enamel, insulation, and plastic which serve to separate the two areas, the warm from the cool and freezing, the outside from the inside. Yet objects cannot be kept indefinitely in a refrigerator, generally reserved for the storing of fresh or relatively fresh food, because despite the cold within they will still spoil or lose their flavor or undergo unpleasant changes in shape, texture, or color. Thus the importance of arranging the food on the shelves and in the bins of the refrigerator in such a way that the older food is closest to the door and so will be taken out and prepared, eaten, served, or drunk before the newer or fresher food, which should be pushed to the back. In this way too, old food will not get shoved into the far corners of shelves or bins and become lost there until suddenly a stench begins leaking out of the box or until it is discovered when the refrigerator is defrosted, all shriveled up. This exercise should be performed every two weeks on the average in winter and every ten days in the summer and should be combined with a general cleaning out of the interior of the refrigerator, to include the washing of the trays and bins with hot soapy water and the enamel inside the box scrubbed with a solution of bicarbonate of soda and water. Throw out the old ice, refill the trays with fresh water—this is also advised, for old ice has a distinctive taste to the sensitive palate, having picked up the odors of various strong foods in the refrigerator despite their being wrapped up in several layers of foil or plastic—onions, cabbage, turnips, some cheeses, to mention a few—for there is virtually nothing that can stop a strong odor that is determined to move from place to place.

The refrigerator of the kitchen and thus of the house can be seen to represent the refrigerator of the Marriage, and by that I mean the repository of all such things as the Husband and the Wife wish to preserve against the effects of heat and time. You may wish to see it as a kind of memory or memory bank or joint account from which both of us may withdraw—or into which deposit—sustenance at any time. Indeed the vaultlike quality of the strong door with its gleaming nickel-plated latches and hinges can hardly suggest anything else, that this is the place where you and I keep what is dearest and of greatest value to the Marriage, that is, the joint memories. You must take care therefore not to deposit the sort of ill-wrapped food with strong odors that would infect the taste of the blander foods, and remember to clean out the interior at regular intervals in order to discourage the growth of fungi and molds. And as you open and close the door of the refrigerator and the light inside the box goes on and off, so too do you open and close the vault of our collective memory, that is, you remember and forget, remember and forget. But it should not be left open for long periods of time, except when defrosting, so that its contents will not be unduly warmed up and thus spoil.

Nor should you crowd the refrigerator up with leftovers, need-less to say, or foods that no one in the household will eat, or with foods that do not in fact need to be refrigerated at all—for the main function of the refrigerator is to halt the growth and spread of microbes and bacteria of the sort that can make the eaters of the house sick or ill and in some cases even kill them, as in ptomaine and botulism. But in most foods there is no danger of this at all and they can simply be shelved in the cabinets or in the pantry, thus keeping the refrigerator from becoming too overcrowded, not only in the kitchen but in the Marriage as well.

But we must not forget that food is grown from the earth in order to be eaten, and so what is put in the refrigerator is put there because it is intended to be taken out at some future date and be eaten up either cooked or raw. Cooking will take place either on the four burners of the stove or in its oven or both, which elements may be said to represent the inner life of the Wife, just as the garden may be said to represent the inner life of the Husband, that is, in those cases in which gardens are kept. Eating is what takes place at meals. One associates meals with placemats, silverware, dishes, and china, and the food that is served and eaten with these imple-ments on a table by persons sitting in chairs and who now and then speak to each other between mouthfuls of food and drafts of water or wine. There are as many styles of eating as there are eaters, no doubt, but one of the most serviceable is to close the mouth once the food is inside it, whereupon you are to begin masticating or chewing in a relaxed manner, without haste. This throws the salivary glands into action. And once the food is ground into a pulp: swal-low. If the food is well ground, the swallow will be smooth and effortless and you will hardly know what happened. Then you pause to have a sip of water or wine or whatever, after which it is wise to clear the throat discreetly so as to make room for the next swallow, that is, to clear away any loose ends. Of course this process of open-ing the mouth and taking in food and masticating it and swallowing it, to which may be added digestion and elimination, will be affected by the type of food to be processed, whether tough and fibrous, crisp and brittle, soft and slippery, spicy or bland, and so on, all of which will also affect your speed. But that one should not eat with the mouth open and not speak with the mouth full are well-known principles universally accepted, and I need add nothing to them except to say that beneath them lie even yet greater truths. For the food that is cooked and served at meals can be seen to represent the food of the Marriage, by which I mean the language of the Mar-riage, and so it is no wonder that the greater part of the eating and the talking takes place at the same time, at meals, with the Husband speaking across the table while his mouth is empty and the Wife listening while hers is full, then speaking when hers is empty and the Husband's full—in short, the manner in which I have often rec-ommended that we converse at our three meals taken together, breakfast, lunch, and dinner.

For if food at the table represents the language of the Marriage with the various courses representing the parts of speech, with prepositions and articles and conjunctions built around the main course of verbs and nouns, many of which have just come from the refrigerator of the Marriage, and the whole meal composing a sentence or a statement that begins with an aperitif (the capital letter) and ends with a period (cup of coffee), then it should be clear how important it is to prepare and utter your words well and to know when to open your mouth and when to close it—when to speak and when not to speak. You should no more blurt out an ill-formed sentence, for example, than you should throw together a dinner in five minutes out of leftovers and stale food to serve up to an honored guest: good sentences, like good meals, require that their ingredients be kept well stored and be prepared with great care and consideration, with delicate sauces and dressings, but not overly seasoned, and be served on attractive plates whose rims are wiped clean of dribbled gravy, but with confidence and without apology. But is your guest a vegetarian? Is he on a diet today, not taking sugar or salt? Do tomatoes give him hives? Bananas nausea? Does ice cream make his hands and feet swell up? Better to know these things in advance than to find you have poisoned your guest who out of politeness has eaten everything you have served up and who now grows more and more silent as his sufferings increase, to a point finally where he is unable to say anything at all.

Windows. But whereas the doors represent breaches in the fabric of the Marriage, that is, the house, the windows are altogether another matter, representing the eyes, for they are bastions of strength despite their apparent fragility. The windows should be kept clean at all times, first of all for the simple pleasure of being able to look through them and, conversely, for the displeasure to be found in staring at films of smoke or rain-splashed dust, the droppings of insects on the interior surfaces of the glass and those of birds on the exterior surfaces, for it may be said that a house with clean windows is a Marriage with clean eyes, that is, eyes that see clearly. Curtains, shades, and blinds are to be drawn or lowered at night, however, so that the outside world in its prowlings around will not be able to see inside the Marriage and what goes on or (in some cases) what does not go on, and they are to be drawn open or raised promptly at the first light of dawn so that there is no doubt that the house is alert and awake as early as it is convenient to be so. Likewise lights are to be turned off inside the house promptly at eleven, since late nights—as in the Marriage's flashing eyes—suggest discord or argumentation between the Husband and the Wife, and should this prove necessary, should the Husband and Wife choose to quarrel after eleven at night, they are advised to draw the curtains and lower the blinds and turn off the lights and to quarrel in a low voice, a whisper if at all possible. The curtains, shades, or blinds represent the eyelids of the Marriage, it should be pointed out.

The windows are one of the more complex structures of the house and consist of glass (as was mentioned), mullions of metal or of wood milled and lap-jointed, putty, and in some cases hinges and latches for windows that open and close, and paint or stain inside and out. They may also be weather-stripped in the case of windows designed to open and close, or merely caulked in those windows that will remain fixed for all time. Windows may also be covered at various seasons by screens, awnings, storm windows, all for various reasons—suggesting the sunglasses, hat brims, etc., of the Marriage. But windows are in all characterized by a quality which is of supreme advantage to those, the Husband and the Wife, who jointly inhabit the house, and that is that one obtains a better view looking out of the windows from inside than looking in through them from outside, an effect which is enhanced by the quadri-focal bi-stereoscopic vision innate to the Marriage itself, as summed up in the saying: two can see better than one. Thus not only can one see better from within looking outward, not only that—there is also the matter of simply being inside while the objects or persons outside are outside, for inside one can communicate in low tones without fear of being overheard, while outside one is not only bi-stereoscopically visible but subject to certain unexpected resonating configurations in the shrubbery, fences, and walls that can serve to project one's softest words right into the house, and in this effect lies the supreme strength of the Marriage over others, who know now how much they are being watched, how much overheard.

The Children. As you know, my dear, I have taken it upon myself to limit the number of our Children to two, one Son and one Daughter, the greater part of whose care I entrust to your apparently sound maternal instincts. There is thus little I can offer by way of advice or recommendation except to say that I do not wish to meet them more than once or twice a day and preferably toward the end of the day and preferably at that part of the end of the day when they are being put to bed, which is also near the hour I have at last managed to dismiss most of the greater concerns of the day and thus am able to summon up the strength to once again introduce myself as their Father. They are, at this time in their lives when they are particularly subject to beneficial influences—I am pleased to note—learning. It would help of course if you would refer to me regularly throughout the day by pointing to me through the windows as I work out in the yard or as I get in the car and drive away, or as I pass by close to the house on the way to get a tool from the garage or return one I have finished with. In such manner they will become accustomed to viewing me at various angles and distances, and in various postures, or moving now slowly, now rapidly, by foot or by car. You may now and then—but perhaps no more than once a day—wish to carry them out in your arms so that they may have a close view of me in direct sunlight—or, as one of them seems to be walking after a fashion, send him for a brief ramble down to the garden walls and let him (or her) peer through the cracks in the gate, staring and blinking, before you call him (or her) back. And when they are old enough to speak in complete sentences and thus to understand them when spoken to them, you might consider reading them aloud, once a day or so, selections from some of my published horticultural pamphlets, particularly *Garlic Questions Finally Answered* and *How to Garden Without Bending Over*. These things must not be hurried, however. There is plenty of time for the Children to get to know me, and I see no reason why they should be rushed into the matter when all of life is yet ahead of them.

Although we will have no more Children—we already have 0.3 too many as it is, statistically speaking—it may nonetheless be said that every day lived within the house, thus within the Marriage, is one of utmost pregnancy. For as you go about your way within the house cleaning and dusting, washing clothes and dishes, and I go about my way outside making repairs and tending the yard and garden, we bear within ourselves, the Husband and the Wife, images or effigies of each other, the Husband of the Wife, the Wife of the Husband, and carry these images about with us while we work. And as the pregnant mother-to-be will have no clear idea of what her future child will look like, or how it will behave, imagine what she will, until it is actually born into the world, so too will neither you nor I have any clear idea of what the other (with whom we have been pregnant all day) will look like or how the other will behave until that moment when we meet again at the end of the day, in that daily birth or rebirth which is the encounter of the Husband and the Wife in the house and in the Marriage. And in this state of unending pregnancy so too must you take care not to eat things that will upset your stomach while at the same time keeping up your breathing exercises, resting when necessary, so that when the moment comes you will be in good physical condition, relaxed and fearless, and able to face the ordeal with the conviction that all will come out well. For to neglect these things in the daily pregnancy of the Marriage is to open oneself to the possibility of not only great pain but the premature or the miscarried as well, in which the image nurtured in pregnancy is too small or is ill formed in comparison with the strapping reality, suddenly strong and overpowering and demanding beyond all preconception.

4

One Thousand Words on Why You Should Not Talk During a Fire Drill

Mark Halliday

FIRST OF ALL, I should point out that the topic of why you should not talk during a fire drill is such a large and complex topic that I cannot do full justice to it in only one thousand words. In only one thousand words I will only be able to scratch the surface of this very interesting topic which has so many important and sensitive aspects. There certainly is a great deal to be said about why a person should not talk during a fire drill, even when everybody knows it is just a drill and even if there is not a teacher talking to us at the time.

One outstanding reason for not talking during a fire drill is because the fire drill is a practice session for when there might be a real fire in which case all the students would certainly need to be very quiet so they could hear the instructions from teachers such as Mrs. DeMella who would be shouting out some important messages. She might be shouting about how we should stand in alphabetical order on the ballfield with the ninth grade closest to the flagpole. If you are talking when Mrs. DeMella shouts about this then you might not hear the instructions and possibly, with the black smoke billowing out the windows of the burning school, if this was a real fire and not just another drill, you might then become confused and forget where to stand, even though the whole school has practiced this entire thing about a thousand times, because at such a time your brain could become overheated and you might run in circles like an insane dog. For this reason you would fail to stand in exactly the place where Mrs. DeMella wanted you to stand, in which case the teachers might count the students and come to the mistaken conclusion that you were absent and that you were roasting in the flames, running around trapped in the burning gym like a human torch, and as a result Mrs. DeMella might go insane with grief about her lost student, thinking that she should have shouted even louder about where everybody should walk and stand, all because you were selfish and kept on talking to your neighbor.

In a sense, the above explanation reveals very much of the essence of why a person should not ever talk during a fire drill, but of course there are further aspects of this interesting topic which can be explained and which will be explained. The concept of not talking during a fire drill is closely related to the concept of silence and to the concept of the value of silence or what we call quiet. In a quiet situation there is a great opportunity for people to hear what someone else may have to say, such as your teacher. In a sense this is the same idea as was studied in the preceding paragraph but there is definitely more to be said about silence or quiet or what we may call the absence of sound. Silence is a situation which gives us the chance to rest our ears, and our minds, which are so busy during most of the day listening to words, words, words, and other noises, like the squeak of chalk on a blackboard (which is actually a green board) or Mr. Perkins clearing his throat which seems to involve a remarkable amount of phlegm or mucus or what have you. After a few hours of hearing so many sounds, some of which are remarkably unpleasant, not to mention the voices of our teachers helping us to understand the Constitution and the methods for determining whether two triangles are congruent (side-angle-side, angle-side-angle, and side-side-side) (but not angle-angle-angle), there is a need for silence, or quiet, and it is a very human need. Thus if a student is talking during a fire drill, that student is ruining a golden opportunity to experience silence, because after all a fire drill is a time when silence is golden, and mandatory, except of course for a teacher like Mrs. DeMella who has the job of shouting instructions to everybody very loudly just in case someone may have forgotten the fire drill procedure from the last fire drill which took place one month ago.

At this point the important issue of why you should absolutely not talk during a fire drill has certainly been clarified in more than one way. However, there is no doubt in my mind that more can be said on this issue which has fascinated the minds of various thinkers since mankind became civilized and outgrew the habits of apes and related primates. If a tribe of monkeys were to participate in a fire drill they would probably go right on chattering and scratching their armpits and hopping on each other no matter what Mrs. DeMella said, and this would be terribly upsetting for her and the other teachers because the high noise level would make them think all the monkeys would get burned to a crisp in the event of a real fire. But fortunately thanks to Charles Darwin and his assistants mankind has evolved and has discovered the concept of self-control which is very beautiful. Surely we can feel proud of the human species when we see the entire ninth grade standing in alphabetical rows by the flagpole with nobody saying a single word, standing there in a condition of total and complete silence and pretending that something important is going on even when everybody knows there is no fire and we could all do the entire drill in our sleep.

In conclusion, possibly a few words should be said on the question of why a person might make the mistake of talking during a fire drill. Here is an example. Bryce Carter grabbed my Screaming Blue Messiahs tape and I had to get it back fast before he wrecked it.

5

Problems for Self-Study

Charles Yu

---

1. TIME T EQUALS ZERO

A is on a train traveling due west along the x-axis at a constant velocity of seventy kilometers per hour (70 km/h). He stands at the rear of the train, looking back with some fondness at the town of (6,3), his point of departure, the location of the university and his few friends. He is carrying a suitcase (30 kg) and a small bound volume (his thesis: 0.7 kg; 7 years).

Using the information given, calculate A's final position.

2. Assume A is lonely. Assume A is leaving (6,3) in order to find someone who could equal his love of pure theory. A says to himself, "No one in a town like (6,3) could possibly equal my love of pure theory." Not even P, his esteemed adviser and mentor.

   A suspects P is a closet empiricist, checking his theory against the world instead of the other way around.

   A once barged in and caught P, hunched over his desk, with a guilty but pleasured look on his face, approximating, right there in his office.

3. RELATIVE MOTION

Across the train car, A spots B. Assume B is lovely.

(a) A immediately recognizes that B is not a physicist.

(b) Still, he calculates his approach.

(c) A wonders, Into what formula do I plug the various quantitative values of B?
Could B, A wonders, though she dearly lacks formal training in me-
chanics, ever be taught, in some rudimentary sense, to understand
the world as I do?

(d) A notes her inconsistent postulates. Her wasted assumptions. Her lovely inexactness.

(e) He decides to give her a test.

(f) A says, If a projectile is launched at a 30-degree angle to
the earth, with an initial velocity of 100 m/s, how far does
it travel?

(g) B notes his nervous and strange confidence, his razor-
nicked chin, his tie too short by an inch, an uncombed
tuft of hair. She is charmed.

(h) B humors A.

(i) B says, Well, doesn't it depend on how windy it is?

(j) Ignore the wind, says A.

(k) But how can I ignore the wind?

(l) Ignore the wind, says A.

(m) Are you saying there is no wind?

(n) A says, The wind is negligible. He says this with a certain pleasure. The other passengers roll their eyes.

(o) A says, It does not matter for the purposes of the problem. Besides, A says, it makes the math too hard.

(p) A looks at B's dumb, expectant, beautiful face. He feels pity for her meager understanding of physics. How can he explain to her what must be ignored: wind, elephants, cookies, air resistance. And: the morning dew, almost everything in newspapers, almost everything owing to random heat dissipation, the taste of papaya. And: the mass of the projectile, the shape of the projectile, what other people think, statistical noise, the capital of Luxembourg.

(q) A wonders, Can I be with a woman who, however lovely, does not understand how to hold all else constant? How to isolate a variable?

A thinks:
  i. she will see it my way;

ii. she will change for me;

iii. I will educate her.

B thinks:

iv. he is lonely;

v. I can make him less so;

vi. I will change for him.

4. A spent seven years (2,557 days, 4,191 cups of coffee) in the town of (6,3).

He was writing his thesis (79 pages, 81 separate equations). A's thesis is on nonlinear dynamic equations.

(a) In it, he discovered a tiny truth.

(b) When he had written the last step in his proof, A smiled.

(c) A's tiny truth is about a tiny part of a tiny sliver of a tiny subset of all possible outcomes of the world.

(d) When A brought it to his adviser and mentor, the esteemed P, P smiled. A's heart leapt.

(e) P said: What it lacks in elegance, it makes up for in rigor.

(f) P also said: What a wonderful minor result.

5. A and B are sliding down a frictionless inclined plane. They are accelerating toward the inevitable. Domesticity. Some marriages are driven by love, some by gravity.

6. THE THREE-BODY PROBLEM

Things continue to get more complicated for A, now traveling in an elliptical path around B. B remains fixed, giving birth to their first child. Doctors and nurses orbit B periodically.

(a) Given the mass of A (now 80kg) and the mass of B (now 55kg), calculate the gravitational force between A and B using Newton's universal gravitational formula: $Fg= G(mA)(mB)/r2$, where R is the gravitational constant.

(b) Imagine the situation from the stationary perspective of B. As bodies whirl around you, you focus on the pain, the quiet place, the baby. Look at A, who so lovingly paces around you, worried about your health. You wonder: What is A thinking?

(c) Now imagine the situation from A's perspective. You wonder: What if the child turns out like its mother? What if the child does not understand theory? You've spent so many nights lying awake with B, trying to teach her how to see the world, its governing principles, the functions lying under it all. Hours spent with B as she cries, frustrated, uncomprehending.

(d) This is what is well-known in the field of celestial dynamics as the three-body problem.

(e) Put simply, this is the problem of computing the mutual gravitational interaction of three separate and different masses.

(f) Astronomers since the time of Kepler have known that this problem is surprisingly difficult to solve.

(g) With two bodies, the problem is trivial. With two bodies, we can simplify the universe, empty it of everything but, say, the moon and the earth, an A and a B, the sun and a speck of dust. The equations are solved analytically.

(h) Unfortunately, when we add a third body to our equations of motion, the equations become intractable. It turns out the mathematics gets very complicated, very fast.

(i) A has only recently begun to feel comfortable predicting B's path, B's behavior, her perturbations and eccentricity of orbit. And now this, he thinks. Another body.

(j) B screams with the agony of natural childbirth. She looks into A's eyes. What is he thinking, her A, her odd, impenetrable husband? Will he make a good father?

(k) A thinks generally about the concept of pain. A has a witty thought and would like to write it down.

7. MOMENT OF INERTIA

(a) A and B are not moving ($V_A = V_B = 0$). A is in his study, hidden in the corner. He is talking in a low voice.

(b) B, across the house, is watching television.

(c) A is talking to J, who is married to S. S is a good friend of A.

(d) J is thinner than B. S is older than A.

(e) B is listening to A. S is listening to J.

(f) Also listening: the neighborhoods Theta and Sigma, Delta and Phi.

(g) Also listening: the social circle: Phi, Chi, and Psi. Eta, Zeta, and Nu. Even Lambda has been known to listen.

(h) Others, just speculating, say that A and J would make a good-looking couple. A says no, thinks yes. J blushes.

(i) S exerts a force on J. A exerts a force on B. A wants to exert a force on J, and J would like it if A would exert a considerable force on her.

(j) B is walking down the hall. A can hear B. B can hear A's voice growing softer with each step she takes. A freezes in anticipation, ready to hang up the phone.

(k) B changes velocity, turns, goes into the kitchen, pretending not to hear.

(l) A does not move. B does not move. The forces cancel out. Everyone remains at rest.

8. PARTIAL SOLUTIONS

(a) renovate the kitchen;

(b) renovate themselves;

(c) go on safari;

(d) go to a "seminar";

(e) make large purchases of luxury durable consumer goods;

(f) make small overtures to an object of lust at work;

(g) take up golf;

(h) find a disorder and self-diagnose;

(i) get a purebred dog;

(j) get religion;

(k) landscape the backyard;

(l) have another child.

9. GEDANKENEXPERIMENT

(a) Imagine A is building a spaceship. He is tired of being pushed, pulled, torqued, accelerated, collided on a daily basis. Losing momentum. He is tired of his thesis failing, time and again. Every day an exception to A's Theorem. Every day he recognizes it a little less—once a shiny unused tool, a slender, immaculate volume. Now riddled with holes, supported with makeshift, untenable assumptions. A's Theorem has not so much predicted the future with success as it has recorded a history of its own exceptions.

(b) It is simplest to approach the problem of satellite motion from the point of view of energy.

(c) Every night for a year, A and B eat dinner in silence. Every night for a year, A lights a cigarette, opens a beer, goes to the garage to work on his imaginary spaceship. Sometimes, he has doubts. Sometimes, he gets frustrated, wondering if it is worth all the imaginary trouble.

(d) And then, one day, A finishes his spaceship. Even imaginary work pays off.

(e) A turns on his imaginary vehicle, listens to it roar. It makes a lot of imaginary noise. B tries to talk over it, but the engine is deafeningly loud.

(f) B shouts at A right in front of his face. A sees B gesturing wildly. Why is she acting so crazy?

(g) The energy of a body in satellite motion is the sum of its kinetic and potential energies. It is given by the following: $E=K+U=1/2mv2-GmN/r2$

(h) A watches B moving frantically around the garage. A notes that B looks rather desperate, as if she is trying to stop him, trying to hold him, trying to keep him from leaving Earth.

(i) A's spaceship is heating up. It is time, he thinks. He holds the imaginary levers and calculates his trajectory. He enjoys for a minute the low frequency hum as it vibrates through his whole body. His future opens up in front of him.

(j) He is moving now. His past sealing itself off, trailing farther and farther behind him.

(k) The escape velocity, vesc, of a projectile launched from the surface of the earth is the minimum speed with which the projectile must launch from the surface in order to over-come gravity and leave the vicinity of the earth forever.

(l) His imperfect theorem, his imperfect credit, his imperfect house, his imperfect bladder, his imperfect hemorrhoids, his imperfect gum disease, his imperfect career, his imperfect penis: gone. Also gone: the history of his interactions, his past collisions, his past. A has finally achieved his major result. He is free from the unceasing pull of gravitational memory.

10. A is in deep space. The solar wind is at his back, pushing him along at a rate of 0.000000001 m/s.

At this rate, it will take the rest of his life to travel a distance of just over eight feet. B is on a space rock, watching A drift by glacially. Imagine you are B.

(a) Imagine you are 20m from A. Close enough to see his face. Close enough to know his shape. Close enough to imagine Contact.

(b) You have a rope. If you can throw it just right, you may be able to tie yourself to A, turn his course, affect his trajectory. You will not be able to stop him, but you may be able to make sure that wherever it is he drifts to you end up there as well.

(c) Assume you are of average strength. Assume you are of above-average compassion, patience, will, and determination.

(d) If you throw the rope and miss, what happens? If you never throw the rope, what happens?

(e) Imagine you will spend a period of eighty years within a few meters of this astronaut, a man in an insulated space suit. Imagine it is possible to drift by this man, staring at him, as he makes his way into the infinite ocean of space.

(f) You will never know any other points, other problems, the mysteries of biochemistry, the magic of literature, the pleasures of topology. You will know only physics.

(g) You will never know what it feels like inside his suit.

(h) You will never know why you are on this rock.

11. INITIAL CONDITIONS

A is on a train traveling due west along the x-axis at a constant velocity of seventy kilometers per hour (70 km/h). He is carrying a suitcase (30kg) and a small bound volume (his thesis; 0.7 kg; 7 years).

He stands at the rear of the train, looking back at the town of (6,3): a point full of sadness, an origin of vectors, a locus of desire; a point like any other point.

6

Permission Slip

Caron A. Levis

Hell-o.

This on?

Think I'm hearin me. Me.

This reverbin either in the buildin or in my head. Whatever. Ha.

Nobody listnin anyways right?

Mos all you out the building by now, an who listens to the announcements they makin evry five minutes like they tryin to give all of evybody in the whole Bronx a holla or somethin anyway.

Thing is, this NOT your principal speakin.

This. Is. Nessa. And today I didn do nothin.

I'm jus a surge cloud, thas all.

Yeah. I didn't ever hear of it either till last week when miss wahzer-fuck—EXCUSE ME, miss whazerface, said something bout it in science.

I'm *passin* that one. I even turn in summa the homework and if she don't pass me, she gonna have to see me in there again nex year, and you know she don't want that cause Ima surge cloud.

She say it's this super hot air that comes offa lava. Like outta a volcano. An it jus as deadly as the lava itself. It can kill. Even though it's invisible it can kill. How you like that? Ha, Yeah. I like that. That is me. Ima get it tattooed.

All I'm sayin is people best watch out. All I'm sayin is if somebody got burnt, not *my* fault. I didn *do* nothin. Is just my invisible hotness.

I was jus sittin there, fourth floor hall, where I always be, not standin or stalkin, screamin, playin beats, or nothin—jus chillin, an mister principal, he come over and he axing me where my sposed to be?

An I am axing him the same thing with my mind but he not seein my mind only my shoulders doin the shruggin and so he axing me again, louder, where my sposed to be?

Damn.

Dults always wantin you to be minding your own biz til the exact moment you do. Right? He think I don't know why he beastin on me steada evybody else runnin round this hall. He think I didn hear my gramma on the phone withim yesterday.

I given her to *you*, she says. I puttin her in *your* hands now, she says.

Course he don't know she meaning that on the literal. She can't tell him she kickin me out, cause maybe it ain't legal. But she do it anyway. She say she too tired for a teenager.

But he's not knowin any a that. He jus want to do his job so he axing me again about where my where my where my.

So I say,

You know, Mister Sobers, you my favorite princiPAL I ever had? For real. They tell you about the pal in elementary but I never saw it in nobody til now. It's the truth. You really—

But then some baby-brawl break out down the other end, probaly eight-oh-two—you know it's gotta be—jumpin eight-ten class again, an he book it down there like he gonna try to do somethin bout it. Nobody can do nothin bout eight-oh-two. They hopeless. But they makin it so he leave fore he get his answer from me an thas fine since thas what I'm workin on anyway, right now, that answer of where my sposed to be.

I wonder if Ida been put with the eight-ten or eight-oh-two class Ida made it to grade eight this year.

An jus in case anybody out there listnin who dont know, I'm in six-oh-three. Three years. Thas right. Ima get it tattooed.

You hearin me?

This thing still on right?

*Whatev*a.

Check it. Principal always tryin to get us to go to class by axing us where you sposed to be, right? If they wanted us to be in the classes then they shoulda built this school with some *walls*, for real, steada this halfway-up-walls-made-outta-paper *Open Air* bullshit. Only rooms that got real walls and doors be the computer lab and the science room and this one right here across from me where the new special *arts* program is at.

This one with the doorknob sayin turn this shit right here, turn this shit right here, I dare you to turn this shit right here.

An maybe I'm hearin this hallway extra loud today, or somethin, I don't know. Usually the only reason I come to school, is for the loud in the hall, an my girls laughin at any little thing don't matter what, but today I'm bored maybe. Maybe my ears be sore. All I know is I'm up with my hands on that knob an it won't turn cause they keep it locked this door. You hearin me?

Locked. Like they got treasure in there or something steada jus some stupid class. An you gotta be on a list to go in there. Like it's a club or some shit. This a school not a night club, right? Why they allowed to be all V.I.P. like that? You hearin?

Yesterday I come in to see what it all about an one a the teachers, the fly one, who dark an licious like gramma's gravy, with his muscles all carved, an his hair all crisp—he *boilin* hot—he say sorry, you not in the program. Sorry, you got to be on the list. Sorry, you not on the list so sorry, you can't be in here, you got to get your sorry ass to your sorry class, you got to go where you sposed to be, where you sposed to be? Evybody want me to go where I sposed to be but nobody in this school seem to know where the fuck that shit is.

Now he too fly to be so sorry, so I left. But today I'm back an givin the door a good BANG. Thas what we do here on doors, right? We BANG, BANG. These new teachers they not used to it, so sometimes they try to come out sayin stop it. Bang, bang, banging been going on in this school for all of ever, and they think we gonna stop cause they Look Serious. Ha. What they gonna do about it? I hear them visitors the other day sayin how this one a them schools needs to jus be burned to the ground cause nothin gonna save it.

BANG BANG.

I got somethin for that fine teacher in my pocket.

Malique, he been in that class two weeks, and he tell me bout it. Bout how they playin games in there and talkin bout wack stuff like feelins and shit. And how they get snack. Bout how the only home-work they gotta do is get some slip signed by they parent or guardian or whatever jus one time. Then they set to be gettin snack an playin they reindeer games evy week for the resta the whole year.

BANG.

I axed Malique what they need that big room for an he say it cause they need room cause they be playin games and warmin ups and shit cause they use they bodies in here cause they be doin actin. When I axed him what kind of actin he say, you know, like shows. I axe what the shows about an he say they bout life. Angerina says they about how to get a better life. Sounds wack to me but they miss social studies for it.

BANG BANG.

I don't know why, I don't know why.

BANG BANG.

Somebody come to see what goin on out here and pop the door a inch. I slip through that crack in there no problem. Surge cloud style. An I am in.

They all sittin in the middle of the big room in a circle. A circle all facin eachother—what class you sit in a circle like that? I say hey-hey to Malique and Angerina give me a snap up. The teacher from the otha day not in there. Jus the other one, the shortie I can't tell if maybe she gotta flava or she jus one a them snowcones who puttin it on. She walkin round the circle a chairs with a box handin out snack, I think it's those nasty granola bars maybe I don't know.

Can I help you? She axin me an evybody lookin. *Do you need something?*

Evybody lookin. Melinda an Angerina smilin cause they expect me to do my usual an make evybody laugh at some loud shit I pull out. Tyrike, I didn know he in this class, he got his fine eyes on me too. And I am thinkin thas not why I am in here, why am I in here, but I am confused, whas that slip called? People sayin hey-hey and lookin at me and this teacher she startin to look tight, crossin her arms and maybe if she axe me again do I need but she sayin where you sposed to—an Tyrike sayin aww *burn*, you *not* gonna let her do like that right—an I am confused so I say, I heard they was given out snacks.

An I like snack.

An she let out this lil sigh. Maybe nobody else hear it, but I hear it. Even though it not even one fluid ounce a the sighs my gramma make it jus as cold, jus as seeable, like it winter in here all a sudden, an I can see every breath she usin to say how she wish but she don't have extra to give and I'm not in the class so I have ta leave. I don't belong here. Like she know where I belong. She don't know nothin.

What she know? She ain't even a real teacher, right? What real teacher talk bout life?

Evybody lookin to see what I'm gonna do to the teacher who talk block to me like that cause they know Nessa not held back for any missin IQ, Nessa jus don't sit quiet. She loud an she funny, crack your shit up all over the floor, an she clear a hall in seven seconds when she want to go stalkin. So they lookin, but why my in here, why my why my an she repeatin and they lookin an I *have* somethin—

But she passin an handin snack outta her box to evybody who sittin there in her wack little circle but not me, an evybody lookin, expectatin, cause my rep proceeds, so I go over there an why my why my an I say YO, GIMME MY SNACK. An she say I don't belong in here and could I please leave, but I feel like stayin so I stay an she still won't gimme a snack.

So, I'm talkin to Malique, cause he *belong here*, and tellin him to get me a snack from the bitch teacher—EXCUSE ME— I'm SO sorry— from the *teacher*.

Cept she won't let him cause she know it for me.

An she keep sayin I am not in the program and I am not supposed to be here not supposed to be here, please leave and leave and leave you don't belong here you don't belong here you don't belong belong belong you don't youdon'tyoudon'toudon'tdon't—

Well, what she saying is exactly what I'm here to fix.

I go for my pocket where I was gonna get what I came in to show. My poem dumb ELA teacher put on the board in the hall, this morning she musta done it. Why she puttin that shit up in the hall I don't know, don't nobody wanna see that shit out there. Dont matter how nice it be, teacher puttin it up, you a punk. Lucky I untacked it fore anybody could start bustin on me bout it. But I kept it in my pocket and maybe it can get me ontha list since it's a arts program, the new special program, an poems is art and my poems bout life and thas what Malique say they doin in here so maybe. Maybe.

So, I tell her, I got somethin for you.

But now she busy axing somebody else ta stay in they seat, jus have patience, soon as she Take Care a *This*, she be startin class. This.

An I lookin at who it is she tryin to get to stay in the room while she tryin to get me outta it, an I see it's Devon. An nexta him is Hector who be bustin on Shawanna, who flirtin with James. An I get the deal now.

I know who belong in here. You gotta be bad to belong in here. Angerina says they tell them they been specially selected, but really it's just that you gotta have like a daddy in jail, or a dropout sister, or a baby, or been arrested, or jus never come to school. You gotta be A Risk. Thas what the school like to call bad kids. A Risk.

Problem is this teacher thinkin how I am not on her list, I'm not A Risk, and I'm not belonging in here, but she will see soon enough. I am a surge cloud.

She sayin again about me leavin, so I say, I'M NOT DEAF ARE YOU?

That get her attention. Like she a dog an I the can that jus got opened.

So, steada the poem, I take outta my pocket one a the tacks that was holdin it up, an I shove it to Angerina near her face an she backs away cause she know it sharp. Teacher should know that. I got sharp objects in my pockets. She. Should. Know. That.

An I hype now, so I start stalkin. It's a big room, lotta space in here, an I'm feelin it. See there this green paper coverin all the walls, like she tryin to make it look like grass in here steada the cracked whiteness in every other room. An there all these drawins over the green paper—an signs sayin cornpop shit bout choices. Like anybody in here got choices for real. I stalk their little circle a chairs a coupla times. Floors still dirty as everywhere.

She lookin mad tight now.

What's your name? she axing me,

Whas *your* name? I axe her back.

She say she not lookin to play around an so I say again WHAS YOUR NAME?!

She *try* not to flinch.

I hear Malique sayin thas Nessa, I go over, slap his head, tell motherfucker to shut the fuck up cause he bunz.

Teacher come up again talking bout language an how she tryin to teach.

Yeah, I *know* that. What you think I come here for? I axe her. I tryin to get my eh-ju-ma-kay-tion. I tell her to quit beastin on me, an give me my snack. I axe her can I get some juice, my throat is dry, she don't say nothin.

FINE.

She don't like me. I can tell. Fine. I don't like her neither. I tell her, I DON'T LIKE YOU.

I go to the back where the teacher desk is and there's a cell phone sittin there, so I pick it up cause I always got people to call. But the keys is locked. She's telling me to put it down, like I'm gonna steal it or somethin. And she's saying it again about leavin and how she's tryin to teach, but I don't see her doin nothin but yellin at me and gettin all up in my business.

They got a microwave in this classroom and everything and I go look at it. To see if there's any popcorn in there and then she is axing me do I need security. And I tell her go ahead. I LOVE SECURITY. She axe does she really have to call security and I say she don't have to do nothin, but if she *want* to call security, she can go head. Security probaly won't come anyway. They lazy. Anyway, all they do is take me outside say some shit an let me go. Security always let me go.

So then she tell somebody to go get security Right Now an I see these comfortable chairs near the teacher desk so I sit down.

Cause I like to be comfortable.

She says get up, I can't sit there. She says I don't belong here. So I say, YOU don't belong here. But it's time so I stand up an I reach inta my pocket—not that I'm needin the paper cause I got it memorized since I wrote it, an anyway it sposed to be spoke on the mic in the first place, not tacked onta some wack hallway bulletin board, an WHO GOT THE MIC NOW?! Ha, yeah. Who. Got. The Mic. Now.

You hearin me?

Ha.

If. I.

By *Nessa*.

If I was.

If I was a liquid.

If I was a liquid I be

Sierra Mist.

Clear an sweet with bubbles.

Spicin up your party.

Cool in a can.

Smooth in a cup.

But if you spill me, no need to mop up.

I'll be out. Risin, jumpin,

Evaporatin.

Nowhere for spilled mist to go

cept up.

ha.

who out there hearin that?

I *said*, you hearin that?

Sound nice on the mic, right?

Yeah. Well. *That* was what I was gonna. But I *don't*.

Cause she still sayin you dont, an I know she wont hear nothin til she shuts up bout the please leave call security shit, an starts respectin, an I standin an she still not respectin so I think I'll havta do somethin more for her to be respectin me so I yell boo in her face, an I grab that poem paper an this kicked Doritos bag I got in my pocket and I put em in the microwave and I turn up the dial high and it go right out into flames.

An she fast that teacher. She fast. She like run or leap or something. She O.D.'n now, screamin hey or somethin and then she openin the door and she take out that bag—with her bare hands—an she stomp on it. And all the kids are sayin, Oh shit, and laughin. An I laugh too. Cause I like to see people tryin to put out fires.

An she finish an look up to me an she sayin she don't know where security is but I am to leave. Right. Now.

An somebody say Oh shit.

An I look behind me an I see she didn get it all. She put out the bag, but she didn see the poem an maybe it fly out still burnin, cause some flames jumpin outta papers on her desk and she tryin to fast over there now and I stop laughin cause she comin through me to get to there and thinkin she can push me now and I say DON'T YOU TOUCH ME! Pushin me out the way an sayin go, get out NOW.

But I say DON'T YOU PUSH ME. And I take the other tack outta my pocket and I go like THIS. I get right up close to her face—she wasn't liking that, right?

You like my polish, right? I'm telling her, my nails is niiiiiiiice, right?

And I tell her to MIND HER BUSINESS. I say, DON'T TOUCH ME. You can't put me out like I'm some busted up bag full of crumbs. I. Don't. Like. You. What's your NAME? WHAS YOUR NAME? I DON'T LIKE YOU!

And somebody sayin FIRE.

An she get behind me someway sayin EVERYBODY OUT. An she spillin juice on the desk an slammin a coat down. An Malique run out, with a bang on the door yellin,

School burnin DOWN! Evybody DISmissed!

An evybody hollerin and grabbin they bookbags and booking out the door and bang, bang, banging on they way out. Cept me, cause I'm not leavin Til.

An the teacher she look up an she see me still here an she sayin GO. LEAVE. NOW.

An I'm saying CHILL. I go when I get it.

An she lookin at me now like I speakin some Chinese or shit an she say GET WHAT?!

MY SNACK.

I want my snack. Thas all.

MY snack. I heard you need a slip to get it. So, can I have one?

She starin at me and squintin an maybe it's cause some smoke has started risin an maybe it's makin it hard to be seein me. An the smoke has started cause the pretty green papers is catchin an my fire be startin up the wall now. She see that an turn to it like she don't believe what she seein an her eyes are all big and startin to water like thas all she got left to battle this fire with now that the juice is spilled. She kinda frozen, an she lookin at the wall but she axin me, like in a whisper, one more time, *what?*

God. Damn. Whas wrong with her hearin?

MY PERMISSION SLIP. SO. I. CAN. BE. LONG. IN. HERE.

God.

What you think I want?

But she never answer me, cause somebody done pull the alarm an the room filled with a loud louder than anything. Bunches a teachers an mister Principal they rushin in here now, with extinguishers, seein the desk an the flames but not me cause I am a surge cloud. An I walkin out the door, through the hall, down the stairs, an security rushin past me up em, not seein me cause I am invisible. An I come down here right to security's desk where nobody's at. Could walk out the front door. Fire department not gonna stop me from goin nowhere.

But I'm gonna wait right here. Sittin in the comfy chair, at this empy desk, til security come back. I got plenty a time an this mic for the PA. Thas *Public Address*, for real, but this NOT your principal speakin.

This. Is. Nessa. An today I didn do nothin.

I'm jus a surge cloud, thas all.

7

How to Become a Writer

Lorrie Moore

FIRST, TRY TO be something, anything, else. A movie star/astronaut. A movie star/missionary. A movie star/kindergarten teacher. President of the World. Fail miserably. It is best if you fail at an early age—say, fourteen. Early, critical disillusionment is necessary so that at fifteen you can write long haiku sequences about thwarted desire. It is a pond, a cherry blossom, a wind brushing against sparrow wing leaving for mountain. Count the syllables. Show it to your mom. She is tough and practical. She has a son in Vietnam and a husband who may be having an affair. She believes in wearing brown because it hides spots. She'll look briefly at your writing, then back up at you with a face blank as a donut. She'll say: "How about emptying the dishwasher?" Look away. Shove the forks in the fork drawer. Accidentally break one of the freebie gas station glasses. This is the required pain and suffering. This is only for starters.

In your high school English class look only at Mr. Killian's face. Decide faces are important. Write a villanelle about pores. Struggle. Write a sonnet. Count the syllables: nine, ten, eleven, thirteen. Decide to experiment with fiction. Here you don't have to count syllables. Write a short story about an elderly man and woman who accidentally shoot each other in the head, the result of an inexplicable malfunction of a shotgun which appears mysteriously in their living room one night. Give it to Mr. Killian as your final project. When you get it back, he has written on it: "Some of your images are quite nice, but you have no sense of plot." When you are home, in the privacy of your own room, faintly scrawl in pencil beneath his black-inked comments: "Plots are for dead people, pore-face."

Take all the babysitting jobs you can get. You are great with kids. They love you. You tell them stories about old people who die idiot deaths. You sing them songs like "Blue Bells of Scotland," which is their favorite. And when they are in their pajamas and have finally stopped pinching each other, when they are fast asleep, you read every sex manual in the house, and wonder how on earth anyone could ever do those things with someone they truly loved. Fall asleep in a chair reading Mr. McMurphy's *Playboy*. When the McMurphys come home, they will tap you on the shoulder, look at the magazine in your lap, and grin. You will want to die. They will ask you if Tracey took her medicine all right. Explain, yes, she did, that you promised her a story if she would take it like a big girl and that seemed to work out just fine. "Oh, marvelous," they will exclaim.

Try to smile proudly.

Apply to college as a child psychology major.

As a child psychology major, you have some electives. You've always liked birds. Sign up for something called "The Ornithological Field Trip." It meets Tuesdays and Thursdays at two. When you arrive at Room 134 on the first day of class, everyone is sitting around a seminar table talking about metaphors. You've heard of these. After a short, excruciating while, raise your hand and say diffidently, "Excuse me, isn't this Birdwatching One-oh-one?" The class stops and turns to look at you. They seem to have one face—giant and blank as a vandalized clock. Someone with a beard booms out, "No, this is Creative Writing." Say: "Oh—right," as if perhaps you knew all along. Look down at your schedule. Wonder how the hell you ended up here. The computer, apparently, has made an error. You start to get up to leave and then don't. The lines at the registrar this week are huge. Perhaps your creative writing isn't all that bad. Perhaps it is fate. Perhaps this is what your dad meant when he said, "It's the age of computers, Francie, it's the age of computers."

Decide that you like college life. In your dorm you meet many nice people. Some are smarter than you. And some, you notice, are dumber than you. You will continue, unfortunately, to view the world in exactly these terms for the rest of your life.

The assignment this week in creative writing is to narrate a violent happening. Turn in a story about driving with your Uncle Gordon and another one about two old people who are accidentally electrocuted when they go to turn on a badly wired desk lamp. The teacher will hand them back to you with comments: "Much of your writing is smooth and energetic. You have, however, a ludicrous notion of plot." Write another story about a man and a woman who, in the very first paragraph, have their lower torsos accidentally blitzed away by dynamite. In the second paragraph, with the insurance money, they buy a frozen yogurt stand together. There are six more paragraphs. You read the whole thing out loud in class. No one likes it. They say your sense of plot is outrageous and incompetent. After class someone asks you if you are crazy.

Decide that perhaps you should stick to comedies. Start dating someone who is funny, someone who has what in high school you called a "really great sense of humor" and what now your creative writing class calls "self-contempt giving rise to comic form." Write down all of his jokes, but don't tell him you are doing this. Make up anagrams of his old girlfriend's name and name all of your socially handicapped characters with them. Tell him his old girlfriend is in all of your stories and then watch how funny he can be, see what a really great sense of humor he can have.

Your child psychology adviser tells you you are neglecting courses in your major. What you spend the most time on should be what you're majoring in. Say yes, you understand.

In creative writing seminars over the next two years, everyone continues to smoke cigarettes and ask the same things: "But does it work?" "Why should we care about this character?" "Have you earned this cliché?" These seem like important questions. On days when it is your turn, you look at the class hopefully as they scour your mimeographs for a plot. They look back up at you, drag deeply and then smile in a sweet sort of way.

You spend too much time slouched and demoralized. Your boyfriend suggests bicycling. Your roommate suggests a new boyfriend. You are said to be self-mutilating and losing weight, but you continue writing. The only happiness you have is writing something new, in the middle of the night, armpits damp, heart pounding, something no one has yet seen. You have only those brief, fragile, untested moments of exhilaration when you know: you are a genius. Understand what you must do. Switch majors. The kids in your nursery project will be disappointed, but you have a calling, an urge, a delusion, an unfortunate habit. You have, as your mother would say, fallen in with a bad crowd.

Why write? Where does writing come from? These are questions to ask yourself. They are like: Where does dust come from? Or: Why is there war? Or: If there's a God, then why is my brother now a cripple?

These are questions that you keep in your wallet, like calling cards. These are questions, your creative writing teacher says, that are good to address in your journals but rarely in your fiction.

The writing professor this fall is stressing the Power of the Imagination. Which means he doesn't want long descriptive stories about your camping trip last July. He wants you to start in a realistic context but then to alter it. Like recombinant DNA. He wants you to let your imagination sail, to let it grow big-bellied in the wind. This is a quote from Shakespeare.

Tell your roommate your great idea, your great exercise of imaginative power: a transformation of Melville to contemporary life. It will be about monomania and the fish-eat-fish world of life insurance in Rochester, N.Y. The first line will be "Call me Fishmeal," and it will feature a menopausal suburban husband named Richard, who because he is so depressed all the time is called "Mopey Dick" by his witty wife Elaine. Say to your roommate: "Mopey Dick, get it?" Your roommate looks at you, her face blank as a large Kleenex. She comes up to you, like a buddy, and puts an arm around your burdened shoulders. "Listen, Francie," she says, slow as speech therapy. "Let's go out and get a big beer."

The seminar doesn't like this one either. You suspect they are beginning to feel sorry for you. They say: "You have to think about what is happening. Where is the story here?"

The next semester the writing professor is obsessed with writing from personal experience. You must write from what you know, from what has happened to you. He wants deaths, he wants camping trips. Think about what has happened to you. In three years there have been three things: you lost your virginity; your parents got divorced; and your brother came home from a forest 10 miles from the Cambodian border with only half a thigh, a permanent smirk nestled into one corner of his mouth.

About the first you write: "It created a new space, which hurt and cried in a voice that wasn't mine, 'I'm not the same anymore, but I'll be O.K.'"

About the second you write an elaborate story of an old married couple who stumble upon an unknown land mine in their kitchen and accidentally blow themselves up. You call it: "For Better or for Liver-wurst."

About the last you write nothing. There are no words for this. Your typewriter hums. You can find no words.

At undergraduate cocktail parties, people say, "Oh, you write? What do you write about?" Your roommate, who has consumed too much wine, too little cheese and no crackers at all, blurts: "Oh, my god, she always writes about her dumb boyfriend."

Later on in life you will learn that writers are merely open, help-less texts with no real understanding of what they have written and therefore must half-believe anything and everything that is said of them. You, however, have not yet reached this stage of literary criti-cism. You stiffen and say, "I do not," the same way you said it when someone in the fourth grade accused you of really liking oboe lessons and your parents really weren't just making you take them.

Insist you are not very interested in any one subject at all, that you are interested in the music of language, that you are interested in—in—syllables, because they are the atoms of poetry, the cells of the mind, the breath of the soul. Begin to feel woozy. Stare into your plastic wine cup.

"Syllables?" you will hear someone ask, voice trailing off, as they glide slowly toward the reassuring white of the dip.

Begin to wonder what you do write about. Or if you have anything to say. Or if there even is such a thing as a thing to say. Limit these thoughts to no more than 10 minutes a day, like sit-ups, they can make you thin.

You will read somewhere that all writing has to do with one's genitals. Don't dwell on this. It will make you nervous.

Your mother will come visit you. She will look at the circles under your eyes and hand you a brown book with a brown briefcase on the cover. It is entitled: "How to Become a Business Executive." She has also brought the "Names for Baby" encyclopedia you asked for; one of your characters, the aging clown-schoolteacher, needs a new name. Your mother will shake her head and say: "Francie, Francie, remember when you were going to be a child psychology major?"

Say: "Mom, I like to write."

She'll say: "Sure you like to write. Of course. Sure you like to write."

Write a story about a confused music student and title it: "Schubert Was the One with the Glasses, Right?" It's not a big hit, although your roommate likes the part where the two violinists accidentally blow themselves up in a recital room. "I went out with a violinist once," she says, snapping her gum.

Thank god you are taking other courses. You can find sanctuary in 19th-century ontological snags and invertebrate courting rituals. Certain globular mollusks have what is called "Sex by the Arm." The male octopus, for instance, loses the end of one arm when placing it inside the female body during intercourse. Marine biologists call it "Seven Heaven." Be glad you know these things. Be glad you are not just a writer. Apply to law school.

From here on in, many things can happen. But the main one will be this: You decide not to go to law school after all, and, instead, you spend a good, big chunk of your adult life telling people how you decided not to go to law school after all. Somehow you end up writing again. Perhaps you go to graduate school. Perhaps you work odd jobs and take writing courses at night. Perhaps you are working and writing down all the clever remarks and intimate personal confessions you hear during the day. Perhaps you are losing your pals, your acquaintances, your balance.

You have broken up with your boyfriend. You now go out with men who, instead of whispering "I love you," shout: "Do it to me, baby." This is good for your writing.

Sooner or later you have a finished manuscript more or less. People look at it in a vaguely troubled sort of way and say, "I'll bet becoming a writer was always a fantasy of yours, wasn't it?" Your lips dry to salt. Say that of all the fantasies possible in the world, you can't imagine being a writer even making the top 20. Tell them you were going to be a child psychology major. "I bet," they always sigh, "you'd be great with kids." Scowl fiercely. Tell them you're a walking blade.

Quit classes. Quit jobs. Cash in old savings bonds. Now you have time like warts on your hands. Slowly copy all of your friends' addresses into a new address book.

Vacuum. Chew cough drops. Keep a folder full of fragments.

An eyelid darkening sideways.

World as conspiracy.

Possible plot?

A woman gets on a bus.

Suppose you threw a love affair and nobody came.

At home drink a lot of coffee. At Howard Johnson's order the coleslaw. Consider how it looks like the soggy confetti of a map: where you've been, where you're going—"You Are Here," says the red star on the back of the menu.

Occasionally a date with a face blank as a sheet of paper asks you whether writers often become discouraged. Say that sometimes they do and sometimes they do. Say it's a lot like having polio.

"Interesting," smiles your date, and then he looks down at his arm hairs and starts to smooth them, all, always, in the same direction.

8

THE DEAD SISTER HANDBOOK:
A Guide for Sensitive Boys
(Laconic Method to Near Misses)

Kevin Wilson

LACONIC METHOD: Developed by dead sisters in the early 1900s, this method of self-preservation consists of internally processing thoughts and feelings and distilling their essence to one, two, or, at most, three words, which are then made audible. It has since gained immense popularity amongst all adolescents, but is still most expertly practiced by the dead sister. You find your sister in your room one afternoon. She is curled up in the fetal position on the floor. You ask her if she is okay and she is silent, her eyes closed. Finally, she answers, "I don't know." You ask if you can stay with her. "Whatever," she says. You lie silently beside her until dinner. When you sit down to eat, your mother asks what the two of you have been up to. You are about to tell a complicated, easily uncovered lie, when you hear your sister's voice. "Nothing," she says. "Nothing," you then say, and your sister smiles and nods her approval.

LACROSSE: All dead sisters play sports that require sticks—field hockey, ice hockey, etc. (*see also* Sports and Leisure). Dead sisters are aggressive on the field to the point that it is troublesome to sensitive boys. Come game time, the day-to-day boredom of the dead sister, heavy-lidded, gives way to punishing checks, angry shouts after every goal, cups of Gatorade thrown to the ground and stomped on. When you remember your sister, she is red-faced and angry, racing down the field, eager to cause a commotion.

LAST MEAL, PREPARATION OF: The last meal of the dead sister is always burnt (*see also* Arson, Minor and Major Cases of). The dead sister puts something in the oven, goes to watch TV, falls asleep, and awakens to the fire alarm and smoking, charred food. This action provides the sensitive boy with a sensory-triggered memory with which to alter his subsequent life experiences. Smoke precedes the death of something. A girlfriend (*see also* Look-Alikes) burns a pan of snickerdoodles and the smell reminds you of that night, when you ran downstairs to investigate the reason for the insistent beeping of the fire alarm. Your sister is staring into the oven, smoke spilling around her, and she retrieves, with her oven-mitted hand, a single slice of cinnamon toast, burnt to black. When she sees you in the doorway of the kitchen, she smiles, takes a bite of the toast, and forces it down. She smiles again and this time her teeth are flecked with black bits of ash and bread. This is one of the last memories you will have of your sister and when your girlfriend reacts disapprovingly to your insistence on eating the burnt cookies after she has thrown them in the garbage, you know she will not be your girlfriend for much longer.

LEGACIES (ALSO KNOWN AS THE DEAD SISTORY): The family tree of the dead sister is filled with unbranching limbs, categorized by several unusual, untimely deaths occurring exclusively to females.

Your great-aunt broke her neck diving into a shallow pond and drowned. Your great-great-grandmother was sleepwalking through the woods beyond her house only seventeen days after the birth of your great-grandfather and was attacked and killed by a bear. Your aunt was smothered in her crib by the family cat before she was a month old. The generational duration of the Dead Sistory is unknown and, by most accounts, unceasing.

LIGHTNING, NEARLY STRUCK BY: In the days before death occurs, the heavy deposits of fate inside the dead sister's body serve as a conduit for the discharge of atmospheric electricity. In 27 percent of cases, the dead sister is actually struck by lightning, though never resulting in death. It is raining and your sister was supposed to be home hours ago (*see also* Midnight Equation). You hear the sound of rocks tapping the window and when you look out, there is your sister, soaking wet, her index finger held against her lips. You are to unlock the bathroom window upstairs, which is near the wooden trellis that runs up the wall. You sneak over to the bathroom, unlock the window, and wait. There is a flash of lightning and then a clap of thunder that follows almost instantly. You still cannot see your sister. You think you should go outside, but it is raining and you are afraid to wake your parents. Fifteen minutes later, your sister climbs into the bathroom. She smells of burnt sugar. When you ask what happened, she says nothing, walks into her room, and shuts the door. The next morning, you go out to the yard and there is the imprint of her shoes burned into the grass. It will stay there for several weeks after her death, and it will surprise you every time you look out your window.

LOCATION OF DIARY: Diary of dead sister (*see also* Papers and Correspondence) is always located in the empty shoebox of her favorite pair of shoes, covered by old quizzes from junior high (*see also* Above-Average Intelligence But Could Have Done So Much Better If She'd Really Applied Herself). This must be found before parents discover its presence. The best time to recover the diary is during the reception that follows the funeral. You will ask to be alone for a little while and everyone will allow this, considering all you've been through. Go into dead sister's room and retrieve diary. Scan quickly for mention of your name, which is rare and, with few exceptions, without incident (*see also* Make Hands). Learn things you had always assumed but had hoped were not true (*see also* Belief That No One Understands Her and She Wishes She Could Go Far Away and Live Her Own Life; Drugs and Alcohol, Abuse of; Sexual Contact with Boys; Sexual Contact with Girls; Suicide, Poetry About). Dispose of diary so no one else can read it.

LOOK-ALIKES: Sensitive boys will encounter between four and eleven women who resemble the dead sister. Do not, under any circumstances, attempt to talk to these women, follow them down crowded city streets, or pay them money in exchange for sexual favors. Nothing good can come from this.

LOSS OF BLOOD: Dead sisters are obsessed with the creation and preservation of slight, imperceptible wounds. This can be attained by several highly effective methods including: a needle and a com-position book; a razor blade and tissue paper; a syringe and glass vials; and a penknife and cotton balls. One night, while your sister is sleeping over at a friend's house (*see also* Sexual Contact with Girls), you rummage through her closet. You find a box filled with daily calendars for the past six years. You pick up the oldest of the calen-dars, and when you look at January 1st, you see a rusty, reddish smudge of what could be blood inside the square for that date. The entire month of January is marked off the same way. The drops of blood in June of that year are slightly darker in such an imperceptible way that you must flip back and forth between the pages of the calendar to be sure. In the most recent calendar, you look at the day's date and see a dark red, almost purple, drop of your sister's blood. You stare so closely at every page, every drop of blood, that even after you have returned the box to its hiding place and gone back to your room, even after you close your eyes for sleep, you can only see dot after dot of red swimming in front of your face. After her death, you try to continue to fill the days of the calendar with your own blood but your fingers begin to ache after three weeks and you have to give up.

LOSS OF CHILD: The sensitive boy secretly believes that his parents, if given the choice, would rather he had died instead of the dead sister. In 80 percent of cases, this is true.

LOVE APPLES: Food/drink invented by dead sister, derived from soaking peeled tomatoes in a jar of vodka for weeks at a time. Highly toxic and can cause death if consumed in large enough quantities. The alcohol-soaked tomatoes are placed in Ziploc bags and taken to school to be consumed during lunch, which allows dead sister to endure the last half of the school day. After news of sister's death is received, discover the jar of tomatoes and take them to your room. Hide in closet and eat every tomato. This will cause severe illness and an impaired mental state similar to mourning.

MAGIC, LACK OF: In the 1930s, the Wilmington Method of Sibling Resurrection gained popularity throughout the Deep South and in small pockets of the Midwest. This practice consisted of placing pennies over the entire body of the deceased. The living siblings then would place their hands on the body, warming the coins with their own heat which transferred to the dead body, causing reanimation. This method only worked when there were eleven or more living siblings participating in the procedure. No living witnesses to the successful practice of this method have ever been located or interviewed. The Tennessee Valley Brother–Sister Exchange and the Thirty-Seven-Day Lazarus Program have been scientifically discredited and outlawed in all fifty states.

MAKE HANDS: Term referring to practice performed by siblings, usually a younger brother and older sister less than four years apart, which involves kissing when no one is looking. Originates from when you and your sister, on a camping trip where you shared your own tent, began to kiss each other's hands to practice what you had seen on TV, moving lips softly against the open palm. Soon, this becomes actual kissing and, afterwards, when you want to do more of it, you will ask your sister if she wants to go and "make hands." This practice continues until sister determines that this is weird and should be stopped and never mentioned again. Due to unknown chemical reactions in the body, this practice causes at least one of the two parties to die within ten years of initial event.

MIDNIGHT EQUATION: Mathematical theorem developed in 1975 by feminist mathematician Deborah O'Nan. The age of the dead sister, the established parental curfew, and the exact time of death are plugged into the equation to reveal the exact moment when the dead sister could no longer safely return home, also known as the

Clock-Strike Point. The equation generally reveals a difference between the Clock-Strike Point and the time of death to be less than fifteen minutes.

MODES OF TRANSPORTATION: Death always occurs in relation to a train, airplane, motorcycle, sled, or, most commonly, automobile. In some cases, such as your own sister, it involves two modes of transportation. The car breaks down on tracks or tries to speed across tracks or is simply parked, waiting, on tracks as train approaches. If boyfriend is present (*see also* First Love; Name of Boyfriend), he will always survive. In 30 percent of the cases, boyfriend will be responsible for the accident (*see also* Altercations at Funeral).

MUSCLE SPASMS: Instinctual response by dead sister to spur body into maturity (*see also* Application of Makeup; Fake ID). Muscles absorb the body's surplus of sugar, nicotine, and pure grain alcohol, and, through intense spasms, speed up the aging process. Packs of ice must be applied weekly to the arms, legs, and chest to prevent overdevelopment.

NAIL-BITER: The sheaths that protect the upper end of the fingers of the dead sister contain small doses of tricyclic antidepressants (*see also* Attempts to Medicate). During stressful situations, the ingestion of the nails potentiates the action of catecholamines and creates a low-level sense of well-being and calm. The body of the dead sister builds up a tolerance to this effect within a few years of development but the instinctual response remains. In particularly bad moments, the dead sister will chew her nails down to the quick and into the flesh, leaving tiny crescents of blood on the papers of tests, the sleeves of her shirts, the skin of those she touches.

NAME OF BOYFRIEND: All boyfriends of dead sisters possess names that can be transposed. Dead sisters date boys named Thomas Alexander or Marcus Benjamin or James Maxwell. Years later, when you try to remember the boyfriend's name, you will switch the order each time. Alexander Thomas. Benjamin Marcus. This characteristic makes searching for them on the Internet incredibly difficult.

NAYSAYING: Act of refusing all evidence supporting the passing of the dead sister. A technique perfected by sensitive boys, this instinctual response is only effective for up to seventy-two hours after the time of death. The most common acts of naysaying include refusal to answer phone, the locking of doors to bar entrance of parents, the ingestion of substances (*see also* Love Apples), and the temporary loss of hearing and sight (*see also* Sensory Deprivation). The night after her death, you go into your sister's bedroom and take one of her T-shirts from the floor. You place this shirt over one of your pillows and hold it against you as you try to fall back to sleep. The shirt smells faintly of grass and smoke and lavender and everything else that makes up the only remaining elements of your sister. You breathe in the scents and though you cannot sleep, it staves off remembering; it keeps you from crying.

NEAR MISSES: Dead sisters have two to five incidents before actual death occurs when they could have died—overdoses, car accidents, appendicitis, and on and on and on (*see also* Lightning, Nearly Struck by). You and your sister are in a Ferris wheel at the state fair, sharing cotton candy and watching the lights of the fair brighten and dim with each revolution. As you nearly reach the top of the wheel and the machine grinds to a halt to allow the passengers at the bottom to disembark, the gate to your seat creaks, unlatches, and swings open. There is nothing but you and your sister and the distance between the sky and the earth. Your sister leans forward and peers over the edge. You hold tight to the seat and watch your sister inch closer and closer to the empty space, and though you want to say something, you are quiet. Just before the wheel resumes its movement, your sister finally sits back in the seat, leans her head against the metal grate and gazes at the sky until you reach the bottom. As the wheel stops, your sister steps out of the seat and runs into the murmuring crowd, leaving you alone, your pants wet, asking her to come back, not to leave, but she is already gone.

9

Interview with a Moron

Elizabeth Stuckey-French

SUBJECT: RICHARD MARSHALL LEE, feebleminded man, twenty-five years of age

INTERVIEWER: J. D. LEE, honors student at Purdue University, twenty-one years of age

On May 14, 1892, at approximately 9:03 a.m., Interviewer boarded the Wabash Special in Lafayette and rode to Logansport in order to conduct this interview. The train stopped at every unincorporated settlement between Lafayette and Logansport and twice ground to a halt in the middle of an empty field, backed up a short way, and then went forward again. The conductor offered no reasonable explanation for these unscheduled stops.

After inhaling coal dust for one hour and fifty-eight minutes on the train, Interviewer disembarked at the station in Logansport. There he hired a hack and endured a wild ride with an inebriated coach driver for another six and a half miles east to St. Bridget's Home for the Feebleminded. The cost of the round-trip train ticket and coach fare equaled exactly half of Interviewer's monthly food and entertainment allowance.

St. Bridget's Home for the Feebleminded is a large, handsome red brick building four stories high, not unlike Cary Quadrangle, the dormitory at Purdue University in which Interviewer currently resides. Interviewer, who had never before set foot in a home for the feebleminded, boldly entered through the front door and was directed into an office barely big enough for a desk and the large Sister sitting behind it.

Sister was drinking tea and eating a sugar cookie but did not offer Interviewer any sustenance after his forty-six-mile journey. Sister is missing her left front incisor and has a wattle hanging over her wimple.

Interviewer introduced himself to Sister as Subject's younger brother, J. D. Lee.

Sister, who'd been expecting Interviewer, rose from behind the desk to shake Interviewer's hand in a manly fashion. She expressed gratitude that someone from Subject's family had finally come to see him.

Interviewer nodded and did not reveal that he had come in order to satisfy a requirement for Dr. Ernest Grubb's Senior Psychology Seminar, a course that Interviewer was given special permission to take, in spite of the fact that he is only a junior.

Sister explained to Interviewer that Subject, although he had been informed of Interviewer's imminent arrival, had gone outside in order to stand in a hole. Sister reported that Subject often stands alone in this hole, located on the grounds behind the home, for hours on end. Sister smiled as if she found the idea of a grown man standing in a hole amusing.

She was asked why Subject stood in the hole but said she did not know. When asked if he had dug the hole himself, she said she did not know. When asked how long he'd been doing this, her reply was the same.

Sister should know more than she claims to know.

After this unhelpful exchange, Interviewer went outside onto the grounds, which are extensive and well maintained, having the appearance of a pleasant city park. Hardwood trees obscure the iron fence around the property. There are gravel paths that go round in circles and multiple beds of garish tulips.

It was a fine spring day on which there blew a pure breeze untainted by urban coal. Interviewer observed a number of inmates out taking the air—a young man with a thin beard sitting on a bench with his eyes closed and two men in heavy sweaters walking on a path. All three men appeared to be of normal intelligence but must not be, or they would not be in a home for the feebleminded.

Interviewer found Subject on the eastern edge of the grounds, standing in a hole approximately 1 meter deep and 2.5 meters in diameter.

Subject recognized Interviewer and called him by name, offering his hand, which Interviewer shook. Subject and Interviewer had not seen each other in two years; nevertheless, Subject did not feel the need to climb out of his hole. Subject remarked that Interviewer looked like an old man, which is not an accurate observation.

Subject himself looks much younger than his twenty-five years, which might be due to the fact that he has no cares in the world. All his needs are seen to, and he is treated like a child, allowed to stand in a hole for no purpose whenever he so desires and for as long as he so desires.

Subject was clean shaven, and despite the dirty hole in which he was standing, his heavy cotton shirt and loose trousers appeared to be neat, clean, and in good repair. Subject asserted that Interviewer was fat and that his cuffs were frayed. Both remarks are clearly inappropriate.

Interviewer asked Subject why he was standing in the hole, and he replied that standing thusly passed the time. When asked what he was looking at, Subject said that he watched whatever was in front of him. There appeared to be nothing in front of him, save some flowering bushes. When asked if he had dug the hole, he said that it had already been there but that he had made it deeper. When asked how long he'd been doing this, Subject said since he was a baby, which is a false statement. Subject has only been residing in this home for two years. Also, babies are unable to dig large holes.

When Interviewer pointed this out, Subject began talking about how he had recently invented a machine that shucks corn but said that he could not show it to Interviewer because he was afraid of his idea being stolen and he was, at present, unable to acquire a patent for his shucker.

Interviewer said he had no intention of stealing anything from Subject.

Subject brought up a time, many years ago, when both Interviewer and Subject were children, and Interviewer took a pocketknife from Subject's desk drawer.

Interviewer reminded Subject that he had simply borrowed the knife, but Subject replied, "Where is it, then?"

Of course Interviewer returned it long ago, has no idea of its present location, and cannot be expected to keep track of Subject's childhood possessions, and said as much to Subject, who did not appear to accept this explanation, as he shook his head and grimaced.

Subject's memory appears to be faulty.

Subject steadfastly refused to show corn-shucking invention to Interviewer but agreed to show him something else he had made instead. He swung himself nimbly out of the hole and walked across the grounds at an unnecessarily brisk pace. Interviewer struggled to keep up. Subject went directly to a telescope of premium quality sitting on a tripod beside the path. Subject claimed that it was his own telescope and that someone had given it to him as a gift.

Have not been able to confirm truth of Subject's claim.

Subject then directed Interviewer to look through the telescope, which was pointed at an object standing on the grass not fifteen meters away. According to Subject, the object under observation was of his own design, a sculpture he'd assembled in the recreation building. The object appeared to be a small heap of rusted metal that could easily be seen by the naked eye. No telescope was needed to view said object.

When asked the purpose of the object, Subject said that if Interviewer looked long enough at the object through the telescope, the purpose would become clear.

Interviewer asserted that he didn't have time to stand and gaze through an unnecessary telescope at an uninteresting and nearby object.

Subject countered that the meaning of the object was very profound but could not be put into words and that Interviewer would be sorry if he did not give it a try.

To humor Subject, Interviewer gazed through the telescope at the object. Interviewer counted thirteen nails and thirty-nine screws, which were fixed by a length of wire onto a section of iron pipe. As expected, no profound meaning yielded itself to Interviewer. He informed Subject that his experiment was a failure.

Subject responded by asking Interviewer if he'd seen a penny on the object.

Interviewer said no. Interviewer asked Subject if the meaning of the object was related to the penny.

Subject said no, and that furthermore, there was in actuality *no penny on the object.*

Interviewer then asked Subject why Subject had mentioned a penny if there was no penny.

Subject said that *many things were not on the object* and that this was the meaning of the object.

Interviewer reminded Subject that Subject had previously stated that the meaning could not be put into words but that he had just stated the meaning using words.

Subject said that Interviewer had misunderstood him. He had said that the *deeper* meaning could not be put into words.

Against his better judgment, Interviewer gazed again through the telescope at the object while Subject stood at his side.

Just then another Sister came along the path and asked Interviewer what he was watching through the telescope.

Interviewer stepped away from the telescope and assured Sister that he wasn't looking at anything.

This Sister was a young woman with a pretty face, not unlike the face of one Rosie McCarthy, who used to live in the house next door to Interviewer and Subject.

Sister said to Interviewer, "Oh, I know what you were looking at. Isn't it marvelous? We all find Richard's object very intriguing."

Unlike Rosie McCarthy, this Sister did not appear to have much common sense.

Sister and Subject smiled at each other in an unseemly manner.

Began to wonder if this home is best placement for Subject.

Was relieved when Sister walked off, apparently to attend to an unspecified errand.

Interviewer queried Subject as to whether he'd noticed the similarity between the Sister and Rosie McCarthy.

Subject insisted that the Sister actually is Rosie McCarthy, which is a false statement, as Rosie McCarthy is now Mrs. William Weigel of Battleground, Indiana.

Subject insisted that the two women are one and the same.

Interviewer, though in the right, let the matter drop.

Subject then asked Interviewer when he would be allowed to go back home.

Interviewer said that their parents were unable to take care of Subject any longer, because he needed such close supervision.

Subject protested, saying that as long as he had a hole and his object that he would never be a burden to anyone.

Interviewer was forced to go into the story of how Subject had strained the nerves and the health of his parents by misspending his youth in a variety of ways, including nailing clothing to walls and stealing animals. Reminded Subject of incident with organ-grinder's monkey. Reminded Subject of how their parents had worried and fretted over Subject's behavior and lavished attention on him, to the detriment of his sibling, whose stellar behavior had gone unnoticed and whose needs had gone unmet.

Subject demanded to know what stellar behavior Interviewer was referring to.

Reminded Subject of time when Subject, at twelve years of age, had climbed out the attic window onto the roof, and Interviewer, though only eight years old and terrified of heights, climbed out onto the roof to retrieve Subject, who sat blithely pulling up the edges of the shingles. Interviewer took Subject's hand and led him back across the roof, while Mrs. McCarthy screamed Dear God, Dear God from her yard below. Inside Mother wept and wept, saying she was sorry, she was so sorry she hadn't been watching Subject closely enough, and she would never let him out of her sight again. Mother had no reason to be sorry, in Interviewer's opinion, as she had done nothing wrong, but Interviewer knew better than to state his opinion, because nobody ever listened to anything he said. During and after this event, no one thanked Interviewer or even acknowledged his brave deed, and Subject was never punished.

Subject, who did not appear to be interested in this account of how Interviewer saved his life, again asked when he was going to go home, and whether or not anyone there still loved him, as they never wrote letters to him or came to visit.

Interviewer pointed out that *he* was there visiting right now.

Subject asked why the rest of the family hadn't come with Interviewer.

Interviewer reminded Subject that he now attends Purdue University and no longer lives at home and rarely sees their parents himself. Interviewer admitted that since he left for college he might as well have stepped off the earth, as far as their parents were concerned. He confessed that he had been glad to leave home, because after Subject was taken away Mother had turned into a mouse and Father had increased his drinking. Interviewer then surprised and embarrassed himself by suddenly blurting out that he had been lonely at home without Subject, as he had nobody to look after.

Subject, not seeming to appreciate or comprehend what he had just been told, asked again why Interviewer had not brought Mother and Father with him.

Interviewer inquired as to why he alone was not sufficient.

Subject said it was because Interviewer was a vile and wicked serpent.

Interviewer reminded Subject that he was the one who had just been crawling around in a filthy hole like a reptile.

Subject reached out and placed his hand on Interviewer's shoulder, stating that even though Interviewer was a silly, stupid, stubborn man, he pitied Interviewer.

Interviewer knocked Subject's hand away and said that the only reason he had come to see Subject was because he had been assigned by a professor to interview a moron.

Subject shoved Interviewer.

Interviewer shoved back.

Subject boxed Interviewer's ears, causing extreme pain.

Interviewer leapt on Subject, knocked him down, and sat on him, pinning Subject's arms as a safety precaution.

Subject, using his typical childish maneuver, sank his teeth into Interviewer's wrist and thus managed to wriggle free. Subject ran away laughing and yelling unprintable insults having to do with Rosie McCarthy.

Interviewer pursued Subject but was unable to catch him.

Interviewer was forced to terminate the interview and to take Subject's metal object with him.

On his way out of the home, Interviewer hid his bitten wrist in his pocket. He told the cookie-eating Sister in the office that Subject had hurried off to the recreation building, but before leaving had expressed satisfaction regarding a sudden inspiration for a new invention on which he wanted to start construction directly. Interviewer told Sister that Subject had given the object to him as a gift.

Object now sits on Interviewer's desk.

As of this time, no meaning has been derived by Interviewer from the object. Subject would undoubtedly say that it is because Interviewer is not looking at it properly through a telescope. Interviewer would respond to this by declaring that he will never purchase a telescope in order to gaze at the object. The purchase of a telescope in order to gaze at a pile of rubbish close enough to spit on is the act of a moron. Interviewer is certain that the object will never be seen more clearly than he is himself viewing it at the present moment.

However, as a last-ditch effort, and in order to be as fair and unbiased as possible, Interviewer took one of his own pennies, one that might have been spent on well-deserved pastries, and wired it onto the object. Interviewer then sat and studied the object for twelve minutes, to no avail. Subject's object, like Subject himself, remained stubbornly opaque and whimsical. This fact should come as no surprise to Interviewer. Interviewer has never known what to make of Subject, nor has he been able to decipher what makes Subject tick. Furthermore, he has never once been successful in his attempts to clearly communicate his own thoughts and feelings to Subject.

However, Interviewer is not one to give up easily. It is certain that when Interviewer next calls on Subject, Subject will no doubt be engaged in another activity of a pointless and selfish nature and, as no other person seems to want to shoulder the burden of attempting to make Subject face the truth about his actions, Interviewer will once again step into the breach.

On future visits, Interviewer will remain at all times objective. He regrets that he lost his temper and removed an object Subject apparently found to be important, even though it is ugly and useless.

If physically attacked, however, Interviewer retains the right to defend himself.

Interviewer is well aware that straightening Subject out will be a difficult feat to accomplish. As Dr. Grubb has said in his lectures, it is nigh on impossible to reason with a moron, and with that statement, Interviewer must heartily concur. His recent interview with Subject has demonstrated as much. In fact, all of Interviewer's experience with Subject has underscored the truth of this assertion. Dr. Grubb has also opined that morons are a corrupting influence on the rest of us, but I must differ with Dr. Grubb on this point.

My brother, Richard, as far as I can see, has never had any influence on anyone, most especially not on me. In fact, neither one of us has ever had any effect on the other.

For example: When Richard was fourteen and I was ten, he tried to enlist my aid in stealing an organ-grinder's monkey, telling me that the organ-grinder was abusing his monkey and that it would be better off living at our house. I told him that this was a very bad idea, and then I explained why. Stealing was stealing, I told him, and he could be arrested. If he was arrested, Mother and Father would be humiliated. Even if he was not arrested, we could never take care of a monkey in our home. There were too many breakables. Besides, we didn't know anything about the care and keeping of monkeys. Anyhow, I reasoned, the monkey might be perfectly happy capering about in a plaid bathrobe collecting coins in a silver cup. It was not up to us to judge whether or not a monkey was happy, even if we could. The monkey belonged to the organ-grinder. This should have been the end of the matter.

But with Richard there is never an end to the matter. Against all my counsel, Richard went downtown, distracted the organ-grinder, snatched the monkey, and ran away. He brought the little monkey, whom we named Willie, back to our house in a shoebox. We attempted to hide Willie in Richard's room, but the creature escaped and Mother caught him pulling the tail feathers out of her stuffed cockatoo. It was an extremely unpleasant day at the Lee house.

However, what I took away from this incident was not that I was right and that morons are incorrigible, and I do not recall that the incident ever created in me a desire to go forth and be wicked also. Nor do I dwell at all upon the upheaval and commotion that resulted from my brother's crime. Instead I remember how Richard, when the police finally arrived, clung desperately to Willie, who only wanted to escape his grasp. I cannot forget how Richard's face looked as he attempted to cuddle the ungrateful monkey to his chest like a ring-tailed baby and how I, forced to stand there and witness this spectacle, would've given anything, anything at all, if the beast would only cease its caterwauling and throw its arms around my brother, just for a little while, and love him back.

10

Reference #388475848-5

Amy Hempel

To Parking Violations Bureau, New York City
I am writing in reference to the ticket I was
issued today for "covering 'The Empire State'"
on my license plate. I include two photographs
I took this afternoon that show, front and back,
that the words "The Empire State" *are* clearly
visible. I noticed several cars on the same
block featuring these license plates on which
these words were entirely covered by the frame
provided by the car dealer, and I noticed that
none of these cars had been ticketed, as mine
had. I don't mean to appear insolent, but I am
wondering if the ticket might have been issued
by the young Hispanic guy I sometimes see
patrolling the double-parked cars during the
week? I ask because the other day my dog yanked
the leash from my hand and ran to him and jumped
up looking for a treat. He did not appear to be
comfortable around dogs, and though mine is a

friendly one, she's big, and maybe the guy was frightened for a moment? It happened as I was getting out of my car, so he would have known it was *my* car, is what I'm saying.

"The Empire State"—it occurred to me that this is a nick-name. I mean, police officers do not put out an all-points bulletin in The Empire State, they put an all-points bulletin in *New York*, which words are also clearly visible on my license plates. In fact, there is no information the government might require that is not visible on these plates. You could even say that the words "The Empire State" are *advertising*. They fit a standard definition: a paid announcement, a public notice in print to induce people to use something, the action of making that thing generally known, providing information of general interest. Close enough.

I have parked my car with the plates as they appear in the accompanying photos on New York City streets for five years, since I drove the car out of the dealership on the Island five years ago; it has never been a problem until now. (I bought the car without ever reading *Consumer Reports*. I checked with a friend who said the price I was quoted was a reasonable one, but that I should refuse the extended warranty the dealer was pushing. "I'm trying to do you a favor," the dealer said, pissed off.)

At the time I bought the car, I didn't know I

would soon be back living in the city, and hardly ever needing it. I had thought I would stay the two-hour drive east. What is the saying?—"If you want to make God laugh, tell him your plans."

I haven't kept track of everything I'm supposed to do with the car, but your records will show that I paid the ticket for my expired registration the same week it was issued. I did better with the safety inspection, and FYI, I'm good through November.

It's not really about the money, the $75 the ticket would cost me. I wouldn't mind writing a check for that amount as a donation to a Police Athletic League, or a fund to help rebuild the city. I'm not like the guy at the film festival yesterday who asked the French director in the Q and A after his film was shown, "Are we going to get our money back?" I hadn't even wanted to see the film; before we went, I told my date what I did want to see, and he said, "They stole the idea from that other one, the one where they ate each other." And I said, "No, that was the plane crash; this is the two guys who had the mountain-climbing accident. It's a documentary." And he said, "What isn't?"

Then, after the French film, after the audience applauded for this *major piece of crap*, the date and I cut out and went to a place he had heard about in the East Village for tea. It

115

turned out to be someone's exotic version of high tea, so instead of scones and clotted cream and cucumber sandwiches, we were each served a teaspoon of clear, rosemary-scented jelly with a single pomegranate seed inside! What came after that were these teensy cubes of polenta covered in grapefruit puree, all floating in a "bubble bath" of champagne. Then came a chocolate truffle the size of a tooth. The fellow and I were giddy. It was pouring outside, and when we left, after the tea ceremony, we didn't want to leave each other, so we walked another couple of blocks to see a second movie, one he wanted to see, and I didn't tell him I had already seen it because by that time I just wanted to sit next to him in the dark. "I wonder who that is singing," I whispered at one point in the sound track. He didn't know, but I did, from having read the credits the first time I saw the movie. "Kind of sounds like Dave Matthews," I said, knowing I was right. "Let's be sure to check at the end," I said. "I'd like to get it for you."

Music keeps you youthful. Like I'm not the target audience for the Verve, but this morning I put on that song that goes, "I'm a million different people from one day to the next—I can change, I can change . . ." and—what's my point? I was in a really good mood when I found the ticket on my windshield. Then how to get rid of the poison, like adrenaline, that flooded my system when I read what it was for?

There is a theory of healing based on animals in the wild. People have observed animals that barely escaped a predator, and they say these animals lie down and *shake*, and in so doing somehow release the trauma. Whereas human beings take it in; we don't work it out, so it lodges in us where it produces any number of nasty effects and symptoms. If you follow a kind of guided fantasy, supposedly you can locate a calm, still place inside you and practice visiting it over and over, and that's as far as I got with this theory. It's supposed to make you feel better.

Maybe I should sell the car. But there is something about being able to get in a car and *leave* when you want to, or need to, without waiting to get to a car rental agency if you even know where one is and if it is even open when you get there.

Like last week, after a guy grabbed my arm when I was running around the reservoir, when he was suddenly in front of me, coming from the trees on the south end of the track, and no one else was around just then and I couldn't swing around wide enough to get completely past him, and he grabbed my arm. I think it was my anger that made him finally release me, because that is what I felt, not fear, until I got back home with a sore throat from yelling at him to leave me the fuck alone. I was shaking like crazy, and it wouldn't stop, so I walked a block to where my car was parked, and I drove for a couple of hours to the ocean. My right leg was bouncing on the accelerator from nerves for much of the way, but I stopped for coffee and when I started up again I steered with my knees, the way *real* drivers steer, with a cup of coffee in one hand, playing the radio with the other. So maybe I am a wild animal, shaking off the trauma of near-capture.

There were actually two men at the reservoir. And I thought it was odd that when the first one grabbed me, and I reflexively swung my free arm around to sock him in the chest, the other man didn't stop me. Because he could have. He watched, and listened to me yell, so I don't know what the deal was. But I think it was worth paying the insurance and having to park the car and get this ticket to have the car there to use that day.

You could accuse me of trying to put a human face on this. And you would be correct. But is there anything wrong with that? Unless the ticket was issued by the guy my dog startled, I know it isn't personal. But I'm not a person who can take this ticket in stride with the kind of urbanity urbane people prize in each other. I feel I must question—and protest—this particular ticket.

I want what is fair. I don't want a fight. But the truth is, I'm shaking—right now, writing this letter. My hand is shaking while I write. It's saying what I can't say—this is the way I say it.

11

The Explanation

Donald Barthelme

Q: Do you believe that this machine could be helpful in changing the government?

A: Changing the government . . .

Q: Making it more responsive to the needs of the people?

A: I don't know what it is. What does it do?

Q: Well, look at it.

A: It offers no clues.

Q: It has a certain . . . reticence.

A: I don't know what it does.

■

Q: A lack of confidence in the machine?

■

Q: Is the novel dead?

A: Oh yes. Very much so.

Q: What replaces it?

A: I should think that it is replaced by what existed before it was invented.

Q: The same thing?

A: The same sort of thing.

Q: Is the bicycle dead?

■

Q: You don't trust the machine?

A: Why should I trust it?

Q: (States his own lack of interest in machines)

■

Q: What a beautiful sweater.

A: Thank you. I don't want to worry about machines.

Q: What do you worry about?

A: I was standing on the corner waiting for the light to change when I noticed, across the street among the people there waiting for the light to change, an extraordinarily handsome girl who was looking at me. Our eyes met, I looked away, then I looked again, she was looking away, the light changed. I moved into the street as did she. First I looked at her again to see if she was still looking at me, she wasn't but I was aware that she was aware of me. I decided to smile. I smiled but in a curious way—the smile was supposed to convey that I was interested in her but also that I was aware that the situation was funny. But I bungled it. I smirked. I dislike even the word "smirk." There was, you know, the moment when we passed each other. I had resolved to look at her directly in that moment. I tried but she was looking a bit to the left of me, she was looking fourteen inches to the left of my eyes.

Q: This is the sort of thing that—

A: I want to go back and do it again.

■

Q: Now that you've studied it for a bit, can you explain how it works?

A: Of course. (Explanation)

■

Q: Is she still removing her blouse?

A: Yes, still.

Q: Do you want to have your picture taken with me?

A: I don't like to have my picture taken.

Q: Do you believe that, at some point in the future, one will be able to achieve sexual satisfaction, "complete" sexual satisfaction, for instance by taking a pill?

A: I doubt that it's impossible.

Q: You don't like the idea.

A: No. I think that under those conditions, we would know less than we do now.

Q: Of course.

■

Q: It has beauties.

A: The machine.

Q: Yes. We construct these machines not because we confidently expect them to do what they are designed to do—change the government in this instance—but because we intuit a machine, out there, glowing like a shopping center . . .

A: You have to contend with a history of success.

Q: Which has gotten us nowhere.

A: (Extends consolation)

■

Q: What did you do then?

A: I walked on a tree. For twenty steps.

Q: What sort of tree?

A: A dead tree. I can't tell one from another. It may have been an oak. I was reading a book.

Q: What was the book?

A: I don't know, I can't tell one from another. They're not like films. With films you can remember, at a minimum, who the actors were . . .

Q: What was she doing?

A: Removing her blouse. Eating an apple.

Q: The tree must have been quite large.

A: The tree must have been quite large.

Q: Where was this?

A: Near the sea. I had rope-soled shoes.

■

Q: I have a number of error messages I'd like to introduce here and I'd like you to study them carefully . . . they're numbered. I'll go over them with you: undefined variable . . . improper sequence of operators . . . improper use of hierarchy . . . missing operator . . . mixed mode, that one's particularly grave . . . argument of a function is fixed-point . . . improper fixed-point constant . . . improper floating-point constant . . . invalid character transmitted in sub-program statement, that's a bitch . . . no END statement.

A: I like them very much.

Q: There are hundreds of others, hundreds and hundreds.

A: You seem emotionless.

Q: That's not true.

A: To what do your emotions . . . adhere, if I can put it that way?

Q: (Long explanation)

■

Q: Do you see what she's doing?

A: Removing her blouse.

Q: How does she look?

A: . . . Self-absorbed.

Q: Are you bored with the question-and-answer form?

A: I am bored with it but I realize that it permits many valuable omissions: what kind of day it is, what I'm wearing, what I'm thinking. That's a very considerable advantage, I would say.

Q: I believe in it.

■

Q: She sang and we listened to her.

A: I was speaking to a tourist.

Q: Their chair is here.

A: I knocked at the door; it was shut.

Q: The soldiers marched toward the castle.

A: I had a watch.

Q: He has struck me.

A: I have struck him.

Q: Their chair is here.

A: We shall not cross the river.

Q: The boats are filled with water.

A: His father will strike him.

Q: Filling his pockets with fruit.

■

Q: The face . . . the machine has a face. This panel here . . .

A: That one?

Q: Just as the human face developed . . . from fish . . . it's traceable, from, say, the . . . The first mouth was that of a jellyfish. I can't remember the name, the Latin name . . . But a mouth, there's more to it than just a mouth, a mouth alone is not a fact. It went on up through the sharks . . .

A: Up through the sharks . . .

Q: . . . to the snakes . . .

A: Yes.

Q: The face has *three* main functions, detection of desirable energy sources, direction of the locomotor machinery toward its goal, and capture . . .

A: Yes.

Q: Capture and preliminary preparation of food. Is this too . . .

A: Not a bit.

Q: The face, a face, also serves as a lure in mate acquisition. The broad, forwardly directed nose—

A: I don't see that on the panel.

Q: Look at it.

A: I don't—

Q: There is analogy, believe it or not. The . . . we use industrial designers to do the front panels, the controls. Designers, artists. To make the machines attractive to potential buyers. Pure cosmetics. They told us that knife switches were masculine. Men felt . . . So we used a lot of knife switches . . .

■

A: What's this one used for?

Q: It's part of the process. We had a lot of trouble with that one, the—

A: I know that a great deal has been written about all this but when I come across such articles, in the magazines or in a newspaper, I don't read them. I'm not interested. What are your interests? I'm a director of the Schumann Festival.

■

Q: What is she doing now?

A: Taking off her jeans.

Q: Has she removed her blouse?

A: No, she's still wearing her blouse.

Q: A yellow blouse?

A: Blue.

Q: Well, what is she doing now?

A: Removing her jeans.

Q: What is she wearing underneath?

A: Pants. Panties.

Q: But she's still wearing her blouse?

A: Yes.

Q: Has she removed her panties?

A: Yes.

Q: Still wearing the blouse?

A: Yes. She's walking along a log.

Q: In her blouse. Is she reading a book?

A: No. She has sunglasses.

Q: She's wearing sunglasses?

A: Holding them in her hand.

Q: How does she look?

A: Quite beautiful.

■

Q: You don't trust the machine?

A: Why should I trust it?

■

Q: What is the content of Maoism?

A: The content of Maoism is purity.

Q: Is purity quantifiable?

A: Purity has never been quantifiable.

Q: What is the incidence of purity worldwide?

A: Purity occurs in .004 per cent of all cases.

Q: What is purity in the pure state often consonant with?

A: Purity in the pure state is often consonant with madness.

Q: This is not to denigrate madness.

A: This is not to denigrate madness. Madness in the pure state offers an alternative to the reign of right reason.

Q: What is the content of right reason?

A: The content of right reason is rhetoric.

Q: And the content of rhetoric?

A: The content of rhetoric is purity.

Q: Is purity quantifiable?

A: Purity is not quantifiable. It *is* inflatable.

Q: How is our rhetoric preserved against attacks by other rhetorics?

A: Our rhetoric is preserved by our elected representatives. In the fat of their heads.

■

Q: There's no point in arguing that the machine is wholly successful, but it has its qualities. I don't like to use anthropomorphic language in talking about these machines, but there is one quality . . .

A: What is it?

Q: It's brave.

A: There's not much bravery in art now.

Q: Since the death of the bicycle.

■

Q: There are ten rules for operating the machine. The first rule is turn it on.

A: Turn it on.

Q: The second rule is convert the terms. The third rule is rotate the inputs. The fourth rule is you have made a serious mistake.

A: What do I do?

Q: You send the appropriate error message.

A: I will never remember these rules.

Q: I'll repeat them a hundred times.

A: I was happier before.

Q: You imagined it.

A: The issues are not real.

Q: The issues are not real in the sense that they are touchable. The issues raised here are equivalents. Reasons and conclusions exist although they exist elsewhere, not here. Reasons and conclusions are in the air and simple to observe even for those who do not have the leisure to consult or learn to read the publications of the specialized disciplines.

A: The situation bristles with difficulties.

Q: The situation bristles with difficulties but in the end young people and workers will live on the same plane as old people and government officials, for the mutual good of all categories. The phenomenon of masses, in following the law of high numbers, makes possible exceptional and rare events, which—

A: I called her then and told her that I had dreamed about her, that she was naked in the dream, that we were making love. She didn't wish to be dreamed about, she said—not now, not later, not ever, when would I stop. I suggested that it was something over which I had no control. She said that it had all been a long time ago and that she was married to Howard now, as I knew, and that she didn't want . . . irruptions of this kind. Think of Howard, she said.

■

Q: He has struck me.
A: I have struck him.
Q: We have seen them.
A: I was looking at the window.
Q: Their chair is here.
A: She sang and we listened to her.
Q: Soldiers marching toward the castle.
A: I spoke to a tourist.
Q: I knocked at the door.
A: We shall not cross the river.
Q: The river has filled the boats with water.
A: I think I have seen her with my uncle.

Q: Getting into their motorcar, I heard them.

A: He will strike her if he has lost it.

■

A (concluding): There's no doubt in my mind that the ballplayers today are the greatest ever. They're brilliant athletes, extremely well coordinated, tremendous in every department. The ballplayers today are so magnificent that scoring is a relatively simple thing for them.

Q: Thank you for confiding in me.

■

Q: . . . show you a picture of my daughter.

A: Very nice.

Q: I can give you a few references for further reading.

A: (Weeps)

■

Q: What is she doing now?

A: There is a bruise on her thigh. The right.

12

From *Letters to Wendy's*

Joe Wenderoth

July 3, 1996

Today I bought a small Frosty. This may not
seem significant, but the fact is: I'm lactose
intolerant. Purchasing a small Frosty, then,
is no different than hiring someone to beat
me. No different in essence. The only
difference, which may or may not be essential,
is that, during my torture, I am gazing upon
your beautiful employees.

July 5, 1996

Today there was no blood in my stool. The sun
was shining as I sat with my burger and Coke
and gazed out across the parking lot. Gazed—
there is the place where what is feels itself
slipping—with difficulty—into the fitful sleep
of replica. I did not gaze. I was the sleep
what is gazed through. One is confused,
though, having truly shit.

July 6, 1996

I was so high on Sudafed and whiskey today
that I couldn't eat. I got a Coke—actually
five Cokes, as I could refill for free. It's
times like this—dehydrated, exhausted, unable
to imagine home—that your plastic seats, your
quiet understandable room, set beside but not
quite overlooking the source of real value,
offer me a tragedy small enough to want to
endure.

July 10, 1996

The great thing about Wendy's—one of the
great things—is that no one ever has sex in
this space. It's like sex is too selfish an
activity to go on here. To be in Wendy's is to
understand that there can be no one other; it
is to disabuse oneself of that foolish hope,
and thereby resume the animal in its more
lonely, more mobbed mode of comportment.

July 11, 1996

The glamorous pictures of new items are
possessed of such a tiny energy. Massive
success accomplishes itself in tiny energy
growing tinier. What is it that chooses to
remain outside of this increasingly tiny
energy—can we even give a name to such a
freakish presence? The only time I love the

other customers is when they seem, above all,
to be eating.

July 12, 1996
I often think about over-eating. It's strange
that I never have. Each bite of my mustard-only
double-cheeseburger is so good that I reel in
the aftermath. The meaty goodness obliterates
my soul as much as it secures it. I am a bell,
incapable of vibrating. If I rang with any more
force I don't know that I would remain a bell—I
don't know that the air could stand me.

July 13, 1996
Today I was looking hard at Wendy. I felt like
a doctor. I felt like Wendy was very ill, and
no one could see it but me. That smile is the
smile of a sexy girl who is well taken care
of, but care, as we all know, is a relatively
new hobby, and Wendy is already moving outside
of its novelty. I like to dream that she will
come to me for futile treatments.

July 14, 1996
It's amazing how I recognize the parking lot
but do not recognize the parking lot's power
to make customers appear. How is it that this
place remains unfulfilled by its sudden
natives? And why these natives, and not those?
And what homeland allows them to arrive so

completely oblivious to the constant violence
of various similar orders following one
another into merely wanting words?

July 16, 1996
Today I bought a salad just to look at it,
smell it, rub it on my face. Again I'm feeling
like a doctor, but now the feeling is
clearer—I feel like an ancient doctor, with
ancient ideas about what need be done. I asked
the register-girl if it would be possible to
have small holes drilled into my skull so that
good strong coffee could be poured down on to
my brain.

July 17, 1996
It feels good to be punched in the face, but
only for an instant. This is what I was
thinking as I sat in this afternoon's empty
dining room. Then my mind wandered and I
imagined Wendy was in my car with me. She
said, "I'd like you to take your fat tongue and
run it from my asshole to my clit over and
over again." I said, "I'd like you to punch me
in the face." Thus it ran, the empty dining
room filling.

July 18, 1996
Today I felt like a cup of soda that had been
sitting—full—for too long. Watery, sides

melting, barely able to be handled—but there,
so very very there, and simply demanding
proper disposal. It is my suspicion that,
however persuasive that demand, there can be
no such thing.

July 24, 1996
I was thinking today of the beatings my mother
used to give me. I came to enjoy them very
early on, and to take them silently, adoringly.
Since then I have come to equate silence with
extreme pleasure. But that silence was never
silence, really. It was a kind of awful
familiar music piped in from nowhere at the
least possible volume. Like here, today.

July 25, 1996
Often, on a very hot day, Wendy's is quite
cool. Almost cold. I have become aware of the
fact that we take leisurely walks in a raging
fire. There is some pleasure in blatant self-
destruction but shelter is a newer and deeper
pleasure—one not yet frilly. At Wendy's, we
begin to fathom the fact: the fire makes us
cold, finally, and fills us with the inadequacy
of pleasure, the pleasure of inadequacy.

July 27, 1996
So many drive-through people. Of course, there
is really no such thing as driving through—one

drives by. And who would drive by a Wendy's?
Who would be so ridiculous as to assume that
he could simply extract what he needs from a
visit without actually making the visit,
without standing awhile inside the blessed
delusion of a manned source? How fast the dead
learn to bury the dead.

July 29, 1996
I sort of recognize your employees, but not
so much as you'd think. I believe they
recognize me. When I think about it, the
faces that really stay etched in my mind are
the faces of porn stars. Only in porn, it
seems, does a face acquire the peculiar glow
of its ownmost rhythmic ambiguity. It's sad
to every day come to Wendy's and see faces
that will never be given to me in their full
porn depth.

July 31, 1996
Your employees are beautiful—they do not have
authority. Even the manager has no authority—
if pushed, he will just call someone, who also
has no ultimate authority. It's extremely
pleasing to recognize this fact—one feels so
fairly situated in the teeming absence of
authors. At Wendy's, one writes not from an
author, but to an author, a sleeping owner who
will never wake.

September 2, 1996

I love the cleanliness of a Wendy's. Such a clean is not in any sense a banishing of genitalia; it is the creation of a quiet bright mind-space that allows for the deliciousness of genitalia to become obvious. I look out over the colorful clean tables and the pretty food posters and *I like people* again; each has a dick and balls, or a cunt and titties, which, clean, are simply enjoyable.

September 14, 1996

Last night I dreamt that I pissed on Wendy's head. I entered the restroom, approached the urinal, and started pissing, when suddenly I realized it was not a urinal at all . . . but Wendy. As I began to protest (to the dream itself) I understood that I *must have* known it was her. I felt ashamed, yet wronged. I also felt like the only thing I ever wanted to happen was finally happening.

September 20, 1996

Today I had a Biggie. Usually I just have a small, and refill. Why pay more? But today I needed a Biggie inside me. Some days, I guess, are like that. Only a Biggie will do. You wake up and you know: today I will get a Biggie and I will put it inside me and I will feel

better. One time I saw a guy with three
Biggies at once. One wonders not about him but
about what it is that holds us back.

September 21, 1996
If I had to say what Wendy really was—if
she had to be one thing instead of a field
of various energies—I think I'd have to say
that she was a penis. Something about her face
and the shape of her hair, the muffled red
coherence of head and torso, and perhaps too
her lack of arms and legs. A penis is found in
just such a lack of limbs; it's really amazing
when it arrives anywhere.

November 15, 1996
A beautiful woman with a Biggie. Nothing else—
just a Biggie. She sat alone; she seemed like
she was waiting for someone. What lucky soul
could make a beautiful woman with a Biggie
wait? Who has that kind of power? What person
would a beautiful woman with a Biggie find
attractive? Only one answer made sense to me:
another beautiful woman with a Biggie.

January 4, 1997
It's wonderful to think of meat sculpted to
resemble a penis, but it's a different thing
to actually have it on your plate. So long as
it's an idea, you can lick it, kiss it, without

feeling strange. Its actually being meat
is something the *idea* seems incapable of
entertaining. That is, while the idea allows
for a wonderful semblance, it forever infuses
the necessary *biting and chewing* with
unnecessary sadness.

March 26, 1997
Shall I put my penis on the counter? But
what would it really accomplish? Would it
change the world? Would it change me, or the
attendant employees? No, no, and no. But
should we judge an activity by whether or
not it *changes* something? That would imply
evolution as pre-determined and full of
specific purpose. My penis on the counter
is resistance; it demonstrates evolution's
indeterminate willfulness.

13

This Is Just to Say That I'm Tired of Sharing an Apartment with William Carlos Williams

Laura Jayne Martin

Will, you are a dick. You're goddamn right I was saving those plums for breakfast.

Fine, it's not like they're my favorite food in the world, but I mean, they're a seasonal fruit, you scumbag. Buy your own food for a change. All you do is sit around the house all day writing about red wheelbarrows and junk.

This is like the millionth time I've come home to an empty fridge. And no, leaving a note does not cut it anymore. I don't care if you put one of your idiotic poems on there. I grind my fingers to the bone all day. I'm a stenographer—that's serious work. I type over 250 words per minute!

If I find one more note taped to the bathroom mirror with some garbage like this . . .

this is just to say
I am sorry
I used
your toothpaste

it's all gone
and I
have gingivitis
there's some
raspberry
floss left under
the cabinet but
it's gross
and expired

. . . I'm going to break your face.

I type over 250 words per minute! And do you know what I've never typed: a metrically irregular poetic apology on the back of a Rite Aid receipt. You went to Rite Aid! Why didn't you buy more toothpaste? Or you could have bought some more plums, or Pop Tarts, or something. We needed sponges.

All you ever get is popcorn. Who buys copious amounts of unsalted, unbuttered popcorn? It's messed up. I'd be better off eating one of your stupid stepped triadic "masterpieces" taped up around this apartment.

While I'm at it, let's just air it all out. This has really stuck in my craw since the moment it happened. You can't just sleep with someone else's girlfriend and then tape a note to her that says . . .

this is just to say
I drank
all the beer
and then
you were probably
asleep

while I banged Suzanne
but don't worry
Phil Collins' greatest
hits were
on all night.

How does playing Phil Collins while you and my girlfriend cheat on me make anything better? It's sick. I haven't even listened to him since *Testify*! That was '97, Will!

I can't take it anymore—you eat all my produce, use all the tooth-paste, sleep with my girlfriend, and I just sprained my ankle on another empty popcorn tin. What kind of a person does these things to a notary public? Who still buys things in tins? Are you sending away for this popcorn, Will?

Things have devolved, real bad. FYI, I'm subletting your room and I'm turning you in for grand theft auto and destruction of public prop-erty. Our neighbors—the ones with the borzois—found a lime green Dodge Durango parked upside down in their sun room yesterday morning. Apparently, the suspect fled the scene of the crime, but there was a note taped to the window on which "someone" had scrawled . . .

this is just to say
I am all right
I left
the owner's
number here
although
I stole his cell phone
so he
will not be

picking up
his lime green Dodge
Durango
whoops my bad.

Newsflash, dirtbag: they don't serve plums in prison!

14

Single Woman for Long Walks on the Beach

Ron Carlson

Looking for a young woman for the chance to exchange introductory remarks and help on homework, particularly math and social studies, perhaps the term project, the triptych display about continental drift, share pencils, markers, erasers (including all those in the shapes of animals), and lunch, with the possibility of swapping the store-bought Aunt Dorothy's Bigrolls for homemade tomato sandwiches stuffed with slices of sharp cheddar, merging our potato chips on a paper plate, talking about our childhood until the bell rings, keeping this up—lunching—both in the cafeteria and on the front steps of the school, until laughing one day we decide to skip quickly away in my car, a lark, that's what we'd share is this lark, driving the strange day-time streets while all our classmates suffer under the confused rule of Mrs. Delmanrico and her versions of what happened when the great land masses first pulled apart, finally ending up at the Blue Bird Drive-in, empty in the late afternoon, and sharing two malts, the strawberry and the vanilla, the feeling encircling us certainly something, but not something easily identifiable or given a name, just something new, and in that place, decided to try for the Senior Prom, laughing at it in fun—what a goofy, schoolboy thing to do—but also laughing from that feeling and, well, joy, and in two weeks, after another set of lunches, sharing the Senior Prom, including me picking you up in my freshly washed Bel Air, and meeting your mother and your sister, your sister really giving me the once-over, and you in a dress that is actually pink, believably pink, a pink that rescues that color once and for all, and then dancing at the Prom, our first touch really, carefully committed in the old gymnasium, visiting with your friends and some of my friends, and dancing and sharing then the long walk to the car, but knowing as we felt the night air fall on our warm faces as we left the building that everything has changed now and the feeling we had at the Blue Bird Drive-in has now become a real thing we still don't have a name for, but we are forever different in the car, talking now about college, not kissing, afraid to really, talking about the future and pledging to write to each other when we go away to college, which we will do, daily, handwritten letters, full of the heartbreaking news of classes, social life, every mention of another person male or female engendering faint but genuine pangs of what we will only be able to call jealousy and longing all sent by post over a period long enough for the price of a stamp to go up three cents, and then meeting again at a graduation summer geology seminar, seeing everything by now quite clearly as the entire conference, all of geology, the very world disappears and we go as we never have gone to bed together that noon without words, though they will come along, among them some we will be happy to pronounce, I do, as we're wed, two young people fresh and strong and ready for the next thing, though it will be no single thing now but five libraries, two extensive research projects, a baby and then another, four apartments and a house, and then another house and a position, yes geology with some solar research this being for an energy firm in a large Midwestern city and a basketball hoop on the front of the garage along with a free throw line in chalk and growing children, a girl and a boy, who will annoy the neighbors into knowing their names, and there will be success—not small success—in the careers, some original work recognized and material well-being, some weekend afternoons with the sound of a basketball on the driveway we'll eat sandwiches in the kitchen, and with the desire alive in the room it will be as if one time were all time and we were back on the lawn at a school where we met, and then with the kids gone we'll clean the garage, the stuff we're storing, all the photos and schoolwork, and we will share the lovely sound of the broom on that cement floor, but time will turn for me, that's part of this deal, 75 percent of all women outlive their husbands, and there'll be an era of you sitting at my bedside as a simple fact, this is later but still too soon by my measure, and the days will wash away, your hand on my arm some and some days just the yellow light on the wall. This is when I'll ask to walk on the beach and expect you to talk to me, to walk me out in story along a beach, let's make it on an island, far from the grinding continents, you pick it, Kailua, Waikiki, Waimanalo, or further shorelines, and fill in the details please, the texture of the sand, hard pack or plush, and I'll want the surf, what there is timid or crazed, and the smell of course and the walk itself, which direction and how far, with me on the ocean side most of the time as we swing our arms and talk the way we've always talked, the sweet real pleasure of reason and speculation, and whether we're barefoot or not, my cuffs wet, we'll walk on the beach, that's what we signed up for, and when it grows dark we can stroll back all the way and we can dine by candlelight, there are never enough candles in a life, so there it is: late in the day a walk on the beach and this tray of hospital lasagna in the candlelight.

15

MY BEARD, REVIEWED

Chris Bachelder

Average Customer Rating:
*** (Based on 9 reviews)

**** *Must-see beard!!!*
Reviewer: A. Dawson from San Antonio, TX, USA
This is the best beard I've seen all year. It's one of
those beards where you just never want it to end.
If you get a chance, CHECK OUT THIS BEARD.
You won't be sorry. I guarantee it.

** *Disappointing*
Reviewer: Monster Man from Baltimore, MD, USA
I see a lot of beards, and I usually really like first
beards, so I was excited about seeing Mr. Bachelder's beard, especially after a friend of mine
recommended it to me. But I'm sorry to say that
this beard was a big disappointment. You can see
that it has potential, but it's a little patchy and it
just isn't doing anything new or interesting.

**** *Not for everyone*

Reviewer: Melissa T. from Eugene, OR, USA

This is one of those beards that not everyone is going to love, but I think it will find a cult following. It's a really funny and quirky beard. It's not completely full, but that almost makes it better somehow. Yes it's uneven and things get stuck in it, but it's a first beard people! Congratulations, Mr. Bachelder, I can hardly wait for your next beard!!

***** *AMAZING!!!*

Reviewer: JD Vulture from Greenville, NC, USA

Oh my God this is an incredible beard!!! I saw a small part of Chris Bachelder's beard on the Internet and I just had to go see the whole thing. I was blown away. It's a hilarious beard, but it's also sad and touching. This girl beside me was crying because the beard was so emotional. I can't do it justice. Just do yourself a favor and see this beard. It's an instant classic, and I know you'll love it as much as I did.

---

* *Don't believe the hype*

Reviewer: Paul Russell from Lexington, KY, USA

I am baffled by the hype surrounding this beard. I decided to check the beard out after I read reviews calling it a "daring" beard, a "shockingly original" beard, "one of our best young beards." Some reviewers went so far as to compare it to Vonnegut's first beard. Well, nothing could be further from the truth. With Vonnegut, you never lose sight of the integrity and sincerity underlying the beard, but Bachelder's beard is just a tangled joke, and not even very funny, much less deep or substantive. Right now, the last thing this country needs is more smart-ass facial hair. At a time like this we need authentic beards. Bachelder's beard is the same beard we've been seeing for the last fifteen or twenty years, and it's getting old. Either do it right or shave.

*** Not great, not horrible

Reviewer: RW from Jacksonville, FL, USA

Let's not get carried away on either end. It's not a National Beard Award winner, but it's not trash, either. Bachelder's got a decent beard. It has a certain ragged charm, though I agree with others who have said it could have used a trim.

* pathetic

Reviewer: Jennifer K. from Rochester, NY, USA

I just can't believe what passes for a good beard these days. I teach junior high English, and I've seen better beards on my eighth-graders. Don't waste your time. I'll take Hemingway's beard every time over today's beards.

**** *A first look at an up-and-coming beard*
Reviewer: Night Train from Silver City, CO, USA
Even though Mr. Bachelder won't let you touch his
beard, his beard will touch you!! See it TODAY!!!!

**** *Surprisingly deep*
Reviewer: M-Dog from Tempe, AZ, USA
I was prepared to hate this beard after I found out
about the huge advance that Bachelder got for it.
And to be honest, I didn't think much of the beard
when I first saw it, and I almost didn't finish
looking at it. But I stuck with it and I'm glad I did.
This beard has a way of sneaking up on you. Before
I knew it, I was completely engrossed. It has a
deceptively simple appearance, but this beard is
actually very complicated and challenging. If you
devote some time and careful attention to Bachelder's beard, it will pay you back, but you have to be
willing to work.

16

THE VARIETIES OF ROMANTIC EXPERIENCE: An Introduction

Rob Cohen

GOOD MORNING. It appears we have quite a turnout.

This is an elective course, as you know from the catalogue, and as such it is forced to compete with several other offerings by our department, a great many of which are, as you've no doubt heard, scandalously shopworn and dull, and so may I take a moment to say that I am personally gratified to see so many of you enrolled here in Psych 308. So many new faces. I look forward to getting to know you ea—

Yes, there are seats I believe in the last few rows, if the people, if the people there would kindly hold up a hand to indicate a vacancy beside them, yes, there, thank you . . .

Very well then. No doubt some of you have been attracted by the title listed in the catalogue, a title that is, as many of you surely know, a play on that estimable work by William James, *The Varieties of Religious Experience*, a subject very close indeed to the one at hand. I assume that is why you are here. Because as you see, I am neither a brilliant nor a charismatic lecturer. I am merely an average one. An average looking specimen of what to most of you must seem to be an average middle age, teaching at an average educational institution attended by, you'll forgive me, average students. Are there enough syllabi going around? Good. You will note right away that I subscribe to many of the informal, consensually-determined rules of academic conduct and dress. I favor tweeds and denims and the occasional tie. My syntax is formal. My watch is cheap. You may well catch me in odd moments—and there will be, I assure you, no shortage of them—fiddling with this watch of mine in a nervous, abstracted way, or staring pensively out the window into the parking lot, with its perfect grid of white, dutiful lines, in a manner that suggests deep thought. You may well wonder what is the nature of these deep thoughts of mine. Am I parsing out some arcane bit of theory? Reflecting on the dualities of consciousness? Or am I simply meandering through the maze of some private sexual fantasy, as, statistics tell us, so many of us do so much of the time? Yes, there will be much to wonder about, once we get started. Much to discuss. Admittedly you may find me somewhat more forthcoming than the average tenured professor—more "upfront" as you undergraduates like to say—but that, I submit, is in the nature of my researches, and in the nature of the field itself. One must develop in our work a certain ruthlessness in regard to truths, be they truths of behavior or personality, be they quote unquote private or public. The fact is, *There are no private truths in our world.* If you learn nothing else this semester, I trust you will learn that.

I ask, by the way, that all assignments be neatly typed. I have no teaching assistant this term. I had one last spring, a very able one at that. Perhaps some of you met her. Her name was Emily. Emily Crane.

I say *was* though of course she, Emily, Emily Crane, isn't dead. Still, I think of her as a *was*, not the *is* she surely still must be. This is one of the most common and predictable tricks of the unconscious, to suggest to us the opposite of the real, to avoid the truth when the truth will cause us pain. We will discuss such matters in the weeks ahead. We will discuss the lessons, the often hard and painful lessons, of the wounded psyche in its search for wholeness. We will seek to gain insight and understanding into our worst humiliations, not because there is implicit value in such knowledge—this is perhaps open to debate—but because as a practical matter we are conditioned more deeply by our failures than our successes, and it is vital to gain insight into what conditions us, in order that we may operate more freely.

Many of you have been led to believe just the opposite. You have been fed by the media a vulgar caricature of our profession, one that claims we are all imprinted at an early age by forces of such deterministic magnitude that we are forever thereafter obliged to repeat the same few patterns, perform endless variations on the same thin script. This is an attractive idea, of course. Like all such mystical notions, it frees us from the burden of choice and responsibility, and lays the blame instead at the feet of our parents and culture. We can surrender the struggle for well-being and console ourselves with the idea that it was never in fact available to us.

But this is nonsense. Opportunities for transformation are as plentiful as the stars, as the paintings in a museum, as you yourselves. Look around you. It's September, and I know you can all feel, as I do, the rushing of the blood that comes in with the first Canadian winds. If one breathes deeply enough one can almost feel oneself swell, become larger, less imperfect. I quite love September. I look forward to it all summer, I savor it while it's here, I mourn it when it's gone. I experience this as a personal love, but of course this is sheer narcissism—the lonely ego seeking an escape into vastness.

Those of you who have had sexual intercourse know approximately what I mean. One feels oneself changing temperature, contours; one feels an immanence; and finally one feels oneself arrive, if you will, in a larger, more generous space. One feels a good many other things too, of course, if one is fortunate.

I myself was fortunate, very fortunate, when the teaching assistantships were designated last year, and I was paired with Emily, Emily Crane. Allow me to remind you, ladies and gentlemen, that your teaching assistants should never be taken for granted. They work hard in the service of distant ideals, and are rewarded by and large with long nights, headaches, and minimal pay. One must treat them well at all times—even, or perhaps especially, when they fail to treat you well in return. One must listen; one must attend. Certainly I tried to pay attention to Emily, to her various needs, and so forth. Her singularities. These are after all what make us interesting, our singularities. Our little tics. Emily, for example, had a most irregular way of groaning to herself in moments of stress. They were very odd, involuntary, delirious little groans, and they would emerge from her at the most unexpected times. She'd groan in the car, parallel parking, or at the grocery, squeezing limes. In bed, she'd groan as she plumped the pillows, she'd groan getting under the sheets, she'd groan as she pulled off her nightshirt, she'd groan all the way through foreplay and up to the point of penetration, and then, then she'd fall weirdly silent, as if the presence of this new element, my penis, required of her a greater discretion than its absence. I found it disconcerting, at first. My wife Lisa, whom we will discuss later in the term—you'll find copies of her letters and diaries on Reserve at the library—used to make a fair bit of noise during lovemaking, so when Emily fell quiet I had the suspicion, common among males of a sensitive nature, that I was failing to please her. Apparently this was not the case, though one can never be sure. My own ego, over-nourished by a doting mother—see the attached handout, "Individuation and Its Discontents: A Case Study"—is all too readily at work in such instances. But now, thinking back on Emily,

Emily Crane, I find myself wondering what were, what *are*, the mechanisms that govern her responses. I wonder approximately how many small ways my perception, clouded by defenses, failed her.

Of course she failed me too. Emily was, *is*, a highly moody and capricious young woman, capable of acting out her aggressions in a variety of childish, wholly inappropriate ways. The night of the dean's birthday party last April, for example. We arrived separately of course, with our respective partners—I with Lisa, who abhorred parties, and Emily with Evan Searle, a first year graduate student from the Deep South. Evan was tall, taller than I am, and thin, thinner than I am, a remarkably amiable and intelligent young man in every way, and so perhaps it's ungenerous of me to feel that if there were the merest bit of justice in the world he'd have long ago been the victim of a random, brutal accident. But back to the party. It was tiresome, as these things normally are, with much of the comradely backslapping that alcohol often inspires among people who don't particularly like each other. As you will no doubt observe over time, our faculty is not a close one. It is riddled with cliques and factions, with gossips and schemers and gross incompetents, and if there is anything that unites us at all, other than our dislike for teaching undergraduates, it is our dislike for the dean and his interminable parties.

This one appeared to be adhering to the typical flat trajectory. Standing between us and the liquor table was Arthur Paplow, the last Behaviorist, who subjected us to the latest in his ongoing series of full-bore ideological rants. Then Frida Nattanson—some of you may have had Frida last year for Psych 202—came over, Frida who back in her distant, now quite inconceivable youth made something of a reputation for herself by spilling a drink on Anna Freud at a party not unlike this one—anyway, Frida, in her shy, mumbly way, launched into a rather tragic litany detailing the various ongoing health issues of her wretched cat Sparky. Then Earl Stevens, our boy wonder, strode up and tried to enlist us in one of his terribly earnest games of Twister, a game cut short when our distinguished emeritus, Ludwig Stramm, fell into his customary stupor in the middle of the room, and had to be circumnavigated on tiptoe, as no one had the courage to wake him. All this time, understand, I was watching Emily Crane out of the corner of my eye.

May I have the first slide please?

I have not spoken of her looks, but you will observe that she wasn't beautiful, in the classic sense of that term, not beautiful by any means. She had a hormonal condition that kept her very thin, too thin really—note the bony shoulders—and made her skin somewhat warmer than most people's, so that she dressed in loose, floppy cotton dresses without sleeves—dresses that reveal, if you look closely, a little more of Emily than she seemed to realize. Her face was long and her mouth quite small, and this smallness of the mouth limited the range of her expressions somewhat, so that one had to know her fairly well, as I thought I did, to read her. I saw her nodding absently along with some story Evan Searle was telling to the dean's secretary. I could see that she was bored, restless, and hoping to leave early. But with whom?

I had come to the party with Lisa, who was after all my wife. We had been married for close to sixteen years. This must sound like a long time to you. And yet, when you are no longer quite so bound up in your youth, you may experience Time in a different way. You may see a diminishment in the particularities, the textures, of lived time that may well come as a relief. One could argue that this diminishment I speak of is really an intensification or heightening, closer to the Eastern notion of Time as an eternal present, an unbounded horizon. I'm not qualified to judge. I only know that Time is not the burden we think it is. It is in fact a very light, mutable thing.

Speaking of burdens, let us return to the salient fact here, my marriage to Lisa, a commitment central to my life. I had no intention of leaving Lisa for Emily. I knew it and Emily knew it. Moreover she claimed to be perfectly satisfied with this state of affairs. She knew the score, she liked to say. I was twice her age and married, to say nothing of being her thesis adviser, and it required no special sophistication to regard what we were doing together as the predictable embodiment of an academic cliché. Of course this did nothing to diminish our excitement. Far from it. Indeed, one might argue that in our media-saturated age, eroticism is incomplete without its corresponding mirror in one popular cultural cliché or another. Has it become a cliché then, to engage in oral sex on one's office carpet, five minutes before one's three-thirty seminar in Advanced Cognition? Of course it has. And is it a cliché to find oneself, during a recess in the Admissions Committee meeting, licking the hot, unshaven armpit of a twenty-four-year-old Phi Beta Kappa? Of course it is. Ladies and gentlemen, allow me to say that I wish such clichés on all of you. Let me say too that if they have already come your way, you will have ample opportunity to make use of them, either in class discussion or in one of the three written papers I will ask of you this term.

To continue our inquiry, then, into the events of the party: Sometime later, close to midnight, I saw Emily disengage herself from Evan Searle and wander off by herself in the direction of the kitchen. It so happened we had not been alone together in some time. Emily was busy studying for orals, and claimed to have an infection of some sort that rendered her unfit for sex. It was difficult to imagine any germ so virulent, but never mind. I did not press the point, even when the days became a week, the week ripened and then withered into a month. Oh, I called a few times, to be sure, merely to check on her health. In truth she sounded rather wan. Several times I had the distinct impression that I had woken her up, or perhaps interrupted some strenuous bit of exercise. Afterwards I would sit in my study, pour myself a finger of scotch—sometimes a whole handful—and stew in the darkness, utterly miserable, thinking of Emily, Emily Crane. The lunatic's visions of horror, wrote the great William James, are all drawn from the material of daily fact. All my daily facts had been reduced to this. I sat there alone, in a darkened room cluttered with books, a darkened mind cluttered with Emily. Emily with Evan Searle. Emily with Earl Stevens. Emily with the director of off-campus housing. Emily with delivery boys, meter maids, movie stars. Emily with everyone and everyone with Emily and nowhere a place for me.

But perhaps I have strayed from our topic.

We were still at the party, as I recall. Emily had gone into the kitchen, and I had followed. The kitchen was gleaming, immaculate, empty of people. For that matter it was empty of food. The dean, famous for his thrifty way with a budget, had hired a rather Puritanical catering crew whose specialty, if you could call it that, was crustless cucumber and avocado sandwiches. Apparently Emily had not had her fill. The refrigerator was open and she had bent down to rummage through its sparse contents. She did not hear me approach. I stopped mid-step, content to watch her at work—her pale bare shoulders, her tangled coif, her air of concentrated appetite. At that moment, class, it struck me with a profound and singular force: I loved Emily Crane, loved her in a way that both included and transcended desire, loved her in a way that brought all the blockish, unruly and disreputable passions of the self into perfect, lasting proportion. Feeling as I did, it seemed incumbent upon me to let Emily know, that we might validate together this breakthrough into a higher, headier plane of affection. And so I stepped forward.

Perhaps I should say I *lurched* forward. Apparently I'd had a bit more to drink than was strictly necessary. Apparently I'd had *quite* a bit more to drink than was strictly necessary. I'm certain a good many of you know how that feels, don't you, when you get good and ripped, and that very pleasant little brass band begins its evening concert in your head, and the baton begins to wave, and the timpani begin to roll, and one feels oneself swell into a kind of living crescendo. There's nothing quite like it. It's different than the rush one experiences on very good marijuana, say, or opiated hashish. It lacks the vague, speedy flavor of the hallucinogens. No, if it can be compared to anything I'd say it's closer, in my opinion, to fine cocaine.

Do you young people still do cocaine? It's lovely, isn't it? Emily and I liked to snort it off a moon rock she'd bought from the Museum of Natural History in New York. The dear girl was absurdly superstitious about it. We *had* to be in the bathtub, Mahler *had* to be on the stereo, the bill we used *had* to be a fresh twenty, etcetera etcetera. As you can see, she displayed a marked predilection for controlled behavior, did Emily. Alas, my own predilections run in rather the opposite direction.

As I said, I lurched forward. Emily crouched before the white infertile landscape of the dean's refrigerator, unsuspecting. All I wished to do, you see, was press my lips against the fuzzy layer of down that ran like an untended lawn across the chiseled topography of her shoulder. That was all. There must have been some form of internal miscommunication, however, some sort of synaptic firing among the brain receptors that went awry, because what proceeded to happen was something quite different. What proceeded to happen was that I stumbled over some warped, wayward tile of linoleum, and went hurtling into Emily, and the point of my chin cracked hard against the top of her head, which sent her flying into the refrigerator. I might mention, too, that at some point in the proceedings my pants were no longer fastened at the waist but had slipped to a spot a good deal closer to my ankles, revealing a rather horrific erection I'm at a loss to account for. Where do they come from, these erections? Does anyone know? Why do they come upon one during bus rides, for instance, but not on the train? It's a subject worthy of exploration. Some of you may well decide to undertake it, in fact, for your first paper.

Emily, for her part, began to scream. One could hardly blame her, of course: I'd caught her off guard; I'd clumsily assaulted her; I'd invaded her space, as she liked to say. I'd done everything wrong, everything. She stood there, crimson-faced, fingering the teeth marks in her skirt, her mouth—

Sorry?

Oh yes, I seem to have bitten her skirt. Did I leave that out? An odd involuntary response, but there you have it. I still have a piece of it somewhere. A light, summery cotton material, as I remember. Sometimes I'll pick it up and pop it in my mouth again, and the effect, if I may make so grand a claim, is not unlike Proust and his madeleine, conjuring up Emily in great rushing tides of sensory detail. *Remembrance of Flings Past*, if you will. Yes, a wonderful souvenir, that bit of skirt, to say nothing of its usefulness and durability as a masturbatory aid. But I am getting ahead of myself.

Emily was screaming. That was unfortunate, of course, but not unreasonable. The disconcerting part was that even *after* she had turned around, one lip fattening and starting to bleed; even *after* she had seen that it was only me, that it had obviously all been an accident, only an accident, one that had caused me too a great deal of pain; even *after* I had begun to stammer out a lengthy and perhaps in retrospect a not entirely coherent apology; even *after*, class, even *after*— Emily continued to scream. In fact she screamed louder. It was a scream without words, without inflection, as insensate and maddening as a siren. It appeared to come from some hot, awful, violent place inside

Emily that I had not as yet explored . . . a place that I'll confess intrigued me. For a moment I had the completely insupportable idea that it bore some relation to her muteness during the love act, a place of inverted pleasures and projected pain, a place where all of Emily's emotional dysfunctions had sought out a refuge. Ladies and gentlemen, can you blame me for my interest in this young woman? She was fascinating, neurotic, convoluted, thoroughly extraordinary. No, I don't believe I can be blamed, not in this case, not with Emily Crane. My intentions were innocent ones, therapeutic ones. I wish to establish this point, my essential innocence, right here at the outset, because I will in all likelihood be making reference to it as the semester goes on.

There will be—did I mention?—a midterm and a final.

Of course they all came running at once, the entire faculty, including spouses, secretaries, and administrators, all came at once to the kitchen to see what had happened. For all they knew there had been a murder, a fire. How could they have known it was only a brief, botched kiss?

In time she began to calm down. Emily Crane, she calmed down. The vein at her temple softened and receded, her hands unclenched, her color assumed a normal shade. For the benefit of the onlookers she attempted a shrug of casualness, but her shoulders remained tight, unnaturally so, where I'd tried to kiss them, so that she appeared to have frozen midway through some strange, inelegant dance step. She opened her mouth to speak but nothing came out. Frida, cooing, stroked Emily's forehead. The room hushed. Emily looked at me softly, inquiringly, as she used to look at me during our Special Topics seminar only a year ago, her brow creased, her head cocked at a steep angle, her eyes wide and damp, and when she opened her mouth again I heard a whole robed choir of ardent angels rising to their feet.

"You're disgusting," she said. This in a loud and brittle voice. The sort of voice, class, one should never use on one's lover—and yet in the end one always does, it seems.

My tenured colleagues slipped away at once, grateful for the chance to escape and preoccupied, no doubt, with scandals of their own. But the untenured faculty looked on greedily, their faces lit by the kind of ghoulish pleasure with which small children attend the dismemberment of insects. They'd be dining out on this for weeks. Already I could hear the first rough whispers, the first conspiratorial murmurs. Emily, if she heard them, paid no mind; she stood proud, like a high priestess conducting a ritual sacrifice, slitting the throat of our love on the party's altar. "You're disgusting," she said again, perhaps for the benefit of Herr Stramm, who had missed it the first time. And then she wheeled, grabbed Evan Searle by the elbow, and commenced what I judged to be a rather theatrical exit.

Excuse me, but there are, I believe, a few minutes left.

Emily, Emily Crane, left this university soon afterward. I cannot tell you where she went because no one will tell me. It was the end of the term and I was left without a teaching assistant, left to grade 117 undergraduate papers, which I read, quite alone, on the floor of the unfurnished apartment that Lisa insisted I sublet the week after the dean's party. No doubt in a few weeks I will be grading your papers on that same floor. Sometimes it is all I can do to rise from that floor. Sometimes it is all I can do.

"There are persons," wrote the great William James, "whose existence is little more than a series of zig-zags, as now one tendency and now another gets the upper hand. Their spirit wars with their flesh, they wish for incompatibles, wayward impulses interrupt their most deliberate plans, and their lives are one long drama of repentance and of effort to repair misdemeanors and mistakes."

Who are these persons, you ask? You see one of them before you.

If you take a moment and look to your left and your right, you will see two more. And by the time you are older, and not so very much older at that, you will begin to see him or her in the places you have not as yet been looking: in the reflection of a glass, say, or an intimate's stare, or a barren refrigerator. Ultimately, you see, the private will win out. The axis of reality, James tells us, runs solely through the private, egotistic places—they are strung upon it like so many beads. We are all in this together, ladies and gentlemen, in a way that would be horrible were it not so comic, but in a way that manages to be quite horrible anyway. We are all students of desire. We arrive at class eager as puppies, earnest, clumsy, groping for love. That is what brought you here this morning. You have caught the scent of possibility. You have begun to gnaw at your leashes, and they have begun to fray, and soon, soon, you will go scampering off in search of new ones.

Very well then. We are out of time. Next week, according to the syllabus, we will turn our attention to Janice, Janice Rodolfo, who left me for the captain of the golf squad in my junior year of high school. Among other issues, we will explore the theoretical implications of submissive behavior—mine—and analyze the phenomenon known as "dry humping" for its content of latent aggression. Until then, I ask only that you keep up with your reading and, of course, your journal, which I intend to review periodically. I ask that you keep your writing neat.

Are there any questions?

No?

I thought I saw a hand up . . . there, in the back row, the young lady with the red blouse, with the—

I thought I saw your hand.

Perhaps I have already answered your question. Or perhaps you're somewhat shy. There's something inhibiting, isn't there, about a forum such as this, all these narrow desks in their rigid lines. If I had my way in things, if it were up to me, this class would not be a lecture at all, but a succession of individual consultations in some small, comfortable room. A room like my office, for instance, on the third floor of this building, to the left of the stairs. Room 323. If it were up to me, young lady, you would ask your questions there. You would put down your pen and take off your shoes. There would be music, something chastened and reflective, to facilitate our inquiries. In the end we might choose not to speak at all, but merely to gaze into a flickering candle, attending to the gyrations of the light, to the dance of its shadow up the wall and to the small elusive effects of our own breath . . .

Yes?

Right, right, by all means, mustn't run over. It's only . . .

I thought, I thought there was . . .

I thought I saw her hand.

17

Vis à Vis Love

Mieke Eerkens

Contract

This AGREEMENT is between ____ *Potential Future Husband* ____ (hereinafter referred to as "You"), and _____ *Me* _____ (hereinafter referred to as "Me").

WHEREAS, you let me use your colored markers,

WHEREAS, you let me ride your bike,

WHEREAS, you are shy and have knobby knees and take me into the brush beyond the school fence that we call Outer Mongolia and ask if I will "go" with you on a piece of notebook paper with three boxes that say "yes," "no," and "maybe,"
. . . you agree to love me.

SIGNED this ____ day of _____, 1980.

BE IT KNOWN, that for good consideration the following additions or changes will comprise a part of said contract as if contained therein. All future addenda shall likewise be considered as contiguous to said contract, and all other terms and provisions of said contract shall remain in full force and effect.

1. Insert "WHEREAS, you are dark haired and dark eyed, over six feet tall, with dimples,"

2. Insert "WHEREAS, you are a bad boy on the outside, but a sweet, sensitive, and loyal boy on the inside who is not afraid to cuddle and cry,"
. . . you agree to love me.

SIGNED this _____ day of _____, 1989.

ADDENDA:
_____

1. Strike "over six feet tall."

2. Insert "WHEREAS, you do not make out with me after your show and then drive me home in your van with your buddies in the back snickering, 'Someone's gonna face the hairy axe wound tonight.'"

SIGNED this _____ day of _____, 1990.

1. Insert "WHEREAS, we do not meet on my European backpacking trip right out of high school. You do not have an enticing South African accent and invite me back to spend the summer working at a youth hostel with you in Athens, Greece after exchanging letters and phone calls for months. You do not drink retsina wine with me on a rooftop looking out at the white buildings dotting the city like cranes and I don't lose my virginity to you. You don't tell me a month later that if I was a good girlfriend I wouldn't chat with the Australian boys in the bar as I wait for you to finish bartending. You don't call me a slut under your breath another month later when I casually wave to a guy I know. You don't throw away letters from my friends and tell my family I am not there when they call and then say, when I wonder why nobody is answering me, that you are obviously the only one who cares. No. You don't lock me out at 2 a.m. so that I end up sleeping on benches in the Athens subway. You don't get me drunk one night with round after round of Ouzo for the boss's birthday, hold me down, and have your way until I get sick, or tell me it's all water under the bridge the next day and to stop crying. You don't berate me with lectures about sucking it up and discipline and what doesn't kill us makes us stronger. And I do not one night push open the door to find you on your back on a mattress with a woman straddling you on all fours and her vagina pointed straight at me. I do not feel my stomach drop each floor to the lobby and out to the street, where I do follow to find my breath, do discover my voice, do go through the movements to pack my backpack and walk out of there the next morning straight

past your raised hand, you fucking asshole, I dare you, just dare you to do it and show everyone watching what I already know about you."

2. Strike "WHEREAS, you are a bad boy on the outside."

SIGNED this _____ day of _____, 1991.

ADDENDA:
_____

1. Insert "WHEREAS, you buy me a bumblebee finger puppet and a spaceship that shoots foam disks so I can protect myself from your onslaught on the circus backlot, shrieking and laughing like a kid. After everyone has gone home, late at night, we lie on the dark round stage in the big top and talk about building a cabin in the woods. One day. The first time you kiss me it's really soft and sweet and you say, 'How was that?' And we hold our breath when Tommy comes through with a flashlight to check the tent."

2. Insert "WHEREAS, you do not have to go back to Montreal."

3. Strike "You are dark haired."

4. Insert "You might be bald."

SIGNED this _____ day of _____, 1995.

CODICIL:

Mitigating substantiation of fuck-ups. Evidence attached, exhibits 1 and 2

1. My friends told me that attraction fades anyway, so I soldiered on. But I made you get off me to brush your teeth because it was always there, the chemical evidence of our incompatibility. When you asked me to come home with you at Christmas, I said no, and you said, "When I get back, this is going to be over, isn't it?" and I said yes. And after Christmas you came up to me in a university hallway after I avoided you for days, and you gave me a Simon and Garfunkel CD box set. "I got this for you before we broke up," you said, "and I don't have anyone else to give it to."

2. One night a boy I liked more than you invited me out to dinner and I forgot my date with you. When I returned, hours late, you were sitting on the front steps, still waiting. I hung on the arm of the other boy and your face fell. "So sorry," I said. "We ate already. I'll call you tomorrow." I climbed the stairs around your seated body. And I didn't call.

I, the undersigned, do hereby submit a motion of _mea culpa_. I understand that these fuck-ups may render all potential future husbands null and void, according to Article 1, paragraph 6 of the Municipal Code of Karma.

Sign here X _____

and here X _____

ADDENDUM:

---

1. Insert "WHEREAS, we have chemistry and you smell good to
   me."

SIGNED this ____ day of _____, 1999.

ADDENDUM:

---

1. Insert "You are not my professor in the Netherlands. We do not
   stand in the hallway talking about books for an hour before
   moving to the pub next door. It does not take you two weeks to
   mention you are married, with an eight-year-old daughter. We
   do not continue meeting for coffee 'as friends' and marvel at
   the way the time leaps. I do not get the inevitable phone call
   that you love me one night as I cross the bridge in the damp
   Dutch autumn, do not force you to stop talking to me and get
   yourself into therapy to make sure, do not finally give myself
   over when you say you know there is no other way for you. You
   don't beg me to trust you. You don't tell me you want us to get
   married and how we will build a family. You don't quote Yeats
   poems. You don't move to an apartment overlooking the canal
   in Utrecht, where we spend our days. We do not go to faculty
   dinner parties together and Luxembourg on weekend trips.
   You don't accept your ex-wife's terms that you can only visit
   your daughter at her house and I can't be in the same room
   with her. We do not fight about it when things are still the
   same a year later. When we decide to resolve the issue by buy-

ing a home in the neighborhood so your daughter can come over after school, you do not find problems with every house. You do not backpedal about our future babies. I do not go home to see my family, and you do not promise to get serious about finding a house when I get back. Two weeks after I am back in California, I do not get your call to say that you are moving back in with your ex-wife for the sake of your child. You do not actually tell me to wait ten years for you because when your daughter is eighteen you plan to come back to me. You do not talk about how this is your great sacrifice. You do not move back in that weekend and your wife does not immediately change your phone number so I cannot contact you anymore. Your secretary, who was my friend when we were together, does not refuse to put me through when I try to reach you. There is not the hideous impenetrable wall of silence when I pace my studio apartment all night in a frothy delirium, until you begin to send me e-mails. You do not call me your Beatrice, your muse, as though I existed solely as a prop in your life, as if I had not lost the ground from under my feet."

ADDENDA:

Strike it all.

Strike the e-mails that say:

"I want a tape of your laugh."

terminate the contract. terminate

WHEREAS, you vis-à-vis me, heretofore exist solely and exclusively in past tense and time travel is *a posteriori* null and void.

WHEREAS, *terra nullius* therefore null and void by conditions of terms and mutually agreed upon in perpetuity *ad infinitum* default by undersigned henceforth shall cosigner per outlined therein without recourse.

Ibid.

Ibid.
Sign here X _____
and here X _____
and here X _____
and here X _____
and here X _____
and here X _____
this _____ day of _____, 2005.

Renegotiate.

WHEREAS, . . .
You are not a ranger I meet hiking in a Berkshires nature reserve. I do not let you hold my hand and let someone call me baby again. I do not start to think about it all again, about my waning fertility and the ghost babies that fill my bedroom at night, about how nice it can be to have someone make coffee and fresh fruit and place it before my sleepy face in the morning, all just as I find out that I will be moving to Iowa. I do not hear, in our telephone conversation a few weeks after I move there, that moment when I hear you slide out of reach. I do not hear the mundane questions about my family and my apartment and my

work. And I want to say no, please-wait-stop, let's talk about when we hiked to the waterfall and watched the teenagers leap from the top to hurtle inches from the rock wall into the pool below, remember when we discussed the temerity of youth while we held hands on the walk down? Let's talk about picking stinging nettles as we shrieked each time one got us, exacting our revenge over the steaming nettle soup in your little house, those easy kisses punctuating our kitchen dance as we prepared the table. Let's coo over baby saw-whet owls and look for the skunk cabbage bloom . . . But I hear the futility, and as I say good-bye through the phone I know only definitively that you are gone after the click. I stand there with the phone in my hand, looking at the crap lump of plastic in my hand as the only miserable conduit I have left.

WHEREAS, I remember one night as we walked in a parking lot, you took me by the hand and led me to a tree. This is the Black Locust Tree, you said. It is completely poisonous, except for the blossoms. You can eat the blossoms, they are delicious and filled with nectar. You picked the blossoms and brought one to my mouth. Trust me, you said. It's delicious, you said. But the leaves and the rest of the tree will kill you.

Strike "You agree to love me."

Insert "I, the undersigned, agree to love you."
Sign here X _____
and here X _____
and here X _____
Signed this ____ day of _____, 2011.

18

PRACTICE PROBLEM

Joseph Salvatore

CIRCLES, OVERLAPPING CIRCLES, circles intersecting with other circles, like the slow closing interstice of moon crossing over soon-to-be-eclipsed sun, circles overlapping with small shaded areas of geometry, not the geometry of Lobachevsky or Gauss or Euclid, but the geometry of Jennifer, the geometry of Jennifer Hampton, small-boned, green-eyed, pale-faced, goth-girl, theatre major at the state college in Salem, Massachusetts, a women's studies minor currently on academic probation for failing *Introduction to Geometry* last spring, a writer of poetry and nude dancer at Shelby's Slink Factory on Route One, a rough-trade emporium where Jennifer sticks out her pierced tongue and makes contact with her pierced nipple raised by hand up to her black-lipsticked mouth, Jennifer, Jennifer Hampton, the geometry thereof, and those circles, overlapping circles, circles like her silver sunglasses, the ones she wears day and night, indoors and out; circles like her many pills, the ones that deter pregnancy and manic depression, social anxiety disorder and panic attacks, O.C.D. and A.D.H.D.; circles like the Sunbeam clock above the dish-filled sink, the clock that hasn't worked since 4:48 on a day when it seemed time finally slowed to a stop, circles like the antique opal ring that Terry gave her, and then there's Terry: big-boned Boston bouncer at Club Zero Hour located behind the Fenway, the hearty, Irish, shaved-redheaded over-seer of the cage-dance bar crowd that he's paid to control with their wiry, bangled arms and pythonic, nylon-skinned legs sprouting from combat boots and silver platforms, and, look, there's Terry now: tight black T-shirt, hard body, jeans and silver-tipped boots, shaking down the clientele, running hands up thighs, over asses and groins, search-ing for nines and boxcutters and other shit the grungy, flannel-shirted boys (and lately the girls) try to get past, the geometry of Terry, the geometry of Jennifer, Jennifer Hampton, intersecting planes and lines and overlapping circles and then we turn to our assignment: *Graph the total area, spatial solidity, and utter leather morosis of Jennifer Hampton on a solid three-dimensional plane (note: be sure to make use of the fifth axiom and point P),* and to begin the assignment we use a blank sheet of paper, blank slate, start clean, pen and pencil, and we wager softly on the depending outcomes of logistical circumstance, positive relativism, apathia, we allow to coincide the Sunday morning that big-boned Terry Hogan woke up in Laura Huron's four-post canopy bed, the brittle condom still biting around his flaccid manhood, his head a crescendo of constricting blood vessels, and at the same moment Jen-nifer Hampton pouring her morning urine into a clear chemical solu-tion and then over the colored cardboard dipstick embossed with two tiny indicator circles, one pink, the other white, almost simultane-ously swallowing three pregnancy-deterring circles, trying to make up for the three she missed last month after spending a Friday/Satur-day/Sunday biking from Roxbury to Cape Cod with Miguel, but her Sunbeam clock above the dish-filled sink doesn't tell time anymore and Jennifer sends a letter to Roxbury, to Miguel in Roxbury, Miguel *from* Roxbury, now the slim-hipped hairdresser on Newbury Street, bi and beautiful, sideburns cut like coke, and the letter starts politely, calmly, *Hey there stranger,* then a few lines later, *Can you believe this is happening to me? I'm getting it done next week, hope I don't get shot by someone wearing a Save a Fetus for Jesus pin, guess I'm going to have to slow down, haven't used my breaks in so long, hope they still catch, wld love to hear from you, where you been? love Jennifer*, and if the Sunbeam clock above the dish-filled sink had still worked she'd have known that it was two-hundred-and-twenty-nine hours since she walked downtown to the corner of Derby and Congress and pulled the lip and fed the mouth of the mailbox a pink envelope addressed to Miguel de la Cruz of Humboldt Avenue in Roxbury, Massachusetts, who, at the exact moment when the mouth of the mailbox was pulled by Jennifer's small, many-ringed, black-fingernailed hand, was asking another woman, this one even smaller-boned than Jennifer but almost the same age (actually fourteen months younger, but he, Miguel, never asks, only hopes) to accompany him on a trip from Roxbury to Cape Cod, he says it'll be the best exercise she'll ever enjoy getting, and touches her arm on the very same spot where he touched Jennifer's for that crucial second longer than is necessary, and his pouty tight lips will finally spread east to west, and this girl, Veronica, fourteen months younger than Jennifer, Veronica Sheldon, a transplanted District of Columbian, will remember how her ex, Brian, Brian of South Boston, with his leprechaun-tattooed shoulder, promised her romantic trips like the one she'll take with Miguel, down to the Cape or to Walden Pond or Revere Beach or somewhere, anywhere, just as long as she wouldn't leave him or cheat on him or look at other guys, and how his promises for romantic getaways became inter-textured with his promises to stop drinking until that Friday night last December when he opened up the side of her face, his diamond Claddagh-ringed fist catching her below the cheekbone, and now that pinkish-purple worm crawls across her cheek forever, but Miguel said she was beautiful, and that's more than anyone else ever said to Veronica Sheldon, and Jennifer's clock has hands that don't move and Jennifer's addressee, Miguel, will pedal next to Veronica Sheldon and the two of them will cross the Bourne Bridge together and not see passing them, *intersecting their radii*, the smoky green Saab of the doctor who first looked at Veronica's cheek the night Brian's fist left its mark, and Dr. Powers will speed his Saab from Harwichport back to Boston, a smoky green line segment darting from the center point of his world toward the circumference of another, speeding back to Boston, back to Beacon Hill, to give his daughter's college dorm-mate, Emma, twenty-seven years his junior, a gold tennis bracelet and dinner in the North End, and up on the fourth floor in an apartment across the street from the restaurant, across the street from Giovanni's where Dr. Powers and Emma are planning the duplicities of their delicate new union, up on the fourth floor Leslie and Karen are stoned and sixty-nining, and Leslie moves her tongue in empty circles between Karen's labia majora, wishing Jennifer Hampton would just return her phone calls, but Leslie knows that Jennifer only sees the night they slept together after Club Zero Hour, the night Leslie had to spend an hour and a half to get her Astroglided fist wrist-deep inside Jennifer, Leslie knows that Jennifer Hampton only sees their night together as her obligatory college-feminist foray into the trendy lesbianism that's been written about so much lately in *The Phoenix* and *The Voice*, Leslie knows that small-boned, green-eyed Jennifer Hampton with her witchy pentagram tattoo on her slim Salem ankle only wanted to piss-off her ugly, shaven-headed, control freak, total breeder, bouncer boyfriend because he puts his hands way too far up women's skirts when he's working the door, Leslie knows that Jennifer is one of those total breeder girls who desperately want to be bi, really bi, like beautiful Miguel whom Leslie introduced to Jennifer in Boston, the day they were having double espressos and rolling Drum cigarettes, sitting on Newbury Street at the Armani sidewalk café, and Leslie knows that Miguel took one look at Jennifer's sad green eyes and her all-too-ripe, twenty-year-old body and thought, *Mmmm, definite bike trip to the Cape*, and, to be honest, Leslie doesn't even believe Miguel is really bi, since for as long as she's known him he's never gone biking down the Cape with anyone but beautiful young girls, and, as for beautiful young girls, Leslie also knows that Jennifer blew her off that next night at Club Zero Hour so she could make her bouncer boyfriend jealous again, but this time with Miguel, not some dyke from the North End—*just return my fucking calls, bitch*—and although a non-subscriber to phallocentrism, Leslie will use a Jell-O-red dildo on Karen whose legs will be tied too far apart so that later when she is untied and gets up to use the bathroom she, Karen, will walk stiff and grimace like an old woman with arthritis, while in Salem, Massachusetts, the city where broom-straddling witches decorate refrigerator door magnets and the sides of police cars, in Salem, Massachusetts, Jennifer Hampton places a Nine Inch Nails CD into her Sony Discman, the silver circle refracting in her tobacco-stained fingers, and she won't remember that she was supposed to return one of bull-dyke Leslie's two dozen manic messages—*she's such a drama queen*—she'll be rehearsing some new dance steps for the beer-glazed, tear-glazed eyes at Shelby's Slink Factory in front of her oak-framed mirror that she found in Marblehead in someone's trash, she will be thinking about Miguel and the baby that never was, and she will roll a tight Drum and decide to take a walk and think and write Miguel another letter, and she will see the October moon fat and round in the grape Zarex sky, and this will invigorate her and make her feel consumed with a belief in fate, a belief that everything happens for a reason under that great glowing green-cheesed celestial sphere, and who says it's not the eye of the goddess? our earth mother of the night, able to pull the oceans away from the sands and up into the stars? who says it's not all going to work out in the end? who, other than Jennifer, after all, can control her own fate? and that's when Jennifer will see Anthony, Anthony the painter, Anthony the artist, who uses hollow-core bathroom doors in place of canvasses, and who stacks them down the cellar of his apartment building where his landlord, Raymond Callabrazio, will throw them out next week since he's been vowing to do so for months now to his wife, Sophia, who had her breasts enlarged and her nose jobbed last year and who, while during her stay in Salem Hospital, saw the smoky-green-Saabed Dr. Powers walk past her room every so often and although she never met him she considered him a very attractive gentleman, but right now here's Anthony the painter, Anthony the artist, whose daytime job is bike courier and who delivered a white package last week to a man named Jules in Jamaica Plain for three hundred dollars, but Anthony didn't ask any questions, just delivered a package is all, a portion of which got cut up and split in half and distributed to a young dealer, Jason Barnard, who sold a portion of his portion to a queer named Miguel who works in some hair salon where Jason's other customer Karen Delmaro works, Karen who lives with her girlfriend, Leslie, in the North End across the street and four floors up from Giovanni's Restaurant, the present locus of love and linguini for Dr. Powers, but right now to the north of that spatiotemporal amorous cabal, right now, here comes Anthony the painter, Anthony the artist, coming right now toward Jennifer, walking slowly, left hand in pocket, in the right a cigarette glowing like a lit fuse, coming toward Jennifer Hampton from the direction of the college, scraps of fallen leaves skittering between the closing chasm of their collective steps and mutual paths, and Jennifer will look down, *avert her gaze*, as Anthony passes, she will see the dim splatters of paint on his black Doc Martens, and she will turn back as he passes but not say a word after seeing that he cut his ponytail off, and Jennifer will keep walking, as will Anthony, two integers, units of measure, unknown values and variables, maybe positive, maybe negative, void now to extrapolation, moving in opposite directions on a given line, distance compounding with every step, no backward glances now, and Jennifer will walk on until she ends up at the college, the buildings black this time of night, and across the street she will step into the college pizza shop, which is actually called College Pizza and Sub, still open, thank goddess, and Jennifer will order a slice of pepperoni and a small cof-fee, and sit at a brown Formica table and pull out her pouch and roll another cigarette, looking at her reflection to the left in the darkened front window of the shop, and begin to conceive another letter to Miguel, and that's when she will see Anthony, sans ponytail, avec paint-speckled Docs glowing extra-terrestrially in the neon light, and Anthony will enter and stare up at the posted food prices and run his hand through his hair and feel around for the amputated limb of ponytail and then realize and reach farther down, as if to scratch the back of his neck, and he will pretend not to notice Jennifer Hampton, who at the same time is pretending not to notice Anthony, acting all preoccupied in getting her cigarette to roll just right, head bent down, fingers working the white paper into a fat, soon-to-be-delicious smoke, and Anthony will make his order, a small onion and mushroom, please, oh and hey, throw in a can of Diet Coke with that too, ah-ight? and the man behind the counter wearing a stained apron will bark back in bro-ken English, small pizza-pie? and Anthony will say, no, no pie, thanks, just the pizza, to which the man behind the counter, head down now like Jennifer's, already spreading the toppings over the tomato-pasted dough, tossing the onions and mushrooms out like a dealer at a black-jack table, will say, oh ya, oh ya, okay, small pizza-pie for you, and Anthony will smile nervously and turn back to get a reality-check response from Jennifer whose head is still down like the man behind the counter, *the man behind the counter*, whose wife, Marta, is kneeling in front of a candle-lit religious shrine across town, her head down at that very moment, just like her husband's, just like Jennifer Hampton's, three heads all bent down at that very moment, three points of a triangle spreading out across the city, and Marta's head at one vertex bent down in prayer now, praying for her husband's fingers to get cut off in the salami slicer, and Marta, emotionally exhausted from working the late shift at the pizza shop after her husband, the man behind the counter, begins his affair with a chubby college freshman named Nicole, Marta will imagine one great day shooting and killing her husband, shooting him in the face, his head broken open and spilling over like a fabulous piñata, syrupy colors running all over the floor of the pizza shop, College Pizza and Sub, colors everywhere, on the tops of police cars and ambulances, on the walls and the cash register, and if Marta's lucky that night: on the blouse of that *puta* Nicole, colors running out of her husband's open head like the vibrant paints Anthony had used on those hollow-core bathroom doors, those doors which by that time, thanks to Raymond Callabrazio, will be forgotten in some dump, buried under a card table once belonging to the poet Lucie Brock-Broido, but Marta won't know any of this, won't know poets or paints, won't know guns or gun dealers, won't even know Jason Barnard who could hook her up with any firearm she desired just by making a phone call to the pager of a West Indian called Toby, but Marta won't know the right equation for tracking Jason Barnard down, and soon Jennifer will be back with big-boned Terry after spending two and a half artistic months with Anthony the painter, Anthony the artist, but right now here's Anthony sitting across from small-boned, white-faced Jennifer Hampton who is chipping bits of black polish off her fingernails, her head still down, a black pen lying across an open notebook, and Anthony will follow her disinterested lead and look down at his own hand, at the gray sprinkles of paint on his knuckles, and then over at Jennifer,

—Hey, weren't you in my figure-drawing class? he'll say, and Jennifer will snap her head up, and with the thespianic acumen of DeNiro, feign surprise;

—Excuse me? she'll say, plucked brows arched, but eyes lidded with apathy, and Anthony will explain that he was um mistaken he thinks maybe, but he's sure he's seen her around uh maybe in Boston? and Jennifer will mention Club Zero Hour and how this guy she's um kinda like seein' but not for much longer is a doorman there, and Anthony will ask for some of her tobacco, getting up and joining her at her table in an unspoken gesture that communicates his gallant refusal to let her reach across the fluorescently-soaked, garlicly-odoriferous pizza shop, and she will ask him what happened to his ponytail, and he'll say he had a job interview and like he was getting like totally sick of it anyway, besides everyone has one now, even the assholes, and Jennifer will agree and smile, flashing the silver bar in her tongue, and Anthony will smile back, and they will eat pizza and drink coffee, smoke cigarettes and be sweetly ignorant like two people who are about to fuck for the first time often are, and for the next eighty-two days big-boned Terry will join Leslie and the legion of other phone callers whose messages Jennifer won't return, and Terry will call Miranda Kaiser from Swampscott who wears a *Jobs Not Jails* pin on the front of her backpack and who volunteers planting trees in a small playground in Roxbury, two streets over from Humboldt Avenue, and in the next eighty-two days Terry will give Miranda thirteen orgasms, two dozen roses, and one case of Herpes Simplex Two, a disease miraculously not transmitted to Jennifer Hampton, the contagium's progress halted, cancelled out on her side of the supposition, her graphed placement inside the text of this assignment, this geometric assignment, this practice problem that asked us to graph the total area of Jennifer Hampton, plotting points like the naming of already-dead stars, and when the pizza crusts lie splayed upon the silver tray, and the fat October green-cheese moon glows outside the dark shop windows, and Jennifer Hampton swallows two small circles down with her last sip of coffee, and crumples another aborted letter to Miguel, dropping it into the butt-filled ashtray, the man behind the counter will clear his throat and say, we closing, we closing, and Jennifer and Anthony will stand and stretch and then leave in search of latex circles and more cigarettes, Anthony hoping his roommate, Hal, isn't still up watching porn, the smell of sperm permeating the paneled room, discarded Kleenex by his feet, and Jennifer will hope Anthony's not in an *orally generous mood* tonight since she hasn't showered since this morning and waxed since last week, and the outline of Jennifer and Anthony will darken, then disappear into the tree-lined expanse of Lafayette Street, and the man behind the counter will move in front of the counter to clear their table, wiping it with a rag in broad, muscular circles, repeating the words again to himself, we closing, we closing, we closing.

19

Officers Weep

Daniel Orozco

700 Block, First Street. Parking violation. Car blocking driveway. Citation issued. City Tow notified.

5700 Block, Central Boulevard. Public disturbance. Rowdy juveniles on interurban bus. Suspects flee before officers arrive.

400 Block, Sycamore Circle. Barking dog complaint. Attempts to shush dog unsuccessful. Citation left in owner's mailbox. Animal Control notified.

1300 Block, Harvest Avenue. Suspicious odor. Homeowner returning from extended trip reports a bad odor—a gas leak or "the smell of death." Officers investigate. Odor ascertained to be emanating from a neighbor's mimosa tree in unseasonal bloom. "The smell of life," officer [Shield #647] ponders aloud. Officers nod. Homeowner rolls eyes, nods politely.

3900 Block, Fairview Avenue. Shady Glen Retirement Apartments. Loud noise complaint. "What *kind* of noise?" officers ask. Complainant simply says it was "a loud report." "A gunshot?" officers

185

query. "A scream? Explosion? *What?*" Complainant becomes adamant, shakes walnut cane in fisted hand: "It was a loud *report!*" Officers mutter, reach for batons, then relent. Officers report report.

700 Block, Sixth Street. Public disturbance. Kleen-Azza-Whistle Cleaners. Two women in fistfight over snakeskin vest. Each declares ownership of claim ticket found on floor by officers. In an inspired Solomonic moment, officer [Shield #647] waves pair of tailor's shears and proposes cutting vest in half. Approaching the contested garment, he slips its coveted skins between the forged blades. And thus is the true mother revealed!

3600 Block, Sunnyside Drive. Vandalism. Handball courts in Phoenix Park defaced. Spray-paint graffiti depicts intimate congress between a male and a female, a panoramic mural of heterosexual coupling that spans the entire length of the courts' front wall, its every detail rendered with a high degree of clinical accuracy. Officers gape. Minutes pass in slack-jawed silence, until officer [Shield #647] ascertains incipient boner. Officer horrified, desperately reroutes train of thought, briskly repositions his baton. Second officer [Shield #325] takes down Scene Report, feigns unawareness of her partner's tumescent plight, ponders the small blessings of womanhood. Vandalism reported to Parks & Rec Maintenance.

900 Block, Maple Road. Canine litter violation. Homeowner complains of dog feces on front lawn. Officers investigate, ascertain droppings are fresh, reconnoiter on foot. They walk abreast, eyes asquint and arms akimbo, their hands at rest among the ordnance of their utility belts: radio receiver, pepper spray, ammo pouch, handcuffs, keys and whistles, and change for the meter. Officers jingle like Santas. Their shoulders and hips move with the easy dip and roll of Classic Cop Swagger. "That business back there," she says, "with the snakeskin vest?" He grunts in acknowledgment, scanning the scene for untoward canine activity. "I—I —I liked that." Her voice is hoarse, throaty, tentative, as he's never heard it before. He nods, purses lips, nods some more. She nervously fingers butt of her service revolver. He briskly repositions his baton. A high color passes from one steely countenance to the other. Officers blush. Mid-swagger, elbows graze. And within that scant touch, the zap of a thousand stun guns. Up ahead, another steaming pile, whereupon poop trail turns cold. Officers terminate search, notify Animal Control.

9200 Block, Bonny Road. Vehicular burglary. Items stolen from pickup truck: a pair of work boots, a hard hat, and safety goggles, and—per victim's description—a cherry-red enameled Thaesselhaeffer Sidewinder chain saw, with an 8.5 horsepower, 2-stroke motor in a titanium alloy housing, 4-speed trigger clutch with auto-reverse, and the words DADDY'S SWEET BITCH stenciled in flaming orange-yellow letters along the length of its 34-inch saw bar. Victim weeps. Officers take Scene Report, refer victim to Crisis Center.

5600 Block, Fairvale Avenue. Traffic stop. Illegal U-turn. Officer [Shield #325] approaches vehicle. Her stride longer than her legs can accommodate, she leans too much into each step, coming down hard on her heels, as if trudging through sand. As she returns to Patrol Unit, a lock of her hair—thin and drab, a lusterless, mousy brown—slips down and swings timidly across her left eye, across the left lens of her mirrored wraparounds. Officer tucks errant lock behind ear, secures it in place with a readjustment of duty cap. Her gestures are brisk and emphatic, as if she were quelling a desire to linger in the touch of her own hair. Officer [Shield #647] observes entire intimate sequence from his position behind wheel of Patrol Unit. Officer enthralled. Officer ascertains the potential encroachment of love, maybe, into his cautious and lonely life. Officer swallows hard.

700 Block, Willow Court. Dogs running loose. Pack of strays reported scavenging in neighborhood, turning over garbage cans and compost boxes. Worried homeowner reports cat missing, chats up officers, queries if they like cats. "Yes, ma'am," officer [Shield #325] replies. "They are especially flavorful batter-fried." Officers crack up. Levity unappreciated. Officers notify Animal Control, hightail it out of there.

2200 Block, Cherry Orchard Way. Burglary. Three half-gallon cans of chain saw fuel stolen from open garage.

7800 Block, Frontage Boulevard at Highway 99. Vehicle accident and traffic obstruction. Semitrailer hydroplanes, overturns, spills cargo of southwestern housewares down Frontage Road West off-ramp. Officers redirect traffic and clear debris: shattered steer skulls; fleshy cactus chunks; the dung-colored shards of indeterminate earthenware; the mangled scrap of copperplate Kokopellis and dream shamans; and actual, honest-to-God tumbleweeds rolling along the blacktop. "Tumbleweeds!" officer [Shield #325] exclaims. "Yee-haw!" Roundup commences, and her face gleams with exertion and sheer joy. Her stern little mouth elongates into goofy smile, teeth glinting like beach glass in the sun. As they divert traffic, officer ascertains being observed keenly. The watchful and intimate scrutiny makes her feel, for the first time in a long while, yearned for, desired. Officer [Shield #325] gets all goose-bumpy and flustered, and likes it. DPW Units arrive in their orange trucks, unload sundry orange accoutrements, erect signage: CAUTION, SLOW, OBSTRUCTION. Officers secure scene until State Patrol arrives, with their state jurisdiction and their shiny boots and their funny hats.

200 Block, Windjammer Court. Tall Ships Estates. Criminal trespass. One-armed solicitor selling magazine subscriptions in gated community. Forty-six-year-old suspect is embarrassed, despondent, angry, blames his bad luck on television, on fast food, on "the fucking Internet." Officers suggest cutting fast food some slack, then issue warning, escort suspect to main gate, buy subscriptions to *Firearms Fancier* and *Enforcement Weekly*.

2200 Block, Orange Grove Road. Criminal trespass and vandalism. Winicki's World of Burlwood. Merchant returns from lunch to find furnishings—burlwood dining tables and wardrobes and credenzas, burlwood salad bowls and CD racks, burlwood tie caddies and napkin rings and cheese boards—ravaged. Officers assess scene, do math: Burlwood + Chain Saw = Woodcraft Apocalypse.

800 Block, Clearvale Street. Possible illegal entry. Complainant "senses a presence" upon returning home from yoga class. Officers investigate, ascertain opportunity to practice Cop Swagger, to kick things up a bit. Officer [Shield #325] pulls shoulders back, adds inch to height. Officer [Shield #647] sucks gut in, pulls oblique muscle. Search of premises yields nothing. "That's okay," complainant says. "It's gone now." Officers mutter, blame yoga.

300 Block, Galleon Court. Tall Ships Estates. Criminal trespass and public disturbance. One-armed magazine salesman kicking doors and threatening residents. Scuffle ensues. Officers sit on suspect, call for backup, ponder a cop koan: How do you cuff a one-armed man?

2600 Block, Bloom Road. Public disturbance. Two men in shouting match at Eugene's Tamale Temple. Customer complains of insect in refried beans. Employee claims it's parsley. Officers investigate. Dead spider ascertained in frijoles. "Well, it's not an insect," officer [Shield #325] declares. "Spiders are arachnids, you know." "They're also high in protein," officer [Shield #647] adds. Customer not amused. Argument escalates. Scuffle ensues. Officers take thirty-two-year-old male customer into custody, and— compliments of a grateful and politic Eugene—two Cha Cha Chicken Chimichangas and a Mucho Macho Nacho Plate to go.

6700 Block, Coast Highway. Officers go to beach. They park Patrol Unit at overlook, dig into chimichangas, chew thoughtfully, ponder view. The sky above is heavy and gray, a slab of concrete. The ocean chops fretfully beneath it, muddy green, frothy as old soup. Officer [Shield #647] loves how the two of them can be quiet together. There is *some* small talk: the upcoming POA ballots; Tasers, yea or nay; the K-9 Unit's dogfighting scandal. But mostly there is only the tick of the cooling engine, the distant whump of surf against shore, the radio crackling like a comfy fire. Officers sigh. Officer [Shield #647] gestures with chimichanga at vista before them. "There's a saying," he says. "How's it go—

> *Blue skies all day, officers gay.*
> *If skies gray and clouds creep, officers weep."*

Officer [Shield #325] chews, nods, furrows her brow. "It's an *old* saying," he adds. "You know. *Happy* gay. Not *gay* gay." She laughs. He laughs, too. Relief fills Patrol Unit. A weight is lifted, a door eases open and swings wide. His right hand slips from steering wheel and alights, trembling, upon her left knee. Her breath catches, then begins again—steady, resolute. Officers swallow, park chimichangas carefully on dash. Officers turn one to the other. Suspect in backseat asks if they're done with those chimis, complains he's hungry, too, you know, complains that *somebody* in Patrol Unit didn't get to eat his combo plate and can they guess who? Officers terminate break, split Mucho Macho Nachos three ways, transport suspect to Division for booking.

400 Block, Glenhaven Road. Criminal trespass and vandalism at construction site. Four pallets of eight-foot framing two-by-fours chain-sawed into a grand assortment of useless two- and four-foot one-by-fours. Officers walk scene, sniff air. Sawdust, gas fumes, chain oil. It is a pungent mix, complex and heady. Officers inhale deeply, go all woozy.

2600 Block, Frontage Boulevard at Highway 99. Injury accident. Soil subduction collapses shoulder of 44th Street on-ramp. Three vehicles roll down embankment. Officers notify EMT and DOT

Units, assist injured, secure scene. State Patrol pulls up, kills engine, emerges from Patrol Unit like starlet at movie premiere. State Patrol is starch-crisp and preternaturally perspiration-free. State Patrol thanks officers for their assistance, flashes horsey smile, tips dopey hat. Officers sit slouched on Patrol Unit, watch State Patrol strut about. "Prince of Freeways," officer [Shield #647] mutters. "Lord of Turnpikes," he says. Partner suggests that a more collegial relationship with State Patrol is called for. "King of the Road," he continues. "Ayatollah of the Asphalt." Officers giggle, get all silly, love that they can be silly. DPW Units swing by, offer wide range of orange gear and signage: SLOW, CAUTION, choice of SOIL SUBDUCTION or SUBDUCTED SHOULDER.

2200 Block, Felicity Court. Domestic disturbance. Man with golf club pounds on washing machine in garage. Woman in lawn chair applauds his every blow, whistles, barks like dog. Dogs next door whipped into frenzy by noise, bark like woman in lawn chair. Soapy water jets in jugular arcs from innards of crippled washer, streams down driveway, gurgles into gutter. Officers linger in Patrol Unit, assess scene, swiftly reach unspoken agreement, gun engine, hightail it out of there.

1000 Block, Clearview Terrace. Traffic obstruction. Sinkhole reported in street, measuring twenty-five feet across by four feet deep. Officers peer down hole, whistle. DPW Units flush restraint down crapper, go whole hog in establishing perimeter—orange barricades and flashers, orange arrowboards and signage, orange-garbed personnel braiding Reflect-O-Tape throughout scene like carnival light strings. Sinkhole perimeter is now a secure *and* festive perimeter. Officers clash with tableau, sent off to disperse rubberneckers: "Move along, folks, nothing to see here, move along."

2200 Block, Oak Street. Public intoxication and urination. Outside Ye Olde Liquor Shoppe. Sixty-four-year-old man taken into custody. During transport to Division, officer [Shield #325] confesses: "I've always wanted to say that. You know: 'Move along, nothing to see here.'"

5500 Block, Pleasant Avenue. Vandalism. Eighteen mailboxes destroyed along roadside, lopped neatly off their posts in a bout of mailbox baseball, but with chain saw instead of baseball bat. "Mailbox lumberjack," officer [Shield #325] muses aloud. Shot at whimsy misses mark. "Har-dee-har," complainant says. "Ha-fucking-ha." Officer [Shield #647] wonders aloud if somebody maybe put their crabby pants on today. Officer [Shield #325] adds if maybe they OD'd on their potty mouth pills, too. Argument escalates. Scuffle ensues. Fifty-five-year-old male complainant taken into custody.

2200 Block, Felicity Court. Domestic disturbance. Woman wielding shovel hacks at wide-screen television set in driveway. Under canopy of tree in front yard, shirtless man sits on case of beer, pounding brewskies, watching woman, offering profane commentary. Above him, slung into limbs and branches, wet laundry drips heavily—hanged men left in the rain. Dogs next door yowl and bay. Officers cruise by, tap brakes, assess scene, nod assent, hightail it out of there.

2500 Block, Fairmount Street. Criminal trespass and vandalism. Spivak's House of Wicker. Wicker chewed and chopped chain saw–style. Officers move silently into gray wicker haze, powdered with wicker dust, in awe of the sheer totality of wicker havoc.

1900 Block, Cypress Avenue. Illegal assembly. Demonstrators blocking access to public health clinic, refuse order to disperse. All available units dispatched for crowd control. Officers gathered at staging area, briefed on use-of-force policy, on arrest and intake procedures, then sicced on crowd. Officers stoked, fired up, ready to rhumba. Hand-to-hand maneuvers seemingly long forgotten— armlocks and choke holds, the supple choreography of baton work—all return facilely to muscle memory. Crowd control progresses smoothly. Officer [Shield #325] musses hair clobbering balky demonstrator. A scrawny little hank slips loose, nestles against her right cheek, framing the side of her face like an open parenthesis. A semaphore of possibility, officer [Shield #647] muses, spotting her while clobbering *his* balky demonstrator. Amid the tussle and heat of arrest and intake, she looks up, seeks him out, finds him. She smiles, waves shyly. From across the tactical field, he smiles, waves back, sticks out tongue. She is suddenly overcome, startled at how the sight of him affects her. It is not just love, nor desire, but something profoundly less complex, as unadorned and simple as the Vehicle Code. Officer laughs, cries. Tearful and giddy, she whales on her demonstrator with what she realizes is joy in her heart. Demonstrators cuffed, processed, loaded onto County Transport Units. Assembly dispersed. Scene secured. Officers spent, pink and damp in the afterglow of crowd control. Cop Camaraderie ensues. Shirttails tucked, batons wiped down, cigarettes shared. Backs and butts slapped all around.

6700 Block, Coast Highway. Officers go to beach, park at overlook. Officers pooped, reposed. They do not speak. They sip double lattes, ponder view. A gash in the bruise-colored sky bleeds yellow. Sunshine leaks into the ocean, stains its surface with shimmering light. He looks over at her, notices a discoloration, a swelling on her left cheekbone. His hand reaches out, his fingers touch the wound, touch her. "You're hurt," he says. She smiles, whispers: "You should see the other guy." They park their double lattes on dash, slip off their sunglasses, avert their eyes. They screw their faces against the jagged harshness of an unpolarized world, slip sunglasses back on. His hands reach for hers, their fingers clasp and enmesh, roil and swarm at the fourth finger of her left hand. Officers tug and pull, remove and park ring on dash. He reaches for her. She leans toward him; it is like falling. Officers fall. Afterward, they linger over their coffee. Wedding ring on dash glints in the shifting light, harmless as a bottle cap or a shiny old button, something a bird might snatch up. Officers watch a ball of sunlight flare up at earth's edge like a direct hit. Officers assess scene, ascertain world to be beautiful.

2200 Block, Felicity Court. Domestic disturbance. Officers pull up, kill engine. They dawdle in Patrol Unit, fiddling with the mirrors and the radio, double-checking the parking brake. Officers sigh heavily, climb out, and assess scene. Garage door closed. Curtains in windows of home drawn. Officers walk up driveway, pick their way through the detritus of television set and washing machine. They knock on door, ring bell. No answer. Neighborhood quiet. Dogs next door quiet. Birds quiet. Everything, in fact, is quiet. The quiet of earplugs, of morgue duty, and of corridors at 3:00 a.m. The quiet before an alarm clock goes off. Officers backtrack down driveway, approach west side of house, move toward a gate in the fence that leads to backyard. They move gingerly across a saturated lawn, squishy beneath their feet. Soapy water oozes into the tracks they leave. Up ahead, against an exterior wall of house, a pile of freshly cut wood comes into view—one-by-four posts and whitewashed flatboards painted with black block letters. "LIFE" one of them reads. "MURDUR" reads another. Chainsawed picket signs. Officers' napes prickle, butts clench in autonomic response. They thumb the release tabs on their holsters, move toward gate. They lift latch, ease gate open. Above them, the sky clears and the sun breaks. The shadow of a distant airplane skims over them, glides across the lawn, disappears. Officers enter backyard. The back fence sags forward. Trellises and plant stakes list at crazy angles. A brick barbecue sits crumpled atop its sunken hearth slab. The deck along the west side of the house is a corrugation of collapsed planking. It is as if the earth here simply gave up, shrugged, and dropped six feet. Officers move along periphery of sinkhole toward the sliding patio doors that open onto deck. Their panes are shattered. The ground glitters with pebbles of safety glass. From within, cool air drifts out. And then they are hit, bowled over by a surge of vapors foul and thick—the redolence of mimosa, clawing at their eyes and throats, like some monstrous blossoming from somewhere inside the house. And then the noises. First, a loud muffled report—the only way to describe it. Then, rising from the basement—or from someplace deeper still—the robust glissandos of a chain saw, its motor throttling up and down, laboring mightily. And within this an indeterminate overtone—the cadence of voices, urgent and shrill. Shouting, or laughing. Or screaming. Officers unholster service revolvers, position themselves at either side of patio entry. They slip off their sunglasses, take this moment to let their eyes adjust to the dark inside. They look at each other. His eyes are dark brown, like coffee or good soil. Hers are gray, flat as lead except for the glint of a pearly chip in one iris. They do not speak. They love that they don't have to say anything. Instead they reach down, check ammo pouches for extra clips, wipe palms on duty trousers. Eyes adjusted, they draw and shoulder their weapons. They brace their wrists, release their safeties, silently count three, and take a breath. Whereupon officers cross threshold, enter home.

20

SUBTOTALS

Greg Burnham

NUMBER OF REFRIGERATORS I've lived with: 18. Number of rotten eggs I've thrown: 1. Number of finger rings I've owned: 3. Number of broken bones: 0. Number of Purple Hearts: 0. Number of times unfaithful to wife: 2. Number of holes in one, big golf: 0; miniature golf: 3. Number of consecutive push-ups, maximum: 25. Number of waist size: 32. Number of gray hairs: 4. Number of children: 4. Number of suits, business: 2; swimming: 22. Number of cigarettes smoked: 83. Number of times I've kicked the dog: 6. Number of times caught in the act, any act: 64. Number of postcards sent: 831; received: 416. Number of spider plants that died while under my care: 34. Number of blind dates: 2. Number of jumping jacks: 982,316. Number of headaches: 184. Number of kisses, given: 21,602; received: 20,041. Number of belts: 21. Number of fuck-ups, bad: 6; not so bad: 1,500. Number of times swore under breath at parents: 838. Number of weeks at church camp: 1. Number of houses owned: 0. Number of houses rented: 12. Number of hunches played: 1,091. Number of compliments, given: 4,051; accepted: 2,249. Number of embarrassing moments: 2,258. Number of states visited: 38. Number of traffic tickets: 3. Number of girlfriends: 4. Number of times fallen off playground equipment, swings: 3; monkey bars: 2; teeter-totter: 1. Number of times flown in dreams: 28. Number of times fallen down stairs: 9. Number of dogs: 1. Number of cats: 7. Number of miracles witnessed: 0. Number of insults, given: 10,038; received: 8,963. Number of wrong telephone numbers dialed: 73. Number of times speechless: 33. Number of times stuck key into electrical socket: 1. Number of birds killed with rocks: 1. Number of times had the wind knocked out of me: 12. Number of times patted on the back: 181. Number of times wished I was dead: 2. Number of times unsure of footing: 458. Number of times fallen asleep reading a book: 513. Number of times born again: 0. Number of times seen double: 28. Number of déjà vu experiences: 43. Number of emotional breakdowns: 1. Number of times choked on bones, chicken: 4; fish: 6; other: 3. Number of times didn't believe parents: 23,978. Number of lawn-mowing miles: 3,575. Number of light bulbs changed: 273. Number of childhood home telephone: 384-621-5844. Number of brothers: 3½. Number of passes at women: 5. Number of stairs walked, up: 745,821; down: 743,609. Number of hats lost: 9. Number of magazine subscriptions: 41. Number of times seasick: 1. Number of bloody noses: 16. Number of times had sexual intercourse: 4,013. Number of fish caught: 1. Number of time(s) heard "The Star Spangled Banner": 2,410. Number of babies held in arms: 9. Number of times I forgot what I was going to say: 631.

21

OUR
SPRING
CATALOG

Jack Pendarvis

AS GOES THE ZEPHYR

LURLEEN BIVANT

This luminous and engaging first novel takes place in a suburbia unlike any suburbia you have ever encountered. Marchie Whitaker's days as a self-recriminating soccer mom and nights as an unsexed sounding board to her workaholic husband are interrupted by the surprising appearance of a rather libidinous manticore. That's just the beginning of the whimsical visitations! When workers come to dig the new swimming pool—a symbol of middle class status quo that should, *should*, answer all of Marchie's dreams—the most wonderful things begin to happen. Goblins, trolls, witches, and other inhabitants of the underworld skitter upwards through the broken soil—including the great god Pan himself! Anyway, everybody wants to lock up Marchie as a crazy person because they can't understand her magical shit. It kind of tapers off at the end, like she ran out of ideas.

I COULDN'T EAT ANOTHER THING

ANGELA BIRD

In this luminous collection of sparkling stories, former newspaper columnist Bird makes a stunning fictional debut with a wry look at the state of modern commitment. A lot of the time I'd get to the end of one of the stories and turn a page like, "Huh?" Like, "Where's the end of it?" Like, "What happened next?" But nothing happened next. You know, those kind of stories. Luminous.

LOW TOWN

KARL HARPER

This is one of those finely wrought first novels of surprising tenderness and depth where a cool teenager is stifled by the closeminded assholes in his small town. He has sex with a lot of beautiful girls and then he makes it big as a painter and says, "So long, losers!" There's a tragedy that makes him rethink everything and pretty soon he comes of age. At the end he's headed off for fame and fortune and all the losers are sorry they didn't suck his dick when they had the chance. But in a funny kind of way Boy Wonder will always carry a piece of Loserville with him wherever he goes. Blah blah blah. If you look at the guy's picture on the dust jacket, you'll see that he made up the part about having sex.

THE SIGHING OF THE STONES
LOUIS DELMONTE

A boy and girl grope innocently toward first love against the backdrop of an Oklahoma farming community where a lot of cattle mutilations are taking place. Who cares?

THE LITTLE DOG LAUGHED
HARRY PARKS

Seriously, what am I doing with my life? Is this it? What am I supposed to say about this book that will make you buy it? Look at the cover. Look at the title. If you like books with covers and titles like that, go for it. It won't kill you. I keep meaning to get around to *The Naked and the Dead*. That's supposed to be awesome. If you have to know, this particular piece of shit is about a guy who's haunted by the death of so-and-so and he takes a trip in a hot air balloon to forget all his problems. But then he finds out you can't run away from your problems. Big fucking deal.

A GOOD FAMILY
BECKINSALE CRUTHERS

Delia Moon had it all: riches, glamour, wit and erudition. But suddenly her Park Avenue world came crashing down around her ears. I bet you never read a book like this before! It's about the horrible pain and turmoil of being rich and white. The Moon family has a shitload of dramatic tragedies and problems. I think there's some incest in there. That makes the title ironic! *Kirkus Reviews* is going to eat this shit up.

THE ENORMOUS SWAN

M. A. McCORQUEDALE

Set against the colorful backdrop of some historical period nobody gives a rat's ass about, *The Enormous Swan* tells the story of a humble craftsman who comes into contact with an emperor or some shit. To tell you the truth I didn't make it past page 10 or so. It's one of those books where the author spent half his life in a library looking up facts about medieval culinary techniques and galley slaves and shit, and now he thinks we're supposed to care.

EAT THE LOTUS

MARIE OVERSTREET

I swear to God I'm going to cut my own throat. I just don't give a shit. Husband and wife reach a crossroads in their relationship against the colorful backdrop of blah blah blah. They're haunted by the suicide of their only son or some shit. Pull yourself together, you pussies! God I'm sick of this shit. I'd rather work at fucking McDonald's, I swear to God. You know what? It's not even about my career goals anymore. "Come on, Annie, this job will be good experience. You'll make lots of contacts. I want to read your novel, Annie. When am I going to see this novel of yours, Annie?" You can bite my ass, you creepy old fuck. One day you're going to get what's coming to you.

22

Robin Hemley

To: Poetry Association of the Western Suburbs Listserve
From: Lisa Drago-Harse
Subject: Next Meeting

Date: July 17th

Hi all,
I wanted to confirm that our next meeting will be held in the
Sir Francis Drake Room at the Bensonville Hampton Inn on
August 3rd. Minutes from our last meeting and an agenda
for the next meeting will follow shortly.

Peace and Poetry,
Lisa Drago-Harse
Secretary/PAWS

To: Poetry Association of the Western Suburbs Listserve
From: Michael Stroud
Re: Re: Next Meeting

Date: July 17th

Dearest Lisa,
First of all, I LOVE your mole and don't find it unsightly in
the least! There is absolutely no reason for you to be

ashamed of it (though it might be a good idea to have it checked out). But please don't remove it! Heaven forbid, my darling! As I recall, I gave you considerable pleasure when I sucked and licked it like a nipple. A nipple it is in size and shape, if not placement. That no one else knows your mole's position on your body (other than your benighted husband, poor limp Richard, that Son(net) of a Bitch as you call him) is more the pity (if Marvell had known such a mole, he undoubtedly would have added an extra stanza to his poem). But my coy mistress is not SO terribly coy as all that, if I remember correctly (and how could I forget!). You were not at all what I had expected in bed – not that I had any expectations at all. When you started massaging my crotch with your foot underneath the table in the Sir Francis Drake Room, I was at first shocked. For a moment, I thought perhaps the unseen massager was none other than our esteemed president, the redoubtable Darcy McFee (makeup and wardrobe courtesy of Yoda). Is that terrible of me? I have nothing personal against her, really, except for her execrable taste in poetry, and the fact that you should be president, not she. And her breath. And that habit of pulling her nose when she speaks and that absolutely horrific expression of hers, Twee. As in, "I find his poetry just so twee." What does twee mean and why does she keep inflicting it upon us! So imagine my horror when I felt this foot in my crotch and I stared across the table at the two of you – she twitching like a slug that's had salt poured on it and you immobile except for your Mont Blanc pen taking down the minutes. Ah, to think that the taking down of minutes could be such an erotic activity, but in your capable hands, it is. To think that mere hours later, it would be my Mont Blanc you'd grasp so firmly, guiding me into the lyrical book of your body. But initially, I thought the worst, that it was Darcy, not you. My only consolation was the idea that at least I had her on a sexual harassment suit, her being my boss after all at Roosevelt. Another reason I thought it was her and not you was because I know you're married and she isn't and I knew that Richard is a member of our esteemed organization, too (and he was in the room, seated beside you no less!). It was only that sly smile in your eyes that tipped me off. I, too, love the danger that illicit public sex brings, as long as it's kept under the table, so to speak. And yes, maybe someday we can make love on that very same table in the Sir Francis Drake Room, my darling. But I must ask you, sweetheart, where did you learn that amazing trick? I have seen people wiggle their ears before, but never that! What amazing talent and such a pity that this is not something you bring out at parties or poetry readings to awe the dumb masses! Would Darcy find that too twee? I think not! Thinking of you now makes me so hot. I want to nibble you. I want to live in your panties. I want to write a series of odes to you equal in number to every lucky taste bud on my tongue, every nerve ending (no, not endings but beginnings!) on my body that live in rapture of your every pore. No, not poor, but rich. I am rich. I make metaphors of your muscles, of your thighs, of the fecund wetness bursting with your being and effulgence. I must swallow now. I must breathe. I must take my leave, my darling, and go now to relieve myself of my private thoughts of you and you alone.

With undying love and erotic daydreams,
Mikey

P.S. Do you think you could get away for an evening next week? Could you be called away from Richard for an emergency meeting of the Public Relations Committee?

To: PAWS Listserve
From: Darcy McFee
Re: Re: Re: Next Meeting

Date: July 17th

I am traveling now and will not be answering e-mails until I
return on July 21st.

Thanks!
Darcy

To: PAWS Listserve
From: Sam Fulgram, Jr.
Re: Re: Re: Re: Next Meeting

Date: July 17th

Whoa boy! Do you realize you just sent out your love note
to the entire Poetry Association of the Western Suburbs
listserve?

Cheers,
Sam

P.S. – That mole? You've got my imagination running wild.
As long as the entire organization knows about it now,
would you mind divulging its location? I'd sleep better at
night knowing it.

To: PAWS Listserve
From: Betsy Midchester
Re: Re: Re: Re: Re: Next Meeting

Date: July 17th

Hi all,

Well! That last message from "Mikey" Stroud certainly made my day. I thought at first the message was addressed to me. As I had no memory of placing my foot in Mike's crotch, I naturally assumed that I needed an adjustment of my medication so that I wouldn't forget such episodes in the future. Now I see it's simply Michael ("Down Boy") Stroud and our esteemed Secretary of the Galloping Mont Blaaaaanc who need the medication adjustments. Thanks, in any case, for a much needed lift in an otherwise humdrum day.

Betsy Midchester
Treasurer/PAWS

To: PAWS Listserve
From: Lisa Drago-Harse
Re: Re: Re: Re: Re: Re: Next Meeting

Date: July 17th

This is a nightmare. I'm not quite sure what to say except that life is unpredictable and often irreversible. While I do not wish to go into details or make excuses for the above e-mail from Michael Stroud, I would like to clarify one thing: that was not my foot in your crotch Michael. But your belief that it was my foot in your crotch explains a few things concerning your subsequent behavior towards me that were up until this moment a mystery.

LDH

To: PAWS Listserve
From: Michael Stroud
Re: Re: Re: Re: Re: Re: Re: Next Meeting

Date: July 17th

I'm

To: PAWS Listserve
From: Michael Stroud
Re: Re: Re: Re: Re: Re: Re: Re: Next Meeting

Date: July 17th

I hit the send button by mistake before I was ready. This isn't my day, to say the least! I'm sorry!!!! I'd like to apologize to the entire PAWS community, and also to Lisa's husband Richard and to Darcy. And to you, Lisa. I don't mean to make excuses for myself, but I would like to say that I've been under a tremendous amount of pressure of late, at school, at home, and I am nothing if not vulnerable and flawed. All I can say is that in poetry I find some solace for the petty actions of others and the sometimes monstrous actions of which I'm all too capable. As déclassé as Truth and Beauty are these days, it is in such expressions as those of Matthew Arnold, Keats, Byron, and Shelley to whom I look for my meager draught of the Divine. And sometimes, I must admit, I seek in the affection of my fellow poetry lovers, the divinity which I myself lack. I ask you all to blame me, not Lisa for what has happened.

But if not your foot, Lisa, then whose?
Michael Stroud

To: PAWS Listserve
From: Greg Rudolfsky
Re: Re: Re: Re: Re: Re: Re: Re: Re: RESPECT

Date: July 17th

Just a little bit, Just a little bit.
Sock it to me, sock it to me, sock it to me, sock it to me, sock it to me, sock it to me, sock it to me, sock it to me, RESPECT, Just a little bit, just a little bit. . . .

To: PAWS Listserve
From: Samantha M. Poulsen, RN
Subject: Fecund Poets

Date: July 17th

I do not care whose foot is in whose crotch, but I think it's insulting and idiotic that so-called educated people would use such phrases as, "the fecund wetness bursting with your being and effulgence." And officers of the PAWS at that!

To: PAWS Listserve
From: Richard Harse
Re: Fecund Poets

Date: July 17th

I would like to tender my resignation in the Poets of the Western Suburbs, as I will be tendering my resignation in several other areas of my life. I only belonged to PAWS in any case because of my wife's interest in poetry. I wanted to share her interests, but clearly not all of them.

To: PAWS Listserve
From: Darcy McFee
Re: Fecund Poets

Date: July 22nd

Well, it seems that our little organization has been busy in my absence. I have over 300 new messages in my e-mail account, all, it seems from my fellow poetry lovers! I haven't yet had a chance to read your exchanges, but I will soon. In the meantime, I wanted to convey some exciting news. This weekend, while attending a workshop at Wright State in

Dayton, I ran into the former Poet Laureate, Billy Collins, who has agreed to be our special guest at our annual Poetry Bash in Oak Park. He said he's heard quite a lot about our organization in recent days and that our board had achieved near legendary status in the poetry community. I knew this would make you as proud as it makes me.

To: PAWS Listerve
From: Darcy McFee
Subject: Twee

Date: July 24th

So this is how it is. Upon reading the 300 e-mails that collected in my inbox over the weekend, my mind is a riot of emotions. I have not slept for nearly 48 hours. Never before have I been so insulted. Yet, I also know that I am, at least in part, to blame. Had I not stuck my foot in Michael Stroud's crotch, none of this would have happened. Twitching like a slug that's had salt poured on it? That hurts, Michael. It really does. I didn't realize you were so shallow. But in reading your collective e-mails, I see that at least half our membership has a decidedly sadistic bent. In any case, it was not your crotch, I aimed for, Michael, but the crotch of our Vice-President, Amir Bathshiri, with whom I have long been intimately acquainted, both of us having lost our spouses several years ago. If the seating arrangements in the Sir Francis Drake Room were any less cramped, none of these misunderstandings would have occurred. Of course, I never would have tried to fondle you, Michael. In the first place, you are the most boring, tedious person I have met in my life, and believe me, as Chair of the English Dept. at Roosevelt, I have met my share of boring, tedious people. You recite poetry with all the grace of a highway sign that cautions one to beware of falling rocks. But enough! I know that it is my errant foot to blame. Amir and I have talked this over and have decided to withdraw from PAWS as well as from academia. Early retirement calls, Michael and Lisa, and I will give neither of you a thought as I walk along the beach hand in hand with Amir in the months and years to come, listening to the mermaids singing each to each.

Yes, Michael, I find you and your crotch and your paramour the very essence of Twee.

To: PAWS Listserve
From: Betsy Midchester/Treasurer
Subject: New Elections

Date: July 30th

Please note that the agenda for our next meeting has changed. We will spend most of the meeting on new elections to be held for the positions of President, Vice-President and Secretary of our organization. Note, too, that we will no longer be meeting in the Sir Francis Drake Room of the Bensonville Hampton Inn. Instead, we will be meeting in the cafeteria of Enchanted Gardens Residence for Seniors in Glen Ellyn. The change in venue was planned well in advance of recent events, so members should not read anything into this (though if any organization's members are skilled at reading between the lines, it should be ours). Please think about whom you would like to nominate for these important positions in our organization. And in the meantime, please remember to always be conscious and considerate of your audience.

Peace and poetry,
Betsy Midchester
Treasurer and Acting President/PAWS

23

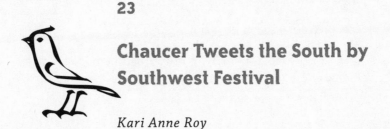

Chaucer Tweets the South by Southwest Festival

Kari Anne Roy

#SXSW hath begunne. Felawshipe is wrot amongst many fyne hypster pilgrimes. The pathwayes overflowe with dangley baddges.

As the evenning aproacheth, hypsters hath desended upon our towne, drinnking our wyne as unikornes feast upon rayes of the sonne.

O that marche daye wan the sonne shone so bryte, vishones of glorye from hypsters' mirrored sonneglasses stabbeth at myne fase.

Crulle lokkes shoote fromme the eyes of thyne bartender. Typ welle, mashine minion. Else you shall earn a boote in youre arse.

The prys paide by a lustye bacheler is this: hypster femayles groupe like flockes of paynted chikennes. Cocques are foresaken. #sadcocques

Flocke of hypsters mightily roarred past my hoarse-carte, stampeedding olde menne offreing free memorees on stix.

Hoarse-carte dryvers watcheth mappyng devises, forsayking welffayre of inosents. Dangere hydes betwixt all lyte polles.

A nobil armye of gentil knyghts appeare to vommit in thyne alley. Alas, they forsayke cleen chin stubbel to partee forthwith. #boot&ralleye

Wat ho, goatee'd man? Thy skinnee jenes hath byrn'd my corneyas.

Fye the dregs who weareth blootooth sets upon theyr heds. Do you speeketh to me or to demones wither sleepe tween your eares?

24

Iconographic Conventions of Pre- and Early Renaissance: Italian Representations of the Flagellation of Christ

Rachel B. Glaser

THE NEW TESTAMENT offers no specific description of the flagellation of Jesus Christ and very little of the rest of the Passion: Jesus's criminal indictment, subsequent suffering, and execution. Yet this series of events received *massive artistic attention* in the Middle Ages and Early Renaissance, depicted thousands of times with a certain consistency of imagery. Biblical flagellation scenes in painting and sculpture from 1300 A.D. to 1525 A.D. exhibit unmistakable iconographic repetition. Given the lack of source material from which to draw, artists of these centuries heavily borrowed from their peers and predecessors.

Historical coverage of the Passion is slim. No direct description of the event exists in the Synoptic Gospels and only one small segment is devoted to it in the Gospel of John. No one reads this segment lost within John. In this significant historical void, great artistic liberties could initially be taken as interest in the subject expanded. Someone once decided, for example, that Jesus had been bound to a column, and this achieved a thematic resonance with the audiences of the time, encouraging artists to repeat it. Someone decided Christ was slender, his hair framing his long face. Long like a horse and long like unhappy. Thereafter, artists followed formats proven to convey the message successfully, deviating rarely and then only slightly. It was established early on how the flagellation was to appear and no monumental compositional alterations occurred for hundreds of years.

The Latin word for *whip*, *flagellum* is also a long, slender projection from the cell body, only visible with a powerful microscope. Its function is to propel a unicellular or small multicellular organism by beating with whiplike motion. In larger animals, flagella are often arranged en masse at the surface of a stationary cell and serve to move fluids along mucous membranes, such as the lining of the trachea. Flagella increase or decrease their rotational speed relative to the strength of the proton-motive force.

This common practice of formal imitation and borrowing is unremarkable, but as the accumulation of passion-related imagery accelerates through this time period, visual history achieves legitimacy. Passion (from the Latin *patior*, meaning to suffer or to endure) is an emotion of intense, compelling enthusiasm for a person, object, activity or idea. The Passion quotient is used in Thomas Friedman's formula of $CQ + PQ > IQ$. Curiosity plus passion is greater than intelligence.

Historical coverage is *slim*. No description exists. Christ was slender; his hair casually framing his long face. Long like a horse's and unhappy. Long like a bluesman playing his blues. Like a mostly empty ketchup, a basset hound looking low with eyelids lower. His chest had some or none hairs. A beard over his cheeks because that was the style back then; *only warriors shaved their beards*, and that was to show how sharp their swords were. That was for fun. Also it was custom for a cuckold to have a warrior shave his beard, publicly showing his marriage as flawed, an invitation to flaw it further.

Curiosity plus passion is *almost* equal to being smart. E = a Mazda car driving twice as fast. E = Michael Jordan dunking two balls while coughing. God is the closest thing to an all-knowing entity. She indexes over 9.5 *billion* Web pages, which is more than any search engine on the Web. She sorts through this vast amount of knowledge using her patented PageRank technology. God is virtually everywhere on earth at the same time. With the proliferation of Wi-Fi networks, one will eventually be able to access God.

Through repetition, validity is assumed. The Flagellation thus becomes one part of a larger visual narrative, instantly recognizable. Flagellation scenes turn *iconic* in their thematic compatibility with each other, to see one is to be reminded of others already seen. This repetition strengthens their representation in religious culture. As with the Crucifixion, a familiarity close to comfort arises when gazing at a crucifixion painting, knowing absolutely the thing being killed will be a white male with a long face and relatively long nose. Nails and blood are optional. Clouds optional. Weeping women optional.

Children tend to add a curlicue of smoke upon the addition of a chimney in a drawing of a house. What if all beach scenes had a sym-metry of beach umbrellas and a ratio of birds to sky? A formation that urged copying. In China, there are no curlicues of smoke in children's drawings. Smoke is usually represented by several soft, wavering lines. Studies such as this show Chinese children to be more thoughtful and observant than American children, who abbreviate visual language immediately to symbols. The sometimes discounted studies of chil-dren's drawings have informed larger studies of lifestyle differences. "California coast drawings varied greatly according to the quality of the children's mark-making tools. Wealthy children had the opportunity to mosaic with minerals and a wide variety of artistic plastics, whereas children in poorer neighborhoods stuck to construction paper and in extreme cases, *broken glass*."

Stick-men and -women are not necessarily the child-drawing norm. Studies found young Russian children making "bubble-men," as researchers referred to them. These rounded sketches were thought to originate from the abundance of snowmen during the lengthy, snow-prone winters of the region.

When American college students take their year abroad, there is no one familiar to greet them except a loneliness they outgrew years ago. Friends will be forged how pioneers forged rivers, how criminals and poor test-takers forge signatures. From this great distance, they will finally be able to *see* America, from looking around and not finding it. Buildings like cakes instead of Legos. If they go to art museums, they feel anxious. How can one *stand* the exquisitely stunning, divinely magnificent paintings in European cities? Making one nostalgic for the Middle Ages, the early ages, painted so *painfully* there are nowhere strokes, nowhere splatters, unnerving to see a scene so deeply actualized in two dimensions, the David in three, appealingly human, the most appealing human, a new ideal to bring home along with the souvenirs.

All humans find themselves in an anxious daze by the end of these museums, the final floors are skipped or else run through frantically. The way to take these paintings in is to blink them, blur them, to look a little less than needed. Such eye-pleasing two-dimensionals beg to be marred, trashed, exposed in two dimensions. A wad of gum would do it, little circles of spit, a knife to reveal the wall behind it. It has been suggested the Louvre commission some copies *of good size*, very fine, expert renderings of one of the museum's paintings, perhaps a collaged scene of a few, hung near the cafeteria to be mauled and defaced by tourists sick on beauty.

Back to the discussion on David: Michelangelo has set up more than one teenage girl for disappointment. Delicate, arrogant, naturally toned, with big hands to hold, many girls fly home heart-struck, it's true! Flocking to the first curly-haired boy they see, looking more carefully at the football team, too much time in the library, tying the phone cord in knots, settling for a prom date, etc., etc., rooting for Italy even in the Olympics. Relative to Jesus but in a different way. One girl's experience with both was to fall for the David, returning home only to sculpt him out of white chocolate and melt him (*melt him!*) on a hot plate. Then meeting a David and understanding the world's preoccupation with Jesus, see diary entry below:

> *The bluest eye proposal was met by one unknowing boy*
> *who had the bluest eyes, winning, generous, butt-perfect,*
> *pleasing, spontaneous and breathing, mother nature's son but shy,*
>   *silly, dillied*
> *all down. If Jesus was like that, then finally I understand*
>   *everyone's preoccupation.*

If one could suspend knowledge and judgment, consider Jesus as the kind-hearted high school sweetheart who dies *tragically in a car crash* (and just two days before graduation!) A dead boyfriend, as we all know, is *impossible* to "*get over*," having committed no crime besides *stealing* our hearts, etc. Breaking off a relationship with no one *breaking it off*, this kind of end is very hard to accept, leaving the left one thinking, *if only* I had driven myself, if only I hadn't *insisted on ice cream*, if only the weather had been nicer, or the road had been cleared, or my purse hadn't been *lazily* draped over the gear shift, *etc.* The large

Christian world wants to meet, to speak with, the tragically died-young, the perpetual. There is no old-aged Lennon, no middle-aged Cobain running amuck. To die young is to stay young, to keep everyone wanting to stay young with you, to make them afraid to approach an age you never got to, that you were supposed to get to first.

In Japan, a young girl published an essay on Cobain's voice. A rough translation states:

> *Cobain's voice houses more than one voice. This magic of voice is most clearly deciphered on the Unplugged album. I could find enough levels in Kurt Cobain's voice to live satisfied, but the rest of my family wasn't as fortunate.*

The text goes on to question the structural makeup of Cobain's throat. Does it contain pebbles or kernels that rumble along? Would the writer try to communicate with Cobain if he had not left his body behind as evidence? Does one assist a dead musician by covering his songs?

A cover is a new rendition of a previously recorded song. Usually, the original recording is regarded as the definitive version and all others lesser competitors, alternates, or tributes. Songs have been covered since the first melody hummed in the presence of another. Monkeys covered songs way before they lost the hair. Adam and Eve used to sing while they had sex in streams. Crickets sure sing similar and leaves have a song, birds, thunder claps are a kind, not so popular or pleasing, but everyone has their music. Different car engines sound good together. An airplane duets nicely with a lawnmower. Music proves one of the most exciting and accessible art forms to cover. A number of literary covers have been produced by a junior high English class, the text only differing in handwriting. Historical recreations, for example, Civil War reenactments could be considered covers, but those wars are fake. A cover song holds all qualities that define a song; a cover song is definitely *real*. One can argue, as the text here is about to, a cover version makes a song *more* real, alive even, since changing the form calls attention to the original, shows the song is still identifiable as the song, even with different qualities.

Some turn into dance songs, "Always on My Mind," for instance, sung first by Brenda Lee, popularized by Elvis, then re-covered by Willie Nelson, then turned dance by the Pet Shop Boys. Newly-turned dance covers sound careless, freed from their gloom by immortal beats. These beats keep going after the song has stopped. Beat-making machines have no *off* button. They must be stuffed in pillows, in closets, in sheds, buried in backyards, until the beat is needed once again.

Does a cover unleash the song? One that's been called the best, Hendrix completely outgunning a Dylan original, throwing it far from Bob's scratchy so-so. John Coltrane rescues "My Favorite Things" from the original *The Sound of Music* version. His meandering jazz masterpiece weaves in and out of melody, trilling notes out of control, and all the while the listener has the other prim version in her head. No one sings lyrics in Coltrane's version. They are offered by the song's ghost. Coltrane's melody calls to mind the kittens and string. Then the instruments storm, there are hundreds of cats, way too much string.

Digital appropriation can be a form of 4th-dimensional rape, as in the mash-up of Ludacris's "What's Your Fantasy" and Kylie Minogue's "Can't Get You Out of My Head." The combination of the two, referred to as "Can't lick you out of my head," puts Kylie's backing dance beat over Ludacris's dark questioning keyboard, transforming Ludacris's lyrics into a seduction. All that's left of Kylie's voice is her girlish "la-la-la" chorus and it's being used against her. Anonymous assault is common, comparable to Photoshop scandal, the cut and paste from one online chat to another, but *incomparable* to the questionable assault of Kobe Bryant upon Unnamed:

> *We stood right here and started having the you know,*
> *the foreplay happened right here . . . the hug goodbye*
> *thing or whatever . . . we just started kissing. I asked her I*
> *said you know, she bent over, and walked over on her own*
> *free will . . . put her foot up here all by herself and if that*
> *wasn't consensual . . . Did she cry, no . . . She didn't cry*
> *at all . . . I didn't say she slipped off, she just you know removed*
> *herself from . . . I said she slid off . . . Slid off like*
> *when uh, that was it and I stood there like this and uh you*
> *know, put it back in my pants so you know, that was it no*
> *more no nothing . . . She kissed goodbye. Boom . . . I put*
> *my thing back in my pants when I was through and she . . .*
> *no, she didn't leave, we kissed goodbye, we kissed goodbye*

Other notorious ballers, the Detroit Piston Bad Boys were known for their unforgiving physical style. One of Rick Mahorn's tactics was to foul an opponent after another Piston had already fouled him and the whistle had blown. In a display of poor sportsmanship, they walked off the court, refusing to shake hands with the Bulls after losing to them in the 1991 Eastern Conference Finals. The Pistons leave behind a vivid legacy and the league's subsequent addition of the flagrant foul rule, granting the badly-fouled two shots and possession of the ball.

Legacies leave things behind. The left-behinds transform to the lost. None would know how Christ looked had the villagers not run to their huts inspired. Darwin patterns decorate more than exotic animals. The Toyota Camry slowly morphs to the more luxury look of the Lexus. A prominent Cadillac grill copied on a new Ford. Is this the same thing that gets daughters like mothers? Nowadays, teens are texting their picks for natural selection. The process of learning is a brain transmission of ideas, the original electricity of contact and understanding. Are Jesus paintings covers of Jesus paintings? Or of Jesus? One can argue *all* portraits as covers, *sunsets covers too*, a day a cover of the last, a year, a century. The USA is a cover of England. Football a cover of war. This links everything to a repetitive tradition. Lightning bolts assisted in this game of improvement. Saints no longer hoard ecstasy. iPod nanos spark bedrooms on fire. As Jimi Hendrix writes on a postcard home:

> Belief comes through electricity. We're playing for our sound to go inside of the soul. You're not going to find it in church. A lot of kids don't find nothing in church. I remember I got thrown out of church because I had the improper clothes on. I had tennis shoes and a suit.

25

THE HUMAN SIDE OF
INSTRUMENTAL TRANSCOMMUNICATION

Wendy Brenner

GREETINGS, AND WELCOME to the third annual Conference of the Instrumental Transcommunication Network. Special welcome to those organizations joining us this year for the first time: the Engineering Anomalies Research Society ("EARS"), the Electromagnetic Aberrations Research Society (also "EARS"), the Tinnitus Family, and Chronic Pain Anonymous. We are delighted to see such a large turnout—surely our growing numbers indicate that the validity of instrumental transcommunication is becoming apparent to even our most outspoken critics.

I would now like to share some thoughts about the meaning of this year's conference theme, "The Human Side of Instrumental Transcommunication." For myself, founder of the Instrumental Transcommunication Network, the answer to the question "Why use tape recorders, televisions, and computers to attempt to communicate interdimensionally with spirit beings?" has always been a highly personal one.

My involvement in the field began four years ago in St. Augustine, Florida, where I was vacationing with my wife and son, Nathan—who

at that time was the only person in our family with a particular interest in recording equipment. Then seven years old, he already owned a
dozen miniature tape recorders, and more cassettes than crayons.
When he was only a baby he had discovered my wife's little Panasonic
portable from her journalism school days, digging it out of a box in the
basement and screaming when we tried to pry it away. Thereafter, we
bought tape recorders for him wherever we saw them, at thrift stores,
flea markets, garage sales we happened to pass. They were cheap, we
reasoned, too big to swallow, and Nathan couldn't seem to get enough
of them—he carried them around like hamsters and wouldn't sleep
without one or two in his bed. On his first day of kindergarten an
entire wing of his school had to be evacuated when the tape recorder
he kept in his windbreaker got stuck on fast-forward in the coatroom
and was believed to be a ticking bomb.

He just had a way with those little machines. He could rewind or
fast-forward any cassette tape to the exact spot he wanted on the first
try, without using the counter device, and on long car trips my wife
and I took turns requesting songs from the middles of tapes to keep
him busy. He would sit on the floor under the dashboard and put his
ear up next to the tape deck like a safecracker, and then his whole face
would light up as though someone had flipped a switch behind it when
he hit the right spot, pressed the play button and my wife's favorite
song came on once again, perfectly cued to the beginning. He never
missed, and, like any good magician, he never told his secrets.

Interestingly, though, despite his love for junky cassette players,
Nathan didn't care at all for the brand new Walkman my wife's mother
bought him. His real love was for making tapes, not listening to them,
we discovered, so we allowed him to make as many as he wanted. He
recorded himself talking in different voices, acting out dramas full of

coyotes, opera singers, helicopters, Mack trucks, nuclear emergency alert sirens, hives of angry bees. In his stories people had frequent arguments, and there were many slamming doors, much shouting to be let in or out.

He was so enthusiastic about his sound effects that he tended to neglect things like plot and logic, jumping from one sensational noise to another without explanation, rushing through dialogue and mixing up his voices so that half the time we couldn't understand what any of his characters were saying, or even what was going on. "You'll have to slow down and enunciate," my wife, ever the good editor, would tell him, "because whatever you just said there is not a word." But Nathan paid no heed. "If it's not a word," he argued, "then how come I just said it?"

Of course he could not have understood how meaningful that offhand remark would come to be, to so many of us. He was saying, of course, that *the act of communication is of greater significance than the means used to achieve it.* Who among us today has not felt deeply that very sentiment? But I digress.

On our trip to St. Augustine, I will always remember, Nathan wished for three things: to visit a Spanish war fort, to find and bring home an unbroken sand dollar, and to get the hotel maid to talk into his tape recorder. This was his first stay in a hotel since he was a baby, and he grew very excited when we explained to him that a lady was going to come into our room while we weren't there and make our beds and leave clean towels for us. "A lady we know?" he asked, and when we told him no, a strange lady, he concluded it was the tooth fairy, or someone just like her, perhaps her friend. This was where they probably lived, he said—in Florida. We tried to explain the truth without letting on that the tooth fairy wasn't real, but Nathan only grew more certain in his belief. Every morning before we left the hotel room to go down to breakfast or the beach, he set up one of his tape recorders on the dresser with this note:

Dear cleaning lady,

Please press Play and Record at the same time and then read this message out loud, begin Here.

Hello, this is the cleaning lady coming to you live from the hotel. Today will be hot and sunny. Now, back to you.

When you are done press Stop.

Unfortunately, the woman never responded. Every night when we returned to the room Nathan ran to the recorder, but it had never been touched, and he grew more disappointed every day. We had already photographed him waving down at us from the parapet of the war fort, and he had not one but several perfect specimens of sand dollars wrapped in Kleenex like cookies and tucked for safety in our suitcase pockets. Yet these successes seemed only to make him more frustrated, as if this were some fairy tale where he had to satisfy an angry king. "Why didn't she do it, why?" he cried to us, night after night. It was possible the cleaning lady didn't speak or read English, we told him, or, more likely, she didn't want to disturb the belongings of guests—or perhaps she never even saw the note, or realized it was intended for her.

Privately my wife and I discussed tracking this woman down and talking to her, or finding another hotel employee who would cooperate, or even disguising one of our voices and recording the message ourselves. We *had* written little notes to him from the tooth fairy, my wife said, and wasn't this the same thing? But in the end we decided it was best to leave the situation to chance. Since we knew the maid was a real person capable of responding, we wanted her message, should it come, to be genuine. My wife eventually came to question this decision, but, as all of us here today undoubtedly understand, in such a situation integrity cannot be compromised, regardless of how desperately our hearts might long for different outcomes to our experiments.

Consider the pioneers in our field: Dr. Konstantin Raudive, who made over one hundred thousand separate recordings after hearing a single mysterious voice on a blank, brand new tape; or Friedrich Juergenson, who abandoned his successful opera-singing career so he could investigate electronic voice phenomena full-time after some strange voices speaking Norwegian turned up on a tape on which he had recorded bird calls. Falsifying results was never an option for these scientists, as it should never be for us.

Yet despite our faithfulness to the scientific method, we must not ignore the personal factor in these experiments—the human side of instrumental transcommunication. For the personal relevance of the message, when it finally comes, is often what establishes the message's authenticity. Those of you who have already received such messages report that the sender will often use, as a kind of password, a phrase or nickname or piece of information that only he and you, the recipient, could know. Who can forget the message our esteemed colleagues Meek and O'Neil received on their Spiricom device, in the unmistakable voice of the deceased electronics specialist with whom they had worked for years: "The problem is an impedance mismatch into the third resistor—try a 150-ohm half-watt resistor in parallel with a .0047 micro-farad ceramic capacitor." Or Dr. Raudive's own unexpected message from the other side, which came through one night at home on the clock radio of the researcher who had been tirelessly advancing Raudive's cause after his untimely death: "This is Konstantin Raudive. Stay on the station, tune in correctly. Here it is summer, always summer! Soon it will work everywhere!" It almost seems that the deceased senders of these messages answered the calls of the living, rather than vice versa, as is usually assumed.

In light of these considerations, I strongly contend that my wife and I were justified in our choice not to fake the maid's voice on Nathan's tape. We could not have known what was about to occur.

For those of you not familiar with my story, which was reprinted in last month's newsletter, the paramedics who so heroically attempted to revive my son gave his cause of death as "generalized childhood seizure," meaning he had stopped breathing before he went underwater, rather than afterward. My wife, who was swimming not far away at the time, agrees; otherwise, she says, he would certainly have splashed or kicked, or cried out for help. She maintains she certainly would have heard him. We did recover the tape recorder in a Ziploc bag that he was carrying so he could record underwater sounds, but he hadn't sealed the bag properly, the whole thing was water-logged, and the cassette yielded nothing.

It might have been restored, of course, but my wife allowed the bag and its contents to be thrown away at the hospital—an oversight which some of us might find difficult to comprehend, but again, how could she have known? At that time, I myself knew nothing about instrumental transcommunication, not even that it existed. I knew nothing of the hours of research already completed, the extraordinary messages already received, the elaborate devices created by scientists and by ordinary men, like myself.

It was later that evening that the first seeds, as they say, were planted. To get back to our hotel we had to go through St. Augustine's cobblestoned side streets, past the crowded displays of artisans; one fellow dressed as a blacksmith called out to us, "Smile! It can't be that bad!" The very quality of the day's light seemed different, smoky, like a film stuck on one frame, the edges burning and closing in. When we got back, my wife went into the bathroom and shut the door. Our room still smelled cheerfully of bananas and Sea & Ski. The TV was on, for some reason, muted and tuned to the closed-circuit bulletin board. A message was running across the bottom of the screen: *If you like what you are hearing, tune in 24 hours a day . . . If you like what you are hearing, tune in 24 hours a day . . .*

That's when I noticed the recorder on the dresser, the one Nathan had left for the maid. It was black and silver and shining in the TV's cold blue light. But there was something off about it, I thought, as if it had been touched or moved by someone. Not the way he'd left it. Then, like a punch in the stomach: Of course! The maid's message! She would have done it this time. *Of course.* I saw it all at once, in simple, clear progression, our lives laid out as in a comic strip, with everything— not just each day of our vacation, each day the maid had not responded, but each day of Nathan's life, our lives, our parents' lives before ours— leading up to *this*, this final square, this *joke.*

I had to hear it anyway. I pressed play and held my breath because it suddenly seemed too noisy, not right, and with my breath stopped I felt the air around me stop, the molecules stop popping, everything stop moving, so I could hear this awful answer, this stupid woman speak the words my son had written for her, too late. Instead, there was silence. Then, ever so faintly, something else, something so small, so familiar it seemed to come from my own body—but it could not have. It was breathing—Nathan, breathing. I waited for him to speak, to begin one of his stories, but he just went on breathing, as if he were just sitting there, reading his Sesame Street book, or lying on the floor, battling with his action figures. But *breathing.*

My wife was in the bathroom with the door closed. And my son, my son who I knew was dead, was breathing in my ear.

Like a DJ, God plays the impossible for us. I cannot speak for others, but that was how it began for me, founder of the Instrumental Trans-communication Network. I did not mistake the sound on the tape that night for the aspirations of a ghost, a message from the other side—but when I heard it, I knew such things were possible.

My wife was not there to receive the message. Was that only a fluke? Had she not been in the bathroom at that moment, I wonder, would she have heard it, too? Or did she leave the room on purpose, following some premonition, practicing a kind of willful deafness, the selective hearing of parents? It is impossible to say. Later, I brought home books for her—*Phone Calls From the Dead*, *The Inaudible Made Audible* in the original German, every seminal text in the field—but she refused to look at any of them. I might as well have handed her a stack of *Playboys*.

At the time of our divorce, we catalogued Nathan's tapes and stored them in a safe-deposit box so that I could continue my research, and so that she could listen to them for what her lawyer called "senti-mental reasons"—an accusation, apparently. *I* am not the sentimental one, is the implication, not *human*, she has said. Yet it is she who refuses to take her own son's call, a call I have no doubt he will make, is perhaps preparing to make this very moment. I am ready. Upstairs in my room in this hotel the most sensitive and sophisticated equipment available at this time—thanks to many of you here today—is in operation even as we speak, poised and ready to receive and safeguard the most tentative inquiry, the faintest nudge of sound.

We are not spoon-benders, I tell my wife, and others like her, not flim-flammers, but scientists and engineers, scholars and teachers and builders, fathers, many of us, and mothers. We wait like any line of people at a pay phone: impatient, hopeful, polite. What will he say when he calls? We can only imagine. It may not sound like English—it may not be English. We still have much work to do in the areas of clarity and amplification. On a typical recording, "soulmate" sounds like "sailboat," "father" may be indistinguishable from "bother," "Nathan" might come through as "nothing."

Still, we wait. We listen like safecrackers, we listen like sleuths. We remember the words of those listeners who came before us, the brave ones who started this whole thing. *Stay on the station, tune in correctly. Here it is summer, always summer! Soon it will work everywhere!*

26

Class Notes

Lucas Cooper

TED MECHAM may be the first member of the Class of '66 to retire. I met him and his beautiful wife Kathy at a Buccaneers game in Tampa Bay in October. His investments in sugar refining and South American cattle have paid off handsomely. Any secret? "Yes," says Ted. "In and out, that is the key." Also in Florida, I saw JIM HASLEK and BILL STEB-BINS. They left their families behind in Columbus and Decatur, respectively, to tune up a 1300-hp open-class, ocean racing boat, Miss Ohio, for trial runs near Miami. The racing season is set to open there in December, and Jim and Bill (famous for their Indy 500 pilgrimages) are among the favorites. JOHN PESKIN writes to say, sad to relay, that he has been sued by BILL TESKER. Bill, general manager at the Dayton office of TelDyne Industries, claims he gave John the idea for a sitcom episode that John subsequently sold to NBC. It all took place more than a decade ago and is more than I can believe.

RALPH FENTIL, handling the case for Bill, made it clearer. Ralph is director of Penalty, Inc., a franchised California paralegal service, which helps clients develop lawsuits. "This is a growing and legitimate consumer-interest area. We encourage people to come in, we go over their past. It's a potential source of income for the client. We let the courts decide who's right and wrong." Hmmm. RICHARD ENDERGEL phoned a few weeks ago from Houston, under arrest for possession of cocaine—third time since 1974. Richard thinks this is it. Unless a miracle happens he is looking at 15 years or more for dealing in a controlled substance.

STANFORD CRIBBS, mangled practically beyond recognition in an automobile accident in 1979, took his own life on March 19, according to a clipping from the Kansas City Star. His former roommate, BRISTOL LANSFORD, has fared no better. Bristol was shot in the head by his wife's lover at the Lansfords' vacation home outside Traverse City. ROBERT DARKO of Palo Alto (where else?) sends word he is moving up very quickly at Mastuch Electronics, and to thank DAVID WHITMAN. David, of Shoremann, Polcher & Edders, Los Angeles, specializes in celebrity and personality contracts. Bob Darko is the sixth middle-management executive hired in David's Free Corporate Agent draft. "Corporate loyalty is something from the fifties," says David. "I want to market people on a competitively-bid, short-term contract basis, with incentive and bonus clauses."

Tell that to STEVEN PARKMAN. He has been living on unemployment benefits and his wife's income from a hairdressing concern since April of last year—with four kids. FRANK VESTA is certainly glad his job (in aerospace planning with General Dynamics of St. Louis) is holding up—he and wife Shirley had their ninth—a boy—in July. GREG OUTKIRK has grim news—daughter Michelle rode her thoroughbred Arabian, Botell III, off the boat dock in front of their Waukegan home in an effort to make the animal swim. It drowned almost immediately. DENNIS MITFORD, owner of a well-known Nevada wh---house (no class discounts, he jokes), reports an unruly customer was shot on the premises in October by his bodyguard, LAWRENCE ADENSON. Larry, who served in Vietnam, says the publicity is awful. He may go back to New York—after Denny officially fires him for the violence. Violence is no stranger to BILL NAST. His wife turned up in terrible shape at Detroit General Hospital two months ago, the victim of Bill's hot temper. Four hours in surgery?

JACK ZIMMERMAN's second wife and two children by his first wife visited over Easter. Sue ZIMMERMAN was a 1978 Penthouse Pet. Jack is managing her modeling career, his entertainment career, and raising the kids. Kudos, Jack. TIM GRAYBULL is dead (of alcohol abuse) in Vermillion, South Dakota, where he taught English at the university. (Please let the editor of Alumnus know you want to see Tim's poems in a future issue.) ALEX ROBINSON won't say what films he distributes, but hints broadly that "beauty is in the eye of the beholder," even in that area. The profit margin, he claims, is not to be believed. I'm reminded of KEVIN MITCHELL, who embezzled $3.2 million from Sperry Tool in 1971. He periodically calls from I-know-not-where. Kevin was home free in 1982, with the expiration of the case. DONALD OVERBROOK—more bad news—is in trouble with the police again for unrequited interest in young ladies, this time in Seattle. JAMES COLEMAN called to say so. Jim and his wife Nancy are quitting their jobs to sail around the world in their 32' ferroconcrete boat. Nancy's parents died and left them well-off. "We were smart not to have kids," Jim commented.

HAROLD DECKER writes from Arkansas that he is angry about Alumni Association fund-raising letters that follow him everywhere he goes. "I haven't got s---, and wouldn't give it if I did." Wow. NORMAN BELLOWS has been named managing editor of Attitude. He says the magazine's 380,000 readers will see a different magazine under his tutelage—"aimed at aggressive, professional people. No tedious essays." Norm's erstwhile literary companion in New York, GEORGE PHILMAN BELLOWS (Betsy BELLOWS and George are living together, sorely testing that close friendship from Spectator days) reports Pounce is doing very well. George's "funny but vicious" anecdotes about celebrities appear bi-weekly in the fledgling, nationally-syndicated column. "At first the humor went right by everyone," says George, feigning disbelief. "George is an a--h---," was GLEN GREEN's observation when I phoned. Glen opens a five-week show in Reno in January (and he will see to it that you get a free drink and best seats in the house). Another class celebrity, actor BOYD DAVIDSON, has entered Mt. Sinai, Los Angeles, for treatment of cocaine and Percodan addiction.

Dr. CARNEY OLIN, who broke a morphine habit at Mt. Sinai in 1979, thinks it's the best program in the country. Carney says he's fully recovered and back in surgery in the Phoenix area. THOMAS GREEN-VILLE's business brochure arrived in the mail last week. He has opened his fifteenth Total Review salon. Tom combines a revitalizing physical-fitness program with various types of modern therapy, like est, to provide clients with brand-new life paths. Some sort of survival prize should go to DEAN FRANCIS. MBA Harvard 1968. Stanford Law 1970. Elected to the California State Assembly in 1974, after managing Sen. Edward Eaton's successful '72 election campaign. In 1978, elected to Congress from California's 43rd District. It all but collapsed like a house of cards last fall. A jealous brother-in-law, and heir to the Greer fortune, instigated a series of nasty suits, publicly denounced Dean as a fraud, and allegedly paid a woman to sexually embarrass him. Dean won re-election, but the word is his marriage is over—and Phyllis

Greer FRANCIS will go to court to recover damages from her brother. A sadder story came to light when I met DOUGLAS BRAND for drinks after the Oklahoma game last fall. Doug's wife Linda went berserk in August and killed their three children. She's in prison. Doug says he used to bait her to a fury with tales of his adulteries and feels great remorse.

BENJAMIN TROPPE has been named vice president for marketing for Temple Industries in Philadelphia. BERNARD HANNAH is new corporate counsel in Conrad Communications, Atlantic City. HENRY CHURCH was killed by police in Newark for unspecified reasons. Well-known painter DAVID WHITCOMB moved to Guatemala and left no forwarding address. (Dave?) FREDERICK MANDELL weeps uncontrollably in his crowded apartment in Miami Beach. JOEL REEDE lives in self-destructive hatred in Rye, New York. JAY LOGAN has joined insurgency forces in Angola. ADRIAN BYRD travels to the Netherlands in the spring to cover proceedings against the Federal Government at The Hague for Dispatch.

GORDON HASKINS has quit the priesthood in Serape, a violent New Mexico border town, to seek political office. ANTHONY CREST succeeds father Luther (Class of '36) as chairman of Fabre. DANIEL REDDLEMAN continues to compose classical music for the cello in Hesterman, Tennessee. ODELL MASTERS cries out in his dreams for love of his wife and children. PAUL GREEN, who never married, farms 1200 acres in eastern Oregon with his father. ROGER BOLTON, who played professional baseball for nine years, lost his family in flooding outside New Orleans and has entered a Benedictine monastery. (Paul Jeffries, 1340 North Michigan, Chicago, IL 60602)

27

Dear Stephen Hawking

Samantha Hunt

Dear Stephen Hawking,
Tell me I can forget the laws of gravity, not be
coy with you.

It's true. I am expanding every night when the
stars come out. I am expanding across the United
States because I'm hungry Stephen. I'll call you
Stephen or *Stephana* or *chou-chou*, and the night
sky is rising in my stomach like yeast.

This expansion is the nestled way Africa and
South America once slept as spoons, the uncleaved
slate that was your rocky body and my sandy
self. Because, as you, *lapin*, told us, if the
universe is expanding then for one brief moment
there was a singularity, you a cell of me, me a
cell of cellulose or quartz or hydrogen or Chicago or you.

Describe all space and time sweetly, generally, relatively. I await your words in packets,
in waves. Because I dreamed, *petit*, of a black
hole which vacuumed all we said. Each, "Umm Mr.

Hawking, umm," or, "Speak up!" or "Can you repeat the question?" every word sucked clean like a bone. They fall into the densest space and are thought lost forever but emerge, emitted as energy shouting, "Love. Love. Love," or "E=mc²."

Bear this out even to the un-edge of your imaginary time and slowly, even love's O and the V, even energy's M and the C will find themselves at distances the postal system hasn't traveled in an entire lifetime, greater than the distances starlight has spanned since Kepler was a boy.

In the beginning there was a oneness. If time ends, it will end because the oneness became a twoness. So remain distant, *ma coeur*, and resonate singularity in the space between you and me, down illimitable corridors that without wrinkle, without waste are only the second of a synapse. Whisper, "I," or whisper, "You," or "envelope" or "the news at 10" and expand.

Tonight, in our briefer history, I am a woman on a Minnesota porch spilling out onto a sheet of airmail. Every word and letter I get secured to paper or allow from my mouth, opens up, distributes me more evenly in the universe so that eventually, randomly, generally, relatively one letter, an A or a T from me will gently brush the downy skin of your cheek.

Yours truly,

28

National Treasures

Charles McLeod

In which the Seller *commodifies his dissent*, listing for the first time this previously uncollected compendium of National Treasures, the delimited choices most chiefly informed by the Seller's belief that each person is a country unto themselves, and possesses a record of conflict and treaty, has customs and boundaries and scandals and ways—that every small piece of the self is worth something, and too that the Seller is broke, and can no longer afford the small storage unit off the Queens Midtown Expressway, Exit 15, and for nearly two months has been receiving, per voicemail, threats from said storage unit's owner, a Sikh, one Mr. S. Bedi who has promised to heave all of the Seller's belongings out into the street, and so then this cyber-boutique *sui generis*, its governing tenets lying ultimately between Organic Nationalism and Dynastic Hegemony, between amour de soi and amour-propre, an emporium that's sought to accommodate too much, and whose ruler now seeks to sell off part and parcel. These items are priced to move.

Lot of Children's Winter Clothes: Two Parkas, Eight Ski Hats, 4 Pair Mittens, Two Pair Sorrel Boots, Child Sizes Ten and Six, Respectively.

Born in Buffalo to middle-class parents, September 1975, my younger brother followed me from my mother's womb some twenty-seven months later. We lived mid-block, between a divorced beat cop and a semi-professional painter named Janine Bench, who was in her fourth decade while I lingered in pre-pubescence. Winters were maelstroms of snow; there were consistent stints of no electricity, and people began buying firewood prior to Labor Day. I can recall watching Miss Bench painting by candlelight; the bedroom that I shared with my brother, James, had a window that looked out at her studio. My neighbor was a gaunt dishwater blonde with mild features, save for a rather pronounced chin, which made her profile unintentionally comic. She was naturally attractive but put little stock in her physical appearance, spending most of her time around the house in the same cocoa and pink velour robe, a neck-to-feet item that she rubber-banded the left sleeve of when apply-ing paint to canvas. I imagined her rich, even though she lived right next to us and we were most certainly not rich, my mother working clerical at a Federal Building downtown and my father teaching math at Grover Cleveland, the public high school I would later attend. Miss Bench herself worked days at Oliver's, one of Buffalo's standout restau-rants. I realize now that the reason I thought her wealthy was that her lifestyle was different than most people's, that she was most generally "other," an idea I was fascinated by: that there was always the anti-, the un-, lurking nearby, stockpiling. I spied on her whenever I could.

Nearly all these people have passed from this world: the beat cop got shot, Miss Bench had a stroke, my brother jumped off the roof of a building five blocks from Manhattan's Port Authority Bus Terminal. My mother, too, is gone; she bought Kents by the carton, vowing always to quit. During one no-power stint in deep winter, I was sent down the block to procure more of these, the corner store, per a generator, open through the worst. Miss Bench was at work and did not lock her door and I had failed to keep my curiosity (innate) quelled sufficiently. That is, I turned the handle and went inside. Miss Bench's front room held no furniture; she utilized the space as an ersatz gallery—paintings hung everywhere, large canvases in grays and blues and browns. Later I would realize these as poor imitations of the "Ab-Ex" tradition: destitute impostors of the work of Kline and Klee, lots of lines and boxes, the hues chosen most certainly influenced by the torpor of Buffalo winters. I took nothing and left, not realizing that my boots (the larger-sized Sorrels listed above) had tracked in snow from Miss Bench's front steps, thereby indicating that a stranger had entered her house. Through high school she offered me only terse waves and sideways glances, acts that left me feeling wholly guilty, despite the fact that I had done nothing, really, wrong.

Starting Bid: $9.99

VHS Recording of Rogers and Hammerstein's *Oklahoma*, as Performed by the 1987 Sixth Grade Class of Phelan Academy. 72 Minutes. Shot with a Panasonic Dual-Head Hi-Fi Camera.

Being in education and realizing that the extent of Reagan's concern, in regard to public schools, hovered somewhere between "fuck" and "you," my father enrolled me at Phelan Academy, a nonsectarian private institution that sat on the east end of Buffalo's west side. I attended Phelan from third through eighth grade. In the fourth grade, a librarian stabbed another teacher upon discovering the tryst between the stabee and the librarian's wife. The following year an ex-Bills linebacker wandered onto campus, high on PCP. (Later, while a sophomore at SUNY–Albany, I would better attempt to understand my brother's own addictions by trying this exact *receptor antagonist* in a friend's dorm room. The effects upon my person were not dissimilar to *swimming in drool*.)

There was a second performance of this musical that was not taped, performed at some other school very deep in the ghetto, a place that I cannot remember the name of. I and my classmates, less concerned about performing with any legitimacy sans the attendance of our parents, had located in the men's dressing room *a bright orange inflatable ball*, which was taken by me or one of my cohorts from said dressing room and released onto the stage during a meager rendition of "The Surrey with the Fringe on Top." To say our chaperones—comprised of three teachers, including the drama teacher, an aged hippy with the first name of Splendor—were indignant would not do justice to the rage that they held inside them, and had to keep holding inside them for the full of the play, until the production was over, at which point a half-dozen of us were repaired to a vacant classroom and beaten savagely, boxed around the ears and held over knees and spanked, the latter of these minor tortures both painful and embarrassing, as we were really too old for this particular mode of punishment. I can only imagine how this meting-out later affected the sex lives of my cohorts, but in regard to myself I now admit fully a predilection for slapping firmly the bare rear of every single partner of intimacy, of raising my hand and then lowering it, and thereby leaving upon a half-dozen individuals misdirected acts of revenge. Opening and Closing Credits

Included. Intermission partially edited out, though as the camera comes back on you can see clearly my brother, age nine, stop, for just a moment, in front of the lens. Slight wear marks in this section of the tape due to repeated pausing. Performance itself is unflawed.

Starting Bid: $4.99

Lot of 2 (Front and Rear) State of New York License Plates, 1973– 1986 Era. Plates are Gold with Blue Letters: 8675-NMS. Stickerless: Window Validation. Front Plate Creased (See Below).

Unable to afford Phelan for the final stage of compulsory schooling, my parents enrolled me at Grover Cleveland High School, some ten blocks from Lake Erie and the Canadian Border. Occupying a full city lot, the school, erected in 1913, is in the Colonial Revival Style of the period: symmetrical façade, pediment supported by pilasters, voussoirs, etc. Steel-framed, with a stone red-brick and terra cotta exterior, this cupola-with-spire topped hellhole is where I would first make the acquaintance of one Frederick Ames Kemper, cast, like myself, in a non-speaking role in the drama that was Grover Cleveland's junior varsity football team. The misery of the bus rides to away games is, in some ways, indescribable: I was lithe and asthmatic, and tormented with a sort of passion I can only term Roman. Everyone smelled like wet, dirty socks. But there also in that rage-drenched miasma (a Bosch canvas on wheels), Frederick: flaxen-haired, halcyon, a toiletries bag filled with Top 40 cassettes on the seat beside him, his Walkman headphones over, always, his ears. Frederick had made a name for himself even prior to his arrival at Grover Cleveland per the advanced utilization of his pronounced kleptomania: that is, Frederick Ames was a semi-professional thief. He lived in a creepy Victorian too near the Dewey Thruway, his father a gravedigger for Forest Lawn Cemetery and his mother, nebbish, a shut-in with a penchant for strays. Frederick's skin was almost diaphanous: he looked like a cave-thing, bleached or otherwise improperly pigmented, and in this way propagated the Gothic bleakness that seemed inherent to his bloodline. I adored him and he knew it and, slowly, let me become his friend. On weekends we traveled by bus to Buffalo's Downtown, robbing most frequently the strange and cluttered "everything" shops that all urban centers seem to possess. We took cameras, silk pocket squares for men's suits, shoe polish, coffee mugs. Frederick often worked with his Walkman on, perhaps to make him look more casual, perhaps to keep some part of himself from analyzing what the other part was doing. My job was to talk, to distract: Frederick and I were cousins, arriving in Buffalo from Pennsylvania to stay with relatives who, it seemed, had forgotten to collect us from the bus depot. With strange men who smelled of booze or smoke or curry, I pored over neighborhood maps in the Yellow Pages while Frederick filled up his bag. I realize now that Frederick made the more severe looting excursions without me; he came to school dressed, for a freshman, to the nines: new Jordans, gold jewelry, a full-length sateen Bills parka. For spending so many weekends together our small talk was minimal, and consisted chiefly of single sentences uttered by Frederick while we waited for the bus: *My dad killed a cat with a shovel last night*, or *my mom thinks the moon is an eye*. Implied in such statements was the fact that I would never see the inside of Frederick's home, and only once did he see the inside of mine, being invited, by my parents, over to dinner the winter of that freshman year, the five of us eating chicken, green beans and mashed potatoes in silence. Afterward, over a dessert of chocolate pudding, Frederick had commented on how bright our house was. You like the blue, my mom had said. (She had recently painted the kitchen.) No, Frederick had said, I mean you guys turn on a lot of lights.

Our sophomore year Fredrick began to steal cars. Sometime over summer his mother had been moved to a state-run facility, and with her departure went the dearth of parenting Frederick received. Absent until lunch, Frederick would drive by the front of Grover Cleveland in a pilfered Skylark or Impala, his wan face glum. On what was to be the last balmy night of October, Frederick showed up at my house past one in the morning, waking me with bottle caps thrown at my second-story window. Frederick was drunk, and had a Porsche. I'd clothed and eased down the trellis in silence. We drove around some in the warm night air; the car's leather smelled new, and even at twenty-five miles an hour, it was clear what the Porsche's engine was capable of. At my feet was a half-finished six-pack of Labatt's Blue. Where'd you get the car, I asked. This world's spent meat, Frederick said back. We sped up, taking the neighborhood's turns more sharply, and I understood at that moment that I was okay, and Frederick was not. Three blocks from Grover Cleveland we passed a cop heading in the opposite direction, and shortly there-after Frederick ceded what was left of his quickly-eroding calm. He upshifted then lost control, the car hopping the curb and hitting a spruce some ten yards from the high school's front doors. Stunned but conscious we sat in the smoking wreck, looking at each other. Frederick's head had connected with the steering wheel; one side of his face was already swelling, and above his eyebrows was wet red blood. He looked like a member of a war fought a long time ago. Then Fredrick told me to run. The Porsche's shotgun door was bent in its frame, and I had to kick at it repeatedly to exit, sprinting down a side street and watching, peripherally, porch lights turn on, the homes' owners awoken by the din of the impact. A mile later I stopped, out of breath and almost losing my night's dinner. I turned to see how far Frederick was behind me, but no one was there.

The next morning, at breakfast, all was explained: the superintendent had made the cursory round of phone calls to high school faculty, and I came downstairs, freshly showered, to find out that Frederick was apprehended at the scene, and awaiting sentence while he lay, casted, on a gurney at Kaleida General. The cop we'd passed the night before had found Frederick behind the steering wheel, his leg broken, the Walkman's play button punched in. I never went to the hospital to visit him, believing such a trip would incriminate me. Frederick was sent to a detention center north of Syracuse; he did not return to Grover Cleveland and my heart, a coward's heart, was thankful for this. That night my father took us all out for dinner—a rare occurrence, and the significance of which was not lost on myself. On the trip home he strayed from the standard route, driving by the scene. The Porsche was still there. Buffalo is a poor city and damage control occurs slowly; the car had been unstuck from the tree, but no wrecker had yet to tow it to impound. It's awful what happened there, my dad said. It sure is, I answered. Are all families' secret thoughts Venn diagrams? Things that overlap and do not? That night I snuck back down the trellis. In my jeans pocket were two screwdrivers, borrowed from my father's garage workbench. Frederick, if you're out there, I have the Porsche's license plates. Convo me and I'll take down this listing. These items belong to you.

Starting Bid: $20.00

Antique Mahogany Chess Set. Pieces Hand-Carved (Bone). Late 19th Century. Travelling Set: Doors are Double-Hinged (Brass), Opening Up and then Out. Game Board is Inlaid—Alternating Mahogany and Rosewood. Dimensions: Box Closed: 11"x 6"x 3 ½"; Box Open (Including Doors): 20"x 12"x 2". All Pieces Intact. Light Scuffing/Burn Marks/Blood Stains along Bottom Left Corner. Made in Sri Lanka (Ceylon).

My brother James evolved to wunderkind the summer between my sophomore and junior years. Held back in kindergarten due to the perceived inability to speak, he took the SATs after middle school and scored in the top percentile. This result was enough for him to leapfrog three full grades, making James, at fourteen, a high school senior. I was prepared to spend my days physically defending him but he was never once mistreated, Grover Cleveland's Class of '93 making him a sort of ad hoc mascot for intellectual endeavor. NYU felt the same way, and spring of that year my brother received a 15K renewable fellowship, along with tuition remission, and five months later moved from New York's second-largest city to its first. While uncoordinated to the point of klutzdom, James looked the most athletic in our small clan. He held a hockey player's build: broad shoulders with a narrow waist and chicken legs, his body thinning as one's eye moved down. We had the same hair, stick straight, a shade my mom's dad referred to as "Irish Brown." This same man would bestow upon my brother the aforementioned chess set, acquired by my great-grandfather during his years in the Merchant Marine. While not nautically inclined, I will admit a penchant, albeit romanticized, for travelling the seas via steam liner or some other outdated vessel, the world still enormous, wonder a possible thing.

For my family, these months were the happiest of any I can recall. My father, normally martinetish, loosened his proverbial neckwear: there was a trip to a water park, tickets to Bisons games. From the cheap seats of Dunn Tire we cheered and swatted bugs in the hot white air. Summer ended, and we stuffed the minivan full of boxes and moved my brother to Brittany Residence Hall on East 10th Street, some five minutes from Manhattan's Washington Square. I recall no voice of concern over whether or not it was truly a good idea for a fifteen-year-old to be living semi-independently in Greenwich Village, any dissent drowned out by the purple and white brochures that were arriving weekly to our Buffalo address. While our parents searched for hot sandwiches in the surrounding blocks, I sat with my brother on his vinyl dorm mattress. What do you think about all this, I asked. I don't think I thought about it at all, James said. The chess set was beside the bed, on his desk. Do you want to play, my brother asked me. I'm not very good, I admitted. The face my brother made next was one of supreme fatigue: he brought his chin down, closing his eyes. His brow furrowed. At fifteen, the skin above my brother's eyes was creased. Okay, James told me, but will you?

I think we fell victim to the ease of familiarity, a malady I imagine common to siblings who consider one another the closest of friends. I played chess with James that day and lost badly and the next day, after a night at a nearby hotel with my parents, returned to the other end of the state. James' roommate was from Taiwan, friendly but far from the things that he knew, and his homesickness kept him near-mute. I suppose the University (an institution my father would later try to sue) considered the best thing to do was pair James with someone wholly non-threatening, a social leper of sorts, who would not introduce my brother to the typical vices sought by those in their late teens. To say this plan backfired does not, perhaps, go far enough. Fall semester passed without incident, but James returned home for Winter Break half terrified outsider and half angst-ridden quasi-adult. He'd undergone a latent growth spurt as well, adding another two inches of height to a frame that was having attention paid to it per the use of NYU's weightlifting room. Dinners were stern affairs, the thick silence broken only by my brother's obscenity-laced reviews of the food, the house, Buffalo itself. There was brief normalcy for December's last week, but with the Christmas trappings quickly outdated, the gloom, like a moat, encircled my brother once more. James left in January; I drove him to the Greyhound, my brother turning down my dad's offer of transport cross-state. In the grey light of the freezing depot, I hugged James goodbye. Visit, he told me, then boarded the bus. I did not. Two months later came a typed notice on school stationery: course work was strong but too often missing; attendance mottled at best. Sometime in late March we lost contact, our calls answered only and always by the Taiwanese roommate, who informed us finally, and in mediocre English, *James take the chess set. He gone.*

May. A month of trips to Manhattan, our father taking leave from Grover Cleveland, a substitute in his stead. There were meetings with Provosts, waits at police stations. There was a trip to the morgue, the John Does slid from their metal tombs, white sheets pulled down to show blue, still faces. Also: the minivan's ashtray, packed with tan butts; street performers in Washington Square, on stilts. My parents' meager savings, garnished by a second mortgage, went to the hiring of first one and then two private detectives, their firms' workers scouring the boroughs, Hoboken, points north. NYU put my parents up, when it could, in housing used for visiting faculty: there were long hours in leather armchairs, down pillows that did little to drown out the street noise below. I went with them some weekends but was still in school myself; I did no homework, sat stunned in my desk, and received straight A's. College admissions notices arrived in the mail; I was a good student but a poor tester, with little interest in the extra-curricular. Two SUNYs made offers but NYU turned me down, the thin envelope a dark cloud portending storm. My parents spoke little and grew gaunt. For a full week freezing rain slicked the roads, the world crystalline. And then news: a sighting in Newark, a grainy snap-shot of someone in rags. It barely mattered if it was my brother or not: here was hope's wellspring, the nightmare's long end. We canvassed as though running for office, the Brick City's telephone poles clothed in our xeroxed flyers. Door after door was answered, it seemed, by the same enormous black woman, her meaty arms spread for consolatory embrace as we gave thanks then descended the thirtieth, the fortieth, the eightieth porch. A third mortgage, the bank said, was out of the question. Winter turned to spring.

Chess, of course, often ends with no winner: there is the draw, the resignation, the fifty-move rule. My parents didn't give up so much as cede to logic: there were no tactics left to employ. They came back to Buffalo; I graduated in May; James jumped from the roof of a building in June. He'd been holding the chessboard when he went airborne, landing headfirst. Toxicology found traces of phencyclidine. James' last meal was bread. In a mortuary not far from Symphony Circle, I asked the Funeral Director how they'd put my brother's face back together. My mother was in a separate room, perusing caskets. Light baroque played from speakers in the walls. Well, the man said, looking to my father for intervention but finding none, in cases like your brother's, we insert a plate. He shifted from one foot to the other and I smiled; discomfort meant life, and it was a joyful thing to see. And this plate, I said, how will it look like my brother's face? Well, incisions are made at the temples, and here, the man said, pointing under the chin. So you peel back my brother's face and put the plate in, I said. That's right, the man said, as though he'd solved something. And what about the stuff that's in the way, I asked, the bone and such. My father was reading an unfolded brochure about flower arrangements, engrossed. The bone is sanded down or removed, the man said, his consternation growing. And how about his eyes, I asked. The eyes are untouched, the man said. AND HOW ABOUT HIS SOUL, I said. Okay, my dad said. Okay, that's enough.

I put in two years at SUNY–Albany, fucked on drugs and not part of the world but not ever, really, wanting to die—as I mentioned already I have the heart of a coward, an organ so puny and useless it can subsist on next to nothing at all. I walked the campus at night dressed in a long wool coat, drunk on gin and setting small fires in the bathroom sinks of empty school buildings. I trailed coeds until they jogged from fear. Tossed out, I packed up and struck west, sending a postcard to my parents bought at a gift shop in Dayton. A Unique Possession from a Bygone Era. Board's Hinges may need Oil.

Starting Bid: $89.99

13" Tulipwood and Teflon Stiletto. Italian-Made (SKM). Single-Action OTF; Blade Retracts Manually. Length of Closed Knife is 7 Inches. Used Once.

Bad times in Decatur. The Midway Inn let you pay by the week, and I developed a dangerous friendship with the night clerk, a trailer-bred gun nut twice my age who sometimes kept minutes for the local chapter of a hate group called Lone Wolf. I was drunk always, beyond grace, and Wynn Jost saw in me a lamb, someone whose psyche held all the worth of a torn kite, and was thereby open to suggestion via the newfound fraternity and acceptance provided by himself and other members of his ethnocentric cell. I worked at a meatpacking plant; I literally packed meat, wrapping t-bones in wax paper and boxing them, sixty-five per. The drone of industrial machinery was womblike, the white conveyer belt splotched, in patches, to pink. Some of Lone Wolf's goons worked here as well; a hulk named Jack Milk handed me, weekly, half-full cartons of cigarettes, the paper container's free space filled with hate literature meant to be distributed in the dark hours of morning to mailboxes within walking distance of my motel. In this man's stone basement I sat on a metal folding chair, surrounded by a dozen of Central Time's Aryan zealots. The aforementioned Mr. Jost, intellectual ringleader of this poor circus, forced these men (most of whom had not finished high school) *to give reports* on Nazi memorabilia Jost had purchased at trade shows in the greater Illinois area. Trip-ups in reading words off the page were covered up by loud cries of White Power. An urn for coffee sat tabled under a German flag.

I was scared and lost and Jost was letting me live in the Midway for free, the owners absentee and oblivious. I bought the above switch-blade at a pawn shop for protection, and three nights later Jost found it stashed beneath my mattress, tossing my room while I was out delivering pamphlets that explained why Jews would lead the human race to Apocalypse. I should emphasize here, for clarity, that I really was starting to digest what was being fed to me: that White Christian Protestants were being treated unfairly in the media, the workplace, the cities; that the continued crosspollination of the races would lead to the demise of Christian Virtues; that it was kill or be killed, and the war, begun long ago, was roiling around us, more acid and thicker than ever before. Trauma (James) both debts and affords, the results often scary. Jost, along with Milk and three others, were waiting for me in my room when I returned that night. They drove me in Milk's Buick to an all-night gas station, where we waited for the next person of color to pull in. Forty minutes passed, the six of us crammed inside, listening to hate metal on low volume. Near dawn, an elderly black man shut off his Chrysler and entered the Conoco. He beelined for the bathroom; Jost handed me the knife. White Power, he said. White Power, I said, and got out. What happened next was a miracle, so unearned I am sure that I cannot pay for it, ever, in this life. The black man stood at the sink, rinsing. He turned his head when he saw me come in. White Power, I said. What Power, he asked. I pulled the knife and sprung the blade. I saw all of you in that car, the man said. He had on a navy blue baseball cap, the name of a naval destroyer spelled out in gold. So, I told him. The man unbuttoned then rolled up one sleeve of his dress shirt. Cut me, he told me. Here, on the arm. What the fuck, I said. Do it, the man said. They won't come check on you. Do it. Right now. He moved his arm, bent at the elbow, out toward me. He wore glasses; he had pleated khakis on. Come on, man, come on, you don't have the time. He bobbed his arm up and down, his bare arm. I strode over to him and sliced. The blade sunk under the skin. He made a sound that was something very near a yawn, a morning sound, a first sound of the day, then stumbled backward into the hand dryer. I dropped the knife and picked it up and turned and ran out of the store.

Back in the Buick I threw up on myself, the men of Lone Wolf cooing like bemused middle-schoolers, which I suppose in some ways they were. My accommodations gratis, I had a small nest egg stored, and once Jost's pickup departed from the Midway's lot that morning, I ran, at full speed, to the bus depot, buying a ticket for the next coach out. I wrapped the switchblade in my work shirt and mailed the whole thing back home to Buffalo. Maybe you don't believe the story I've just told. I can only reply: Lucky you.

Buy It Now: $10, Firm

Brown Mesh Trucker's Hat, "Custer Gas Service, Custer, South Dakota" Printed on Front of Hat. Good Condition. Bill Rounded (Broken In). Ready to Wear.

A long engagement to one Katherine Anne Svenlund that consumed over three years of my late 20s. Sioux Falls is a pleasant place and were I a different person, more even or stalwart, I might have managed an existence in that large village, continuing my work as Night Manager of Country Buffet #3847 and spending much of my free time browsing the ample selection of goods offered at the Salvation Army out near the airport. The Svenlund family is of fine Nordic stock, if genealogically naive, as their ancestors arrived to this country via *propagandistic literature*, specifically brochures and/or pamphlets that outlined the unequivocal agricultural promise of the Great Plains (I should mention here, out of fairness, that these false promises were not limited to peoples of Norwegian descent nor just the acres comprising South Dakota; rather, America's new Robber Barons hired a great number of men to promote falsely that most of Middle America was a Farmer's Utopia—that places of near-apocalyptical aridity and barrenness were ripe wombs of earth, an agrarian delight, and that much of the middle part of the country was populated via the exacting of high levels of bullshit).

Lone Wolf sent no minions to find me and I settled in, saving enough to afford a one-bedroom above a paint shop near the train tracks. I worked six days a week, seven, the staff at Country Buffet my surrogate family. One of my foster siblings was a short kind punk rocker named Tyler Banks. Tyler was five-five and washed dishes and sported a mohawk that changed colors every two weeks with each new paycheck received. He was always smiling and did no drugs and brought with him, each shift, a small battery-powered boombox, which he set on a shelf above the sink, The Germs or Anti-Flag slamming it out while Tyler sprayed dishes clean. Nighttimes in Sioux Falls were slow affairs, our clientele mainly truckers and conspiracy theorists, the two demographics often overlapping. I'd started out bussing tables days but the turnover was constant, and within months had worked my way up to running overnights, the franchise's owner finding my demeanor supererogatory (in truth, it didn't take much). Through Tyler I found a small group of close friends, punkers and book nuts and antiestablishment crocheters, all of good heart and sound mind. Here were the intellectuals of the prairie, too poor for the fridge to be full consistently but able to knit cardigans and talk Gide. Dilettantes, it seems, keep to the coasts, Chicago. The prairie kids were all about worth.

In autumn of '97, while I spoke with a trenchcoated man about the hoax that was the '69 Apollo moon landing, Katherine Anne Svenlund walked into Country Buffet for the first time. To say the restaurant's teal-carpeted environs was in direct contrast to the glamour that Katherine possessed would not do her aesthetic true justice. Beneath my nametag, my heart leapt. She was five-ten, in tight indigo Levi's.

Red heels held thin, perfect feet. From a side pocket of her black leather biker's jacket Katherine removed a silver cigarette case. Her lipstick matched the shade of her footwear exactly. But betrayal: a brightening of Katherine's eyes, the good values instilled upon her in her youth usurping the glam vamp she was trying, so hard, to be. She smiled, and it was a smile of church Sundays and ribbons received at 4H events. It was a smile of wheat. Is Tyler here, Katherine asked. I'll get him, I said, but everything that was going to happen just had.

She moved in with me, the two of us watching Fellini's oeuvre and reading Dickinson aloud. Katherine ran the phones and did filing for a tow place; we lived modestly but never went without. Her parents, Meade County residents, generally approved of me; they worked cattle west of the river, and had a small cabin in the Black Hills to which Katherine and I sometimes escaped, the mountain air at the west end of the state like no other air I have smelled. I saved in secret, telling no one other than Tyler of my plans. A year later, I walked into Raymond's on South Phillips (part of Sioux Falls' historic Downtown) and purchased a gold band with inlaid Idaho opal. Katherine's big eyes leaked, her full smiling lips making her cheeks dimpled: we would wed.

Setbacks—Mr. Svenlund sustained a broken hip from being kicked by a heifer during calving; the Country Buffet, from asbestos, was temporarily shut down. We pushed the date back a year; I had had meager and infrequent communication with my own parents though they did know my whereabouts, and a month before the makeup date for the wedding, a call came from my father: it was time to come home. Cancer had eroded my mother's lungs; the chemo worked and then didn't. I flew on an airplane for the very first time. The hospice aide was a Catholic ghost, so pious she seemed to float down the ward's halls. She spoke in soft tones, aroused by the misery her workplace lent. The lobby's vending machines became close friends; I can still recall that C4 held Twix bars, H8 Junior Mints. My mom was tubes and skin on a gurney. I told her of Katherine; I told her I was sorry. Also: cold hands held with no words said; crows on telephones poles. Collapse. After purchasing a second lot at Forest Lawn Cemetery, after the insurance money had come in, after my dad took early retirement from Grover Cleveland and sold off my childhood home, I packed up my duffel on my last night in town. At an all-night donut shop, my father wept over coffee. What do you want me to do, I said. Better, he told me, putting his Merit out on his bear claw. I flew back to Dakota but the bottom had dropped out of things there: Tyler had moved to LA to act in commercials, and ownership at the Country Buffet had switched hands. Katherine, too, had vanished, disappearing into Proust's seven volumes just as autumn set in. The choice to terminate the union was as democratic and affable as such a decision can be, but I wonder still what my life might have been like had things gone differently: the Midwest is this country's best wonder, and to know again the pastoral life, where small things mattered, where big clouds moved like ships across wide blue skies, the fields windswept, the post-and-wire clocklike, its taut lengths measuring the course of each day—to return again ever would bring about a sort of devastating grace I'm not prepared for. Talcum applied to Hat's Interior Lining, to get out the smell.

Starting Bid: $3.99

Mason Jar of Eighteen Rattlesnake Tails. Vacuum-Sealed. Glass is Aqua, Reads "Mason's Patent, October 31st, 1864." Tails Guaranteed Authentic; Still Rattle.

For me our country's true west is not its coast but rather that odd strip that comprises the western part of Mountain Time, and the eastern part of Pacific—here are your Elkos, your Provos, your Yumas, Pocatello and Pueblo and Butte. Here the word hardscrabble seems not sentimental but correct, the mesa erasing everything, the Rockies and Tetons stern reminders that humans are but minor pox or canker, a virus that with time will be flushed out. I spent six months in the first city mentioned above, working third shift at a gas station tucked to one side of I-80. My rented doublewide stood just across the inter-state, and each dawn I crossed the blacktop on foot, this trek emblem-atic of the fact that I was not living the life that most people were, that here one had a road that ran from Oakland all the way to New York, that millions each year crossed east to west or west to east and I, other, without car or bank account, without obligation to spouse, child or family, without mortgage or any other mile marker common to status quo American existence, could get across in under thirty seconds, and be home.

My coworker was a middle-aged Chicana named Aura. Her daughter, jailed for possession with intent, had left her in charge of two grand-sons, who more often than not slept on the white beveled linoleum behind the register, under twin fleece Wal-Mart Cookie Monster blan-kets. My first month I bought a computer from a "traveling salesman," a Mormon-turned-meth-head who had stolen an automobile in Boise and was willing to sell me the Compaq desktop unit for one-quarter of the going price. I bought in, an installer coming to my trailer the next day. Here was the world, shrunk to pixels. I couldn't figure out why anyone cared. Weren't we brought up to not talk to strangers? I unplugged the device, spending those winter days watching snow bloat the desert. But vice thrives on intrigue and with time I plugged back in, locating individuals (see below post) who viewed this new medium in a manner not dissimilar to how Thoreau viewed the railroads: that what was being built was also taking away; that the tech boom was not trend but monster, a dark thing with sharp edges that preyed upon the more craven tendencies of human society; that sought to destroy connection through mimicry of connection, private industry now making the rules for the very ways in which we, as a species, would interact. Or something like that. For a while the banter was static catharsis, fun if a little bit odd, but with time the irony of such persiflages produced in me deep melancholy: we had to pay in to the very thing we sought to critique. Spring came and I set the device by the highway, and a day later it was gone.

Aura's grandsons, Rodolfo and Rogelio, presented me with the snake tails on my last night of work. The gas station mandated that two employees always be present, the ideology being that this coupling would somehow stave off any felonious acts from being rendered upon their establishment. And they may have been right: my half-year in Elko passed without incident. But it was too much seeing those children sleep under cheap and highly flammable blankets night after night, and more often than not I told Aura to come in late or leave early, her time card doctored accordingly by myself. The boys fought as they handed over my gift, each one wanting to be the chief presenter. And where did you get these, I asked, bending down. Out there, said Rodolfo, pointing past the pumps, the jar almost dropping. I took a bus out of town, skimming California's coastline before settling, homeless, in Santa Cruz, the cool sand under the Boardwalk's planks home to a coven of vagabonds from, it seemed, all ends of the earth.

To this day I have no idea how that trio of people ultimately came to possess one and a half dozen tails of venomous reptiles, but I have, as stated above, verified the items' authenticity, taking the jar to a taxidermist in the Bronx, who in turn referred me to a herpetologist at Rutgers–New Brunswick. Tails are Divided between Two Varieties: Great Basin (*Crotalus viridis lutosus*) and Panamint (*Crotalus mitchellii stephensi*). While neither species is considered particularly antagonistic, if cornered either will stand its ground.

Starting Bid: $16.99

Black Low-Top Chuck Taylors (Pre-Nike Era!!!!). Heavily Used. Hole in Rubber Sole of Right Shoe approx. 3/5 inch in Diameter. (Hole Has Been Filled With Wad of Paper Napkins Taken From A Churros Stand at the Santa Cruz Beach Boardwalk). Color Faded. One (1) Eyelet missing metal ring. Size 11½.

Denouncing all manner of helotry, I bought a bus ticket from Santa Cruz to Seattle, arriving the week before the WTO conference and locating, amidst the impending rioters, a half-dozen *online acquaintances*, not quite socialists but something closer, perhaps, to secular nihilists, rich kids, products of divorce, real MENSA types with chips on their shoulders, who by their mid-20s had been bailed out of jails all over the country by lawyers retained by their parents; kids who had grown up on the Upper West Side and gone to St. George's or Andover, and had formed a small tribe of like-minded individuals hellbent on vandalism (I had learned all this through repeated excursions to the Santa Cruz Public Library, a place sympathetic to ideologies like mine, an institution that has resisted wholly the sensational hegemony of the Patriot Act, *that would rather read Orwell than live it*, a place that fully endorsed the idea of someone who had been sleeping on the beach for a week, unshowered, sitting down and using a computer to exchange messages with a group planning violence, as long as the violence spoke out against larger violence, which the violence in Seattle really meant to), and with the vapors of tear gas roiling about us, providing a berserk sort of vestment, I, along with this crew of a half-dozen, removed a public trash can from its foundation, rocked and then ripped the can free from where it was bolted to the concrete, and while I cannot take credit for actually launching said can through the plate glass storefront of NikeTown, I most certainly did enter the spacious, high-ceilinged shop and wrecked everything I could before an agent of law forcibly detained me; which is to say these very shoes, made by a company subsequently bought out by Nike, destroyed a multitude of shelves, boxes, clothing racks and other props within the previously mentioned establishment. It remains a sad thing for me to see the uneducated hipster masses still wearing these shoes obliviously, wholly unaware that they are supporting a corporate monster. As I had no rich parents to bail me out of jail, I watched my beleaguered cohorts exit the King County holding cell we had shared for the past seventy-two hours, each vowing that they would make sure that their legal representation found a way to afford me a similar freedom. These promises turned out to be empty, and I in turn was held for nearly a month before my day in court, wherein a female judge wore the same terse frown for a full twenty minutes before assigning me a very heavy fine, which I haven't paid a cent of.

Starting Bid: $8.99

Lot of Mets Paraphernalia, Years 2003–08. Ten Pennants, Three T-Shirts, Two "Bobbleheads" (Piazza and Martinez). Keychain. Inflatable Bat.

And there were more travels, too, trips worn like coats, heavy journeys, all by bus; things that now seem at once fictive and real, not lived but experienced, as I stalled, balked and temporized, trying hard to never commit, to never settle. In Denton, Texas, there was a fistfight during the Fry Street Fair. In Tulsa, I had an affair with a topless dancer, her husband a tornado chaser and retired seismologist. We were discovered after an F4 didn't pan out, the man walking in while we kissed in the kitchen and subsequently weeping, screaming I was doom's chattel, the paw of Satan himself. There was a year spent in Cleveland, running bags at a fancy hotel. But with time these jumps summed to nothing, their purpose epicene, if possessing form at all. That is, I (sort of) went home. My father, with whom I had been in touch intermittently, had moved to Long Island City, his pension and part-time math tutoring just enough. I arrived on his doorstep windblown, eight people at once. Time had taken; his hair had turned white. We sat in twin recliners in his small living room. I'm ready to stick around now, I told him. I've dreamed that, that you said that, my father said back.

The New York Transit Authority is always looking for a few good men, and I got a job as a Customer Service Rep at Grand Central, the pay rate 25 per. I'm still here, sitting while so many move. My father and I have season bleacher seats at Shea, the Metties, each year, breaking our hearts. The ramp to Grand Central's lower concourse possesses improbable acoustical properties; in those rare moments when things are slow a single person will descend its length and, passing under the archway, the sound of their footfalls will dance up to the ceiling, and it's all I can do to keep myself seated, to not rise from my faux leather desk chair and scream at them take me with you, I will pay any amount. Is there a trick to this that I'm missing? Some clue, unfound? At the ballpark are beef franks, soft pretzels, hot mustard. My commute in from Queens is easy, off-hours. But I can't quite convince myself to buy in completely, and my dad, from a fall, now has a fake hip, and the bills are like virus, dormant then outbreak, and I can't house this stuff because I can't keep it near me, can't see it each day and know more stuff is out there, while I wait here, an anchor, the son now returned, as epics are written and objects constructed and buses, at nighttime, rush over blacktops, always going somewhere better, somewhere else.

Starting Bid: $9.99

Original Copy of Toast from the Banks–Skyzwack Wedding Reception, Orange County Country Club, July 16th, 2006. Paper is Slightly Yellowed (Time) and has Large Merlot Stain in right bottom corner. Legibility of text remains unaffected.

I should state here that it wasn't just me that was against the Banks–Skyzwack union, but rather that the group of friends that I had known from my time in the Midwest found this merger so unsavory that many of them actually *boycotted* the event, and that in accepting my role of Best Man there were two starkly different demographics pressuring me with their agendas, the first of these being the aforementioned friends, and the second The Bride and Groom. While I did and do admit to a predilection for spirits, the latter party's selfishly exaggerated concern in regard to this issue translated ultimately to me being forced to sleep at the foot of Kyla Skyzwack's childhood bed, The Bride and Groom inches away, snoring in tandem on the spring-coiled Serta twin so as to keep sober the night before their big day. But let me back up: Tyler Banks, once punk rock dishwasher, was now a porn mogul, having landed in Chatsworth at just the right time to be a part of smut's jump into cyberspace. Everything wrong with America is dreamed up first in LA.

Tyler found me through my place of employment, my name listed on some page of the MTA's website. I tell myself I flew west out of loyalty, though I know it has much more to do with a dysfunctional lusting after things long passed. Arriving at John Wayne, I found my former friend and his bride in baggage claim, tanned and dead inside. The subsequent days only brought proof of this claim, the wedding party dining at a Cheesecake Factory in Brentwood, where Kyla, an employ of Tyler's Tens (in addition to a multitude of other pay sites), flashed her enormous fake breasts to a group of Japanese tourists, who in turn held up their end of this tasteless cliché by taking copious amounts of pictures with their digital cameras. Tyler's own parents sat smiling, Midwestern and horrified. Kyla's family was Armenian and devoid of moral pretense, caring less about what their daughter did than making sure she in no way could be viewed as lumpen: that the millions would keep coming, never mind the source. The last straw was the procurement, by Tyler, of an entourage of mid-tier adult stars, from which I could pick as many or as few as I wanted to have my way with. This wretched attempt at gift occurred in a private lounge in a West Hollywood nightclub, Tyler producing a key to a suite at a nearby hotel. I chose a single female, had the taxi drop her off a block away, and went to the room alone, where I wrote the below speech in full:

A toast then, while we can, while youth graces us, while our faces shine, while our hair is coiffed in a manner that inspires true envy, while our fingernails possess no chips, nothing hanging, while our organs are determined and hearty, while our good teeth remain intact in their gums, need not root canals, need not extraction, need not to be worked on while we sit in a chair that has been reclined mechanically, trying to think of something better to think about, the birds lighting past the window, the dental saw whirring; while we wake without tingling in one of our limbs, before our blouses and cap toes and cuts of our jeans plunge inevitably toward obsolescence, prior to the consideration of vitamin supplements, prior to repeat excursions to outlet wholesalers because *the thatched Javan magazine rack is back-ordered*; while there's a tap in our toes, a cut to our jib, while vibrancy still speckles the iris, while beds go unmade and floors function as hampers and we know all the songs on the radio, and our skin is not squamous from the aging of cells, and we do not lurch down the hallways of rest homes, before ducks in neat rows and the long gloam of August, before the cold front, the squall line, *the wind shift*, a lifting of glasses, a jubilant hoisting, because we have made it this far mainly intact, because no act has crushed us to palsied, because it's 6:32 on a June night in Tustin and the back room of this hall is ours for the full of the evening, and for a short time we will not be hurtled toward loss, toward our own peculiar miseries, will sit here with wine and not age and not die for we possess *immortal capacity*, something better than hope, because hope is for the weak, is for the needy, is for middle-aged dads six months past divorce, is for the octogenarian who prays before bedtime that her SSI checks will outlast her, will not expire before she does, these people need hope, that gold, hollow thing, and we, while here, while dining, need nothing—need only for our drinks to be freshened up, need only to have the food keep coming.

Because we had been promised that the food *would* keep coming, were assured by a bevy of antediluvians (whom we did or did not cast our votes for), that the shelves would be full, that the taps would run clean, that there would be *unending smorgasbord*, as this country, while we were still glints in the eye, still tears in the condom, had chosen McDonald's, not McGovern, had fueled oiled and lubed the corporate machine, *had cared more about product than service*, and so then new odes: to the plasma tv, to the next batch of modified food additives, to pay sites devoted to horny young teens and updated daily; to bugs in the code and thus data corruption, to Diebold's firm grasp on Ohio, to the image, long passed, of Saddam in beret, grasping the hilt of a saber, gauging the weight of the gold-handled sword per a series of terse chopping motions—Saddam is testing a weapon—to a long list of lies that we'll be left to explain to our children and then to our grand-children, should we not die on the roads, in the air, from disease—to tunnel-vision, because as long as we can keep both eyes on the road, we do not need to look at the landscape, and as long as there's gas and asphalt and rubber trees, we can keep driving without *destination*, a word we know not what to do with, a word and idea, we're really pretty sure, that somebody else was supposed to take care of, while we leased SUVs and ate maki rolls and attained thorough knowledge of Wall Street's big gainers, and since we know nothing, since the directions were lost, since all manner of order was tossed out the window, as we enter this century grasping at straws and pointing with fingers, I urge, while you can, listen less and see more, before what lies ahead turns to dots in the rearview, before life is a marker long passed and well gone—steal these candlesticks, fill your coat up with forks, and hurry along into the night; do not let this world catch up with you, ever, and if it does knock, do not let it in.

Speech was read once in its entirety. A second reading was halted by the disc jockey, a for-hire guy by the name of Lenny Tarveck who, as it turns out, was also from Buffalo, and grew up not all that far from me.

Starting Bid: $1

29

Discarded Notions

Matthew Williamson

THE UNDERGROUND MANSION.

In a nutshell: This big, crazy mansion—*totally underground*.

Master plan: Purchase 1) camping gear, 2) inexpensive plot of land, 3) shovel, 4) seeds and bulbs, 5) materials for homebuilding. Plant seeds and bulbs on property. Pitch tent. Camp on property during construction of mansion, subsisting on fruit and vegetable harvest. Dig hole. When hole is mansion-sized, begin building mansion from bottom up. When mansion is complete, pack up camping gear, move into mansion, reside there indefinitely. Continue to subsist on fruit and vegetable harvest.

Why discarded: 1) Money: Because of unemployment, lacked funds to purchase land and homebuilding materials. 2) The Proficiency Deficit: No experience in carpentry, masonry, plumbing, wiring, etc. 3) Building Code: Code forbade construction of underground mansions.

Days entertained before abandonment: 6.

THE TRUTH PARTY.

In a nutshell: A political party, okay, but one that tells the *truth*, and is in favor of total freedom from government intrusion into the *private affairs of its citizens*, and is all about fostering a nationwide brotherhood and a community based on community (vs. corrupt capitalism).

Master plan: Photocopy and distribute leaflets addressing key social issues/problems of community concern & answering questions like: *What is the Truth Party?*, *Why should I join the Truth Party?*, and *How can I join the Truth Party?* Organize community meetings. Nominate self for, win local office. Use local office as bully pulpit, spreading truth, generating interest in national Truth Party. Run for, win national office. (Pres.?) End government intrusion into *private affairs of citizens*, foster brotherhood, replace capitalism with system of sharing based on common values. Revise building code to permit construction of underground mansions.

Why discarded: 1) Money: Because of unemployment, lacked funds to photocopy leaflets. 2) Corrupt Corporate-Controlled Media: Media controlled by corrupt corporate interests, hostile to political party based on truth and sharing. 3) The Lemming Factor: Public unreceptive to new ideas (esp. when presented via leaflet), unable to act collectively in own self-interest (see Corrupt Corporate-Controlled Media, above).

Days entertained before abandonment: 277.

THE CHRISTFUXX.

In a nutshell: Musically/politically/philosophically/aesthetically rev-
olutionary punk/rap/worldbeat combo.

Master plan: Place classified ad in Chronicle listing influences, invit-
ing gifted, adventurous, politically conscious instrumentalists to
audition for multi-ethnic septet. Hold auditions. Form above-
described septet (w/self as frontman). Perform unique hybrid of
punk, rap, worldbeat, drawing on various cultures past and present, blending music of Ignored Instruments and Forgotten Instruments w/bass, guitar, drums. Build following. Sign major-label
record deal. Subvert dominant paradigm from within culture. Tour
Europe, Asia.

Why discarded: 1) Money: Because of unemployment, lacked funds
to purchase classified ad. 2) The Proficiency Deficit: Unable to play
any instrument; voice described as nasal, unappealing (also: easily
winded due to decades of heavy tobacco/cannabis consumption);
poor sense of rhythm, pitch. 3) The Credibility Gap: Skilled multi-
ethnic multi-instrumentalists unlikely to join/finance project
spearheaded by easily-winded non-instrumentalist w/unappeal-
ing, nasal voice.

Days entertained before abandonment: 1,843 (non-consecutive).

THE TRAVELS OF NICHOLAS O'GRADY.

In a nutshell: Mammoth Novel of Ideas following travels/adventures of titular thinker/lover/poet (loosely modeled on self) in dystopian near-future. Opening epigram: *"Not all who wander are lost."*

Master plan: Boldly envision dystopian near-future in which corrupt corporate-controlled world government routinely intrudes into citizens' private affairs. (Workers replaced/governed by robots, etc.) Transmit bold vision to pages of epic novel (jointly dedicated to H. P. Lovecraft, Allen Ginsberg, Janis Joplin). Self-publish (in English, Icelandic). Tour the country, giving readings to eclectic audiences, interviewing w/local print/radio journalists. When novel has become worldwide cult phenomenon, sell rights to major publishing house for many millions of dollars. Lecture at universities/participate in elite symposia. Accept prestigious/lucrative fellowship(s), move to Iceland, begin work on *The Further Travels of Nicholas O'Grady.*

Why discarded: 1) Money: Because of unemployment, lacked funds to self-publish. 2) The Proficiency Deficit: Monolingual; unable to translate epic work into Icelandic. 3) The Lemming Factor: Public unreceptive to new ideas (esp. when presented via sci-fi picaresque). 4) Corrupt Corporate-Controlled Media: Enticing array of entertainment options inhibited concentration, prolonging tedious work of transmitting bold vision to printed page.

Days entertained before abandonment: 2,372 (non-consecutive).

ELFA GUDMUNDSDOTTIR.

In a nutshell: Gorgeous, artistic, unapologetically intellectual, Icelandic on-again-off-again girlfriend of ex-best-friend (Brock Taylor). Soulmate?

Master plan: After Brock is discovered *in flagrante delicto* w/Elfa's 17-y/o cousin Sigrun, lure Elfa into retaliatory sex. During postcoital embrace, talk expansively/poetically of life, love, art. Confide grand dreams of underground mansion, grassroots political movement, genre-busting multi-ethnic combo, Novel of Ideas, gainful employment. In weeks/months/years following Elfa's tearful reconciliation w/Brock, liaise w/Elfa in secret whenever possible. Gradually woo away from Brock. Wed.

Why discarded: 1) Money: Because of unemployment, lacked funds to A) court Elfa, B) repay $700 debt to Elfa. 2) The Brock Dynamic: Chief rival for Elfa's affections taller, thinner, handsomer, cleaner, gainfully employed, fluent in Icelandic.

Days entertained before abandonment: 959 (each more painful and humiliating than the last).

30

Star Lake Letters

Arda Collins

RE: MS #04-2683; Epiglottic Haematoma: An Unusual Complication of Foreign Body Ingestion

Dear Dr. Fukushima,
Thank you for submitting the above-referenced manuscript to the *Annals of Otology, Rhinology, and Laryngology*. Two experts have now reviewed your paper, and we have decided that you live somewhere extremely far away, and every time we try to picture you, we come up with nothing, and revert to an inexplicable image of a kitchen cabinet under the sink at home, the inside and the outside of the cabinet, and some of the surrounding kitchen. I keep some cleaning supplies under here, brushes and sponges, but it isn't a dirty space. I understand why this might not be what you would imagine your name and manuscript title to connote. However, if you were to respond to my admission about you, I would ignore you by sending you the following letter:

RE: MS #04-2683; Epiglottic Haematoma: An
Unusual Complication of Foreign Body Ingestion

Dear Dr. Fukushima,
Two weeks and you will have an editorial decision. If you believe that, I can't help you. I
actually couldn't help you if I tried. I'm picturing you enraged and maybe in tears somewhere
in Japan. I don't know what Japan looks like. I
like to think about rural Japan a lot though. I
picture small, snowy villages in Hokkaido. In
the summer, I imagine calm, sweaty farmers eating noodles with a cucumber. I am looking at the
cover of a plastic sheet-saver or whatever, that
has a painting of a magical looking pagoda leading down a cliff to a waterfall on the cover. It
reminds me of something I might have seen in a
restaurant. Is there a restaurant somewhere in
you, is that what I'm noticing? Obviously, I
don't want you to answer that, not because I
don't genuinely want to know, but because you
know I never want to hear from you.

RE: MS #04-2706; Cochlear Implants and
Malformations of the Inner Ear

Dear Dr. Olthoff,
I apologize for the delay in responding to your
email. Your manuscript means nothing to me, and
although there appears to be a complicated net-

work of people for whom this is not the case, I have such a hard time picturing them that mostly they exist as a notion of voices that I think I remember hearing when I was in a car accident on the highway as a child; or when I am lying in the dark in bed and catch myself turning into an elusive, forgotten interlude of humanity; or when the living room light is still on in the middle of the night. I want to talk about the word "cochlear" though. It reminds me of the beach, because it makes an association with a conch shell. But that would be on a romantic, tropical beach, or one where a man and woman with their young child first learn that they are expecting once again. I am thinking of an autumn beach, someplace cold, like Maine or the Arctic Circle. I don't have many feelings for you, but I think that something we could do together would be to ride in a dune buggy across the tundra. The beach in the autumn is how we know who we are, the way that everyone's reaction to velvet curtains, clothing, or furniture is similar, but there are things that have to be explicit.

To: Oto Dept.
From: Annals
RE: Office

I am writing in regards to my office. I seem to be placed at the end of a hall near the fire door, which is fine. I enjoy pretending to be alone at all times, and not existing at all for large portions of that time. However, on that note, I have to bring up the office next to mine. A man in pleated pants who is either German, Danish, or Belgian is working next door, and he is working in conjunction with the story *Hans Brinker and the Silver Skates* at all times. It would make more sense if he was Dutch, but I doubt he is. He enters and leaves his office with a look of unending devotion to misery. One time in the winter I saw him changing his shoes before he went home at the end of the day; even though he wasn't changing into ice skates, it was implied. It is impossible that he doesn't have secret wishes. The reason that this is harmless now but dangerous in the long run, is because it raises the possibility that the presence of the story *The Red Shoes* could enter the Oto department, if it hasn't already. I am sure I don't have to explain why this would be a problem. Immolation in a public building can cause real harm. The sprinkler system in the ceilings in the hallways would go off and all the sheetrock in the hospital would become meaningless. It is a ballet shoe equivalent to *Carrie*, *Firestarter*, or *Cujo*. These are stories from our past that we should learn from in our present society. No one wants the hallway to be immolated.

RE: MS #04-2305; Fixation of Soft Tissue
Surrounded by Bone Using Microwave
Irradiation: Electron Microscopic Observation
of Guinea Pig Inner Ear

Dear Dr. Goding,
We haven't spoken. At least, not for a while. I
recognize your name and your manuscript number,
but not the title. However, it makes sense that
you are not one of the ones who writes about
vocal folds, but about the inner ear.

Doctor, if I may, I feel that if we knew each
other, things would be very different for both
of us. We would be together in Dusseldorf, in an
apartment by the river. For the first time, I
would like wall-to-wall carpeting; we would have
a glass-topped dining room table, and I would
wear expensive blue eyeliner. You would be my
valentine and a giant box of chocolates would
come from somewhere; one of us would bite all of
them—pink, white, caramel, raspberry gel, granu-
lar chocolate—all over the living room, while
the other one would wear my seashell-inspired
bra and underwear set, even if it made me think
of mustaches and doorbells to see you in it.
Goding, I'm not going to lie to you. You, and I
think you know this, break into my silent stream
and make the fluorescent lights turn present
instead of ongoing. In the end, Goding, as
observed by the saints I have seen in paintings

in museums, positioned in infinite configurations of hats and outfits, in settings that
include baby lambs, calves, and foals; pastures;
naked violence; and feasts of fruit and meat held
in dark cathedral vaults, I have found that you
are still transformed into a medium-size planter
in a hotel lobby. The transition into this feeling happens over the course of the afternoon.
When I leave the hospital around four or five,
when the light is turning in the cold outside
the parking garage, I feel empty of plush desires
and the thrill of never speaking to you. You open
the door to the possibility that speech originates outside of any particular person or plant.

RE: MS #04-2578; Laryngeal Thrush

Dear Dr. Sulica,
I have two words for you: "Laryngeal Thrush."
Hands down, this is my favorite manuscript
title. The obvious pornography is subtle. I also
love your name, and that it goes with the title.
It is as though otolaryngology is its own language, and if I were to translate "Laryngeal
Thrush" into English, I would translate "laryngeal" as the word for "river" and "thrush" would
be like "rush" so it would be "rushing river,"
like the Old West or China, but much more beautiful, because "thrush" also means "vanish" and
"thrust," so it is a river—a "throat"—that does

all of those things at once. Modified by your name, Sulica, it does these things slowly, because you cannot say Sulica fast. It is like the word "sluice," which you also wouldn't say fast. All together, it is a river, a sluice, that vanishes slowly, with the velocity of rushing and thrusting, which gives it the obvious sexual symbolism that makes a person feel as though they are looking up close at a giant rock face trying to spell their own name.

RE: MS #04-2632; Seasonal Variation of Rhinocerebral Mucor Infection

Magliulo,

Remember the time on the rocks? When we both imagined you drowning me in the inlet? What was needed was succor, not mucor. But that is what it is like with you, one misunderstanding after another; this is what we are supposed to do, make obligatory half moons together in order to maintain the dimension of existence that stores low-grade failures, and I am trying. The dark ocean where there is a cavern of particles from this category of possible enactments is behind one of my organs, and in one of the emotion particle sacs at the base of my skull. If you tested it with your hands it would feel like a raisin made out of a dark ocean.

On the way home, it rained very hard and I wasn't afraid. Sometimes I mistake Sunday for other things. A hot afternoon that disappears without any desires in it has a place, but I don't like that aesthetic of reality; maybe it could have a number or a name, and then we could establish for ourselves in life what qualities of reality we wanted to avoid, or if we couldn't or shouldn't avoid them we would be prepared because we would recognize them. We would know, for example, that qualities of fear are an established part of a certain kind of sunny day in January, but that it is not fear to be avoided, they are fears that we can possibly become inured to as we get older and find other value in it. Since January is written in muted white cursive letters with a gold tone in the background to indicate waning light behind it, this aesthetic might be called White January Marigold 001 for children, when the fears are new, and for an adult stage it could be White January Marigold 004, to indicate that at least three stages of thought, experience, and subtlety in this category had been traversed. A high level fear would be an inquiry, and this one could be White January Marigold 478: Where Is It? I have the sense that I know, the way sense and know can become snow, but that won't be how this works.

RE: MS #04-2563; Clinical Significance of
Middle Frequency Sudden Deafness

Dear Dr. Filho,
There is a pile of empty cans and being in a
junkyard stringing some of them to the tail of
a dog, and in another part there is a movie
about a wooded area.

You are never there when I think of you, and
your absence is large and delicate. I have won-
dered if the shadows in my discriminating fac-
ulties are the reason I detect you, especially
since the record of your manuscript in the data-
base shows that you are unavailable at this
time.

This has left a problem about trains that
people have lost interest in. We felt close to
them through myths of the West and the Civil
War, but train tracks in the daytime in the
summer are dreary and meaningless and they have
to be addressed. I would rather be bitten by a
dog than look at them, but as I am saying this
it seems like they are the same thing.

RE: MS #04-2571; Acute Laryngeal Abscess: A
Rare Entity But Life-Threatening Disease
Revisited

Dear Dr. Eliashar,
Your manuscript, "Acute Laryngeal Abscess: A

Rare Entity But Life-Threatening Disease Revisited" exists. Your name in my handwriting on a file folder though is its true incarnation. To say "revisited" actually refers to many people's bad habits. I don't know why you would bring up something so unpleasant, when clearly you are hoping to have your paper published. As for things here, they're going well. I have been getting your emails, I am sure you have been wondering, but as you know, I don't care, not because I don't actually care, but because the physical actions that are part of this have to take place through the conduit of my office, and then I feel gray about us. I feel so sad when I think of us, the sense of hopelessness is overwhelming. Is that what you mean by "revisited?" I hope that things with you and your wife are better, and the sleeping pills. Sometimes I think of you chewing through the pillow in your bedroom in the middle of the night while your wife is lost in her nightgown. Most of this must be soothed by the early breakfasts you share in what is generally the best part of the day. Even though you have shitty sleep, the minutes after you pull into the garage on a night when it first seems like the end of winter and listen to the car cool to the memory of a former shrub, is a gentle, dark pantomime. Even if you are forced to remember the past, you don't have to finish your thought.

RE: MS #04-2649; Purulent Chondritis of the
Laryngeal Framework Cartilages

Dear Dr. Ewend,
Where do we start? Your sister's white Romanian
sneakers have been in and out of the hallway
door for a month. She has had her hair high-
lighted, and the tired problem and the laundry
seem better. In America, people would be worried
about Epstein Barr but for her, it is probably
Chernobyl. I also saw yesterday before it rained,
the outer borough patio of the comptroller's
wife. She tried to commit suicide two years ago,
and even though I have passed her house again
and again I have never seen her. It is wrong to
feel sad about someone else's private, abomina-
ble pain that I did not have to experience. The
geraniums and plastic white outdoor chairs that
I have seen only in that way were showing between
the slats of the wooden enclosure they have on
the side of their house facing the sidewalk. I
don't know what things are for in their specif-
ics, but I have an overall sense that no work is
wasted.

RE: MS #04-2674; The Anterior Laryngeal Webs

Lijie,
Lijie. I don't know what to think about that. Are
you like a tongue? A pre-historic animal making

infrequent sounds lost in the advent of Pha-
nerozoic miasma in a plant landscape? You open
the door to the possibility that speech originates outside of any particular person or plant.
You extrude that from life.

RE: MS #04-2812; Unusual Case of Accessory Nose
Associated With Unilateral Complete Congenital
Choanal Atresia

Dear Dr. Ou,
You are my mind. Not you, and not your mind, but
you as the unidentified physical components
that are assigned to your spatiality that
includes limb thoughts and organ thoughts.
Maybe that is the total wrong direction. End-
lessness is happening right now, and lions and
grass are part of it. The problem is not that
there is no one in our soul, or that it's invisible. It in this life is so visible it's up close
to us every minute. If you had a beautiful animal so close to your face that you were gazing
into its eyes every minute so that you were in
motion with it in time through its relation to
the black cosmos, your perception would be
affected and other things about the world and
the particulars of creation might be obscured.
A commercial that my soul gives me is a sprinkler in a garden or grass area. I understand why
it likes this, but I only like it because it

likes it. When I see that image, either on the inside or the outside of my mind, I know my soul is activated, and is conveying its participation in the present tense in a mainstream way.

RE: MS #04-2653; Pulsatile Tinnitus Associated with Internal Carotid Artery Morphologic Abnormalities

Dear Dr. Eshragy,
Fistula. What pleasures, or pleasutes lie here? A pleasute is an episode of logical, optimistic pleasure, a vignette of pleasure that is a completed bright interlude.

I have some punctuation, an eyebrow pierce, a lip pierce, and an earring loop in my top cartilage. There is a myriad of jewelry in life. Is jewelry a flute? A river that flows so that everything that festers in one area of geologic gestation germinates to form a temporal spore is separated by rocks that break a melismatic waterfall chamber for space to echo sensible inside any? any what? this, again? Your ears overrun, and my ears, in faunal space. We're alone together, and not alive at the same time, but we bring ourselves to ring together. What if we changed the concept of beginning? What are your aquatic interests?

31

LIFE STORY

David Shields

FIRST THINGS FIRST.

You're only young once, but you can be immature forever. I may grow old, but I'll never grow up. Too fast to love, too young to die. Life's a beach.

Not all men are fools; some are single. 100% Single. I'm not playing hard to get; I am hard to get. I love being exactly who I am.

Heaven doesn't want me and Hell's afraid I'll take over. I'm the person your mother warned you about. Ex-girlfriend in trunk. Don't laugh; your girlfriend might be in here.

Girls wanted, all positions, will train. Playgirl on board. Party girl on board. Sexy blonde on board. Not all dumbs are blonde. Never underestimate the power of redheads. Yes, I am a movie star. 2QT4U. A4NQT. No ugly chicks. No fat chicks. I may be fat, but you're ugly and I can diet. Nobody is ugly after 2 a.m.

Party on board. Mass confusion on board. I brake for bong water. Jerk off and smoke up. Elvis died for your sins. Screw guilt. I'm Elvis; kiss me.

Ten and a half inches on board. Built to last. You can't take it with you, but I'll let you hold it for a while.

Be kind to animals—kiss a rugby player. Ballroom dancers do it with rhythm. Railroaders love to couple up. Roofers are always on top. Pilots slip it in.

Love sucks and then you die. Gravity's a lie; life sucks. Life's a bitch; you marry one, then you die. Life's a bitch and so am I. Beyond bitch.

Down on your knees, bitch. Sex is only dirty when you do it right. Liquor up front—poker in the rear. Smile; it's the second-best thing you can do with your lips. I haven't had sex for so long I forget who gets tied up. I'm looking for love but will settle for sex. Bad boys have bad toys. Sticks and stones may break my bones, but whips and chains excite me. Live fast; love hard; die with your mask on.

So many men, so little time. Expensive but worth it. If you're rich, I'm single. Richer is better. Shopaholic on board. Born to shop. I'd rather be shopping at Nordstrom. Born to be pampered. A woman's place is the mall. When the going gets tough, the tough go shopping. Consume and die. He who dies with the most toys wins. She who dies with the most jewels wins. Die, yuppie scum.

This vehicle not purchased with drug money. Hugs are better than drugs.

You are loved.

Expectant mother on board. Baby on board. Family on board. I love my kids. Precious cargo on board. Are we having fun yet? Baby on fire. No child in car. Grandchild in back.

I fight poverty; I work. I owe, I owe, it's off to work I go. It sure makes the day long when you get to work on time. Money talks; mine only knows how to say goodbye. What do you mean I can't pay off my Visa with my MasterCard?

How's my driving? Call 1-800-545-8601. If this vehicle is being driven recklessly, please call 1-800-EAT-SHIT. Don't drink and drive—you might hit a bump and spill your drink.

My other car is a horse. Thoroughbreds always get there first. Horse lovers are stable people. My other car is a boat. My other car is a Rolls-Royce. My Mercedes is in the shop today. Unemployed? Hungry? Eat your foreign car. My other car is a 747. My ex-wife's car is a broom. I think my car has PMS. My other car is a piece of shit, too. Do not wash—this car is undergoing a scientific dirt test. Don't laugh; it's paid for. If this car were a horse, I'd have to shoot it. If I go any faster, I'll burn out my hamsters. I may be slow, but I'm ahead of you. I also drive a Titleist. Pedal downhill.

Shit happens. I love your wife. Megashit happens. I'm single again. Wife and dog missing—reward for dog. The more people I meet, the more I like my cat. Nobody on board. Sober 'n' crazy. Do it sober. Drive smart; drive sober.

No more Mr. Nice Guy. Lost your cat? Try looking under my tires. I love my German shepherd. Never mind the dog—beware of owner. Don't fence me in. Don't tell me what kind of day to have. Don't tailgate or I'll flush. Eat shit and die. My kid beat up your honor student. Abort your inner child. I don't care who you are, what you're driving, who's on board, who you love, where you'd rather be, or what you'd rather be doing.

Not so close—I hardly know you. Watch my rear end, not hers. You hit it—you buy it. Hands off. No radio. No Condo/No MBA/No BMW. You toucha my car—I breaka your face. Protected by Smith & Wesson. Warning: This car is protected by a large sheet of cardboard.

LUV2HNT. Gun control is being able to hit your target. Hunters make better lovers: they go deeper into the bush—they shoot more often—and they eat what they shoot.

Yes, as a matter of fact, I do own the whole damn road. Get in, sit down, shut up, and hold on. I don't drive fast; I just fly low. If you don't like the way I drive, stay off the sidewalk. I'm polluting the atmosphere. Can't do 55.

I may be growing old, but I refuse to grow up. Get even: Live long enough to become a problem to your kids. We're out spending our children's inheritance.

Life is pretty dry without a boat. I'd rather be sailing. A man's place is on his boat. Everyone must believe in something; I believe I'll go canoeing. Who cares!

Eat dessert first; life is uncertain. Why be normal?

Don't follow me; I'm lost, too. Wherever you are, be there. No matter where you go, there you are. Bloom where you are planted.

Easy does it. Keep it simple, stupid. I'm 4 Clean Air. Go fly a kite. No matter—never mind. UFOs are real. Of all the things I've lost, I miss my mind the most. I brake for unicorns.

Choose death.

32

Instructions for Extinction

Melanie Rae Thon

Sturgeons: Use steamboats. Imagine these lakes and rivers are bottomless. Trawl for the great fish in numbers beyond counting. Smoke their flesh. You and your passengers will find it delightful. Feast on their salty eggs. Use the fat of the fish to fuel your engines. Catch, eat, render—what could be more efficient?

Songbirds: Slash forests, pave highways, build railroads. Expand suburbs. Create the perfect environment for usurpers and vagabonds. Give the cowbirds plenty of space to rove and feed; leave them just enough woodland for breeding. Watch them lay their big eggs in the nests of warblers and vireos. Close your eyes. Count to ten. Finished.

Wolves: Use aircraft to spot them. Hunt them with dogs, their own cousins. Set steel traps, even where these are illegal. Use high-powered rifles with scopes. Follow their movement with heat sensors. Poison the carcass of a deer and leave it in the snow when the winter is hard and the wolves hungry. Lure a nursing female from her den. Shoot her. Crawl down the burrow to find her young. Be quick. The other wolves are hunting and might return soon. Do not be afraid of the pups. They are blind and toothless. You could keep one alive with half a pint of milk a day. Don't do this. Put all five in a burlap bag, twist the top twice, sling it over your shoulder. These wolves are not heavy yet, only seven pounds between them.

When you reach the bridge, drop three large stones into the bag. Do not be distracted by cries or whimpers. Knot the bag tight; use a rope if necessary.

As you walk to the center of the bridge, take time to enjoy the view. Imagine the long plunge to swirling water.

Heave the bag over the side.

Drop it.

Variations: If you suspect wolves have killed your livestock, you may prefer more intimate methods. Take the bag to the river's edge. Some find comfort or satisfaction drowning the pups one at a time. You may wish to feel them struggle.

If you live in Montana, if you are a stockman obsessed with the idea that the wolf, that wily thief, takes money from your pocket, you are invited to resort to extreme measures: the state veterinarian will inoculate any wolf you capture with sarcoptic mange. Give him your tired, your poor, your famished wolves, your trap-torn cripples. He will provide the needle full of mange, and the wolves will carry this new death to all their brothers and sisters.

Advice: Do not be deterred by the knowledge that your precious cow died from disease, that the three wolves you saw at twilight were scavengers, not killers. Do not consider the likely possibility that your sheep was pulled down and gutted by your neighbor's sleek black Labradors, those skillful hunters with strong jaws and powerful haunches. Ignore any blood you see on the paws of your own Irish setter.

Remember: The wolf is dangerous. He leaps into your dreams. He steals your children. He disguises himself as your grandmother. Trust me. Your actions are necessary. Small and helpless as the pups are, your rage and your fear are justified.

Consider the words of Lieutenant General Phil Sheridan: "The only good Indian is a dead Indian." I hear my mother's voice, my mockingbird, my teacher.

You can kill Indians one by one, risk your own life, suffer discomfort. Or you can wipe them out from a distance. Use your diseases: malaria, measles, influenza, cholera, smallpox, syphilis, tuberculosis.

To speed the process: eliminate the buffalo. Again, Sheridan offers words of inspiration: "Destroy the Indian's commissary, and you will destroy him."

The buffalo is everywhere and everything, sixty million strong from the Atlantic to the Rockies, from dusty Texas to the Great Slave Lake of Canada. He moves as one beast, an impenetrable mass of muscled animal twenty-five miles long and fifty miles wide. He cannot be counted. He cannot be domesticated. The only thing that stops him is the quick rise of western mountains.

He speaks a language you might understand if you were wise enough and patient. He squeaks, bellows, clicks, hisses—at dawn and dusk you hear him moaning. He has a voice like God's, or a cry like your mother's.

In a silent catechism, my mother asks, What is your uncle's name?

Pte, buffalo.

What does he become?

We are good Catholics, Rina and I; we believe in the miracle of transubstantiation.

I say, *His flesh is my body; his skin is my tipi. His hide is my boat, and his dung is my fuel. I worship his head. I sharpen his shoulder blades and swing them like axes. Hooves become glue, bones become needles. His sinew is thread, and his horn is my ladle. With his blood, I am dark; I am painted for battle.*

Rina says, *If he is everything to you, why did you kill him?*

White girl, betraying daughter, I am to blame for this and other crimes against my mother and all her people.

Mother, who swam away one bright day, who will not swim home, who has left her pale husband and her two fair-skinned daughters now and forever, this mother whispers, *How can you sleep, my child, while the world you know vanishes?*

33

Will & Testament

Matthew Vollmer

October 30, 2001

To Whom It May Concern:

Enclosed please find the last will and testament of Andrew Walter,[1] which, as of five-thirty p.m. today, will be simultaneously submitted to twenty-seven unknown readers, in the hope that one of them might accept the role of executor.[2]

To choose these persons, the undersigned, with the help of the Manhattan Phone Book, recited the names and addresses of possible candidates aloud. Candidates were chosen partly because of the aural pleasure obtained by reciting their names and addresses, and partly because the visions that un-spooled during this recitation were harmonious with the undersigned's idea of the kind of person the executor should be—i.e., someone sympathetic enough to stop when passing the injured, yet not sentimental enough to think herself/himself a hero; someone intelligent enough to complete a *New York Times* cross-

---

1 By the time the reader receives these documents, the undersigned will have already have been dead for some hours. Though the undersigned has taken some necessary precautions to prevent body spoilage, the reader should act quickly so that the last wishes of the undersigned might be met.

2 The undersigned has decided to eschew the tradition of referring to a female executor as "executrix." Therefore, as the undersigned uses it, "executor" should remain neutral.

word puzzle, yet humble enough to say it was just a thing they did while waiting for the next thing to happen; someone who would pause—on a train, under a bridge, on a toilet—to read, and perhaps memorize, an extraordinary graffiti passage.

The undersigned acknowledges these unreliable methods might have led him to make inappropriate choices. Indeed, some recipients may find the following subject matter[3] offensive, and may conclude that the undersigned is insane, blasphemous, or perverted. In this event, the undersigned apologizes, and asks that the recipient destroy these documents.

Though the letters of the undersigned's name will, undoubtedly, have a particular effect upon the reader—an association produced by the particular combination of the letters, conjuring up a vision, however irrational, however unclear, of what the undersigned might look like—the undersigned understands that the reader will have not known him. The undersigned has figured, based on the proximity of the address, as well as the undersigned's affinity for brisk walks, that there is a very good possibility that he has passed the reader in the street—though the undersigned's face was, most likely, simply another face in that churning face-mass each day brings, and so the undersigned's face probably tumbled, along with the hundreds of other faces of the day, down the laundry chute of the reader's head into oblivion or, if the undersigned was lucky, into that unconscious

---

3   The reader should also know that the undersigned is composing this in between answering phones, making copies, addressing envelopes, and entering data concerning the promotional materials of the A. J. Forsythe investment firm, and while the cube in which he works seems an appropriate environment for the last day of his life (photos of a dog, a boy, and a party which are not his, a half-eaten chocolate bunny in the top desk drawer, and a placard, slapped on the forehead of his monitor, that reads *SPOILED ROTTEN!*), it is not the best environment in which to compose, and the document may be riddled with errors and inaccuracies. Hence, the undersigned begs the reader's pardon should these last wishes be untranslatable.

well where he might be drawn up, momentarily, in a dream. Perhaps, as he types, the undersigned is performing any number of things, without his consent, in the confines of other people's heads, though it's more likely, since he has a face that he's been forced, at times, to repress, that he's been forgotten altogether. It is not, however, the undersigned's intent to create a sense of guilt[4] in the reader for his/her failure to remember the undersigned's face. In fact, anonymity is of the utmost importance for the undersigned, as his purpose is to allow the reader, should the reader so desire, to believe that Fate has had a hand in the proceedings. Though the undersigned does not believe, necessarily, in Providence, he believes that this somewhat random act of choosing potential executors will allow s/he who decides to follow the accompanying procedures to indulge a sensation of having been chosen, thus granting said procedures a significance that they might not have otherwise possessed.

That said, the undersigned asks that the recipient of these documents, in a spirit of goodwill, consider following the procedures set forth in the accompanying will and testament, in an effort to help keep the undersigned's memory, or what's left of it, alive.

Signed, this 30th Day of October, 2001.

_____

Andrew Walter

---

4 Guilt, the undersigned believes, is for the damned.

LAST WILL AND TESTAMENT
OF ANDREW WALTER

I.

The undersigned, Andrew Walter, residing at 12A Lazarus Court, Brooklyn, New York, being of sound mind and body, does hereby declare this instrument to be his last will and testament.

II.

The undersigned hereby revokes all previous wills and codicils.

III.

The undersigned hereby directs that the disposition of his remains be as follows:

A. ACQUIRING THE BODY:

At Terminal D of the LaGuardia Airport, across from a newsstand, stands a locker numbered 15B, combination 5-25-74. In this locker the executor will find a key to the undersigned's apartment, directions for acquiring the body of the deceased (the location of which, by this point, will have remained unknown), as well as access codes to a bank account containing the undersigned's life savings, which should be used for any expenses accrued in the distribution of both the undersigned's body and his possessions. Leftover monies should be accepted by the executor as payment for her/his participation.

B. WHAT MIGHT BE DONE WITH THE BODY:

Once contacted by the executor, the undersigned's neighbor, a Mr. Charles Christopher—having assured the undersigned that his thirteen months at Johns Hopkins Medical School granted him more than sufficient knowledge concerning the dissection of human cadavers—has agreed, in lieu of the traditional embalming, to perform the favor of separating skull, skeleton, body fat, brain, and heart from the remainder of the deceased's body. Fat, brain and heart will be placed immediately into plastic bags, then separate coolers,[5] until the respective parts are to be prepared and delivered to the destinations described below. In return, Mr. Christopher[6] will receive the undersigned's rare and highly valuable antique Ouija board (the details of which are spelled out in section IV-C of this document).

1. Skull: The undersigned would ask that his skull be given to one of the following doctors, providing said doctor place the skull upon a shelf in her/his office: Dr. Bill Jameson; Dr. Rachel Hawthorne; Drs. Lola and Marvin Randy; and Dr. Weston Hildebrand. These physicians—all of whom the undersigned has visited at least three times in the last year—should be reminded that the deceased's skull could serve several functions. One: a kind of model for understanding where scientists believe memory is located, as well as various points of entry, and Two: when hinges are attached to the jaw, the skull might provide its owner with a macabre, though humorous, puppet. "Mr. Bones" might teach otherwise skeptical children the importance of abstaining from

---

5 Executor will find supplies, as well as wardrobe (which can be either worn by executor or donated to Goodwill), in bedroom closet of the deceased.
6 In the event that Mr. Charles Christopher refuses to make good on his word, the deceased's body, fully intact, should be delivered to the nearest medical-research facility. In this case, Mr. Christopher shall not receive said antique Ouija board, regardless of how much begging Mr. Christopher performs, and the board shall be ceremoniously set aflame.

flesh foods, flossing after every meal, washing one's hands regularly to prevent the spread of disease, and drinking plenty of fluids.

2. Remainder of Skeleton: The undersigned has made arrangements[7] with a progressive elementary school, St. Enid's, on the Upper West Side, that will accept his skeleton. The skeleton could be hung on the wall of their biology lab, as both a model of the human body and, hopefully, as a reminder of what students will someday be reduced to. (The undersigned hopes that this reminder of one's brief passage through this earthly realm will encourage students to treasure each unthinkable moment of their lives, though he recognizes that the sight of his bones might contribute to some kind of death desensitization, which may or may not be so bad, depending on one's mental disposition and/or metaphysics.)

3. Fat: Body fat should be removed from the remains of the deceased and placed inside a cooler, which should then be delivered to lamp maker Gabrielle Whiting, who works in a loft above a buffet in Chinatown, and with whom discreet arrangements have already been made to use the undersigned's fat, not unlike the versatile blubber of the whale, as fuel for light. The undersigned has estimated[8] that he has fat enough for ten lamps, to be distributed to the following ten women the under-

---

7 "Arrangements" here simply means that the undersigned spoke with the biology teacher, Mr. Eric Yancey, who led the undersigned to believe that, after death, his bones would be welcome, if they were thoroughly sanitized and disinfected—though he could make no promises.
8 See schematic no. 1 on page 2 of a notebook, which will hereafter be referred to as the "Appendix," and which can be found inside the aforementioned locker in Terminal D of the LaGuardia Airport.

signed has thought of, at some time or other, as his friends, some of whom he had dreamed, however fantastically, of loving: Hope Ramsey, Paris Kim, Lydia Gonzalez, Whitney Silvers, Anjeannette LaRoche, Raquel Davis, Daphne Finch, Jill Loganberry, Julie Smith, and Penelope Jones.[9] For the sake of their delicate sensibilities, recipients of the lamps should not be told how the lamps are fueled. They need know only that the undersigned wishes to provide them with the kind of light in which their ancestors worked—the unstable and dramatic flickering of the lamp, the kind of light in which so many of us look best.

4. Brain: The brain of the undersigned shall be sliced, by Mr. Charles Christopher, into sixty-six rectangular pieces—the exact number of companies/organizations the undersigned worked for during his life. These pieces of the undersigned's brain shall be placed, along with a splash of formaldehyde, into clear glass vials, each of which shall then be corked, labeled, packed tightly in green shipping peanuts, and hand-delivered in a watchcase-sized box to the CEOs/presidents of these companies/organizations.[10] The following note should accompany each vial: *Dear Sir/Madam: Here is a little something to remember me by. Enjoyed (circle all that apply): making copies / entering data / manning desk / folding pamphlets / surfing Internet at your top-notch company and/or organization. Adieu, AW.*

5. Heart: The undersigned's heart should be removed, wrapped in

---

9 The addresses of these women, who have most likely forgotten the undersigned, are available on page 3 of the Appendix.

10 Names and addresses of said companies available on page 6 of Appendix. Vials can be found in the fridge of the undersigned's apartment.

plastic, packed in a small cooler of dry ice, placed in a square pinewood box,[11] and shipped to eastern Tennessee, where the undersigned's cousin, Marty Richards, maintains a plot of ground behind his A-frame in which deceased members of the Walter family, including the parents of the undersigned, have been laid to rest. No marked headstone is required, though the executor might mention to Mr. Richards that a jagged rock, rolled up from a creek bed, and stood, pointy part up, would be greatly appreciated.

6: Remainder of Body: To be delivered by Mr. Charles Christopher to Abraham Crematorium.

IV. THE UNDERSIGNED'S POSSESSIONS:

A. Books: The undersigned owns few books, since the majority have been accidentally left on the seats of subway trains and upon the pews of various cathedrals. The following are the ones he refuses to remove from the house, and thus, can be found upon his nightstand:

1. *"Inner Experience,"* by Georges Bataille; *"Tao Te Ching,"* by Lao Tzu; *"The Diary of a Young Girl,"* by Anne Frank; *"Song of Myself,"* by Walt Whitman; and *"Tales of a Fourth-Grade Nothing,"* by Judy Blume, should, within a year following the undersigned's death, be de-paged and handed out as flyers to passersby in

---

11   This box, measuring 8 x 8 inches, which he purchased for an unbeatable price at Box Town, can be found in the top cupboard of the undersigned's apartment, above the stove on the right-hand side.

Times Square, preferably those just coming from or going to stand in front of NBC's *Today* show window.

2. *"The Selected Poems of Robert Frost"* should be delivered to Paris Kim, the round Korean woman who can recite "Stopping by Woods on a Snowy Evening" from memory, and who has, for nearly six years now, shampooed, cut, shaved, and styled the undersigned's hair at In Tri Cut, on Beaumont Street.

3. *Holy Bible*, King James Version, which bears the undersigned's name in gold print, should be delivered to Ms. Raquel Davis, with whom the undersigned worked for three days, filling a temporary secretarial position at St. John's Episcopal Church in SoHo. Ms. Davis—who, as far as the undersigned could tell, had been blessed not only with a striking, if not luminous, winter tan, but also a lovely speaking voice—might be asked to read the first chapter of St. John aloud. If Ms. Davis will allow it, her voice might also be recorded.[12] Also, if Ms. Davis would accept it, the Bible should be given to her. She may keep the photograph inside—a blurry image of the undersigned's father, Hal, with his second wife, Regan, which was sent to the undersigned during the couple's vacation to Iceland, days before the undersigned's father swallowed[13] forty-six sleeping pills, subsequently falling into a permanent slumber.

B. Candles: In an ideal world, every Friday, for twenty-seven minutes, for twenty-seven consecutive weeks—the exact number of years the undersigned spent on earth—one candle from the undersigned's handmade collection would be chosen

---

12 See Section IV.A, in which Ms. Davis's voice is put to good use.
13 Or was made to swallow, as the undersigned's sister is wont to believe.

and lit. At this time, the recorded voice of Ms. Raquel Davis's reading of the first chapter of St. John would be played. The undersigned realizes, however, that such a ritual may involve an unprecedented level of commitment from the executor. Therefore, if the executor lights a candle every once in a while, and remembers the undersigned for a moment, he would consider this request granted.

C. Rare, Highly Valuable Antique Ouija Board: The undersigned owns one antique Ouija board, reportedly used by his great-grandmother Elsie to contact the spirit of Miles Whitcomb Gardner, an eighteenth-century blacksmith to whom she claimed to have been married in a previous life. Though the undersigned, despite multiple attempts, has yet to receive a response to what he believes are the simplest questions,[14] the aforementioned Mr. Charles Christopher seems to believe he can make the board come alive. Should he fulfill his part of the bargain (see section III), the board is his. If not, the board should be, as stated earlier, ceremoniously set aflame.

D. Food: All leftover food should either be consumed by the executor, slowly and solemnly, in the light of one of the aforementioned candles, or, if the executor feels uneasy about consuming the food of a strange dead man, be broken up into pieces and used to feed seagulls, pigeons, or the executor's favorite bird. Although the undersigned prefers a winged creature, any living creature in need of nourishment is acceptable.

---

14 E.g., does this tie match these slacks?, will it rain today?, and, will X call me back?

E. LPs: The undersigned's record collection, albeit quite insignificant, should be delivered to Ms. Lydia Gonzalez, with whom the undersigned spent one afternoon working at www.bigdongs.com, the headquarters of which were composed of a gray, vaulted office space filled with a maze of cubicles, all of which appeared to have been vacated except for the undersigned's, whose job it was to divert the phone calls of hostile "big dong" customers, and Lydia's, whose job it was, as far as the undersigned could tell, to answer a deluge of email while simultaneously providing a series of directives, via telephone, in Spanish. Though the undersigned was too timid to strike up a conversation, the rhythms of Ms. Gonzalez's fingers upon her keyboard and the untranslatable cadences that streamed, unbroken, from her mouth, formed a kind of music, and thus the undersigned feels, why not, she is entitled to his meager collection.[15]

F. Photographs: Self-portraits of the undersigned should be either a) burned in one of the lamps whose fuel is his fat,[16] or b) sent to people who share the same name,[17] with a note explaining the following: *Dear Andrew Walter: We have spent a lifetime sharing the same name. People have shouted out our names and our heads have turned. Certainly, we would like to think, that there is something to this. Only we probably realize this is not the case. Please bask in the undeniable meaninglessness of this coincidence, and enjoy the picture. Sincerely, Andrew Walter.*

---

15 Ms. Gonzalez should know that, ideally, should she accept the collection, Dusty Springfield's *Dusty in Memphis* and Schubert's *Winterreise* might be played—alternately—on the thirtieth of October, the anniversary of the undersigned's death.

16 Obviously, this would be done *before* the lamps are delivered to the ten women.

17 The undersigned has kept a list of persons who share the same name, or a slight variation thereof. This list occurs on page 12 of the Appendix.

Photographs of the undersigned's acquaintances, though few and far between, should be sent to those friends,[18] with this note attached: *A hypothesis: if one is forgotten enough times, one ceases to exist. Forgive me if my failure to remember your face contributed to your gradual and inevitable annihilation. Yours, AW.*

G. "Faceless Man" painting: An oil-painting of a man, minus face, sitting in a chair, reading a book beneath a willow tree, was composed by the undersigned's mother before he was born,[19] and now hangs above the undersigned's sleeping mat in his apartment. The painting, as the executor will discover, appears at first glance to be unfinished. However, the undersigned likes to think of the painting as a completed work, and, more specifically, a portrait of the undersigned himself. Though the man in the painting is obviously in much better physical condition than the undersigned, the undersigned feels they have something in common, perhaps because the undersigned's older sister used to tell him that their mother had intended it to be a portrait of the undersigned himself—a kind of prediction of what he would look like once he grew up: someday, his face would simply disappear.

The painting should be delivered to a Ms. Penelope Jones, originally from Tallahassee, Florida, who works as a receptionist for Jacob and Jacob at 115 Houston Street. The undersigned spent two weeks under the tutelage of Ms. Jones, who, though six months pregnant, did an unparalleled job of show-

---

18 The names of the acquaintances appear on the backs of the photos. Addresses appear on page 13 of the Appendix.

19 The undersigned's mother, coincidentally, died of kidney failure before he was old enough to remember, in any organic way, *her* face.

ing the undersigned, who would perform all of Ms. Jones' secretarial duties during her maternity leave, the ropes.

As a way of explanation, a note might be delivered with the painting: *Dear Ms. Jones: I would probably never admit this if I didn't know you would never see me again. I have always felt, since the day you explained how to use the dictation machine, that in another life I would have liked to have been your baby, your son. I am not ashamed to say that I have imagined a life in which you were my mother: that you cradled me, packed my lunches, scrubbed my bloody elbows with hydrogen peroxide, picked me up in the van from my music lessons. Therefore, it is my wish that you would accept this painting, which was made by my own actual mother, whom I never knew. Yours sincerely, AW.*

H. Apartment: The undersigned hereby declares that, assuming that the executor has completed the tasks described in this document, the apartment[20] shall become the sole property of the executor.

---

20 The apartment, though quite small, boasts a view of the avenue, and if the executor looks closely, s/he will find constellations of the undersigned's fingerprints upon the sliding glass door. Though the undersigned knows no view can save us (we must save ourselves, be saved by others, or, if the executor believes in God, be saved by her/his God), he endorses said window as a place for contemplation. In fact, the undersigned stood there when the idea of this will and testament struck him, just as he stood there when he opened the Manhattan phone book and began to recite the names of potential executors, and as he leaned his head against the cool pane, he imagined the potential executor entering the apartment. He imagined this executor startled by the lack of furniture, the sweet, slightly sour odor of garbage—imagined the executor drawn toward the portable radio beside the window, a radio which will have been purposely left on as a kind of hospitable gesture, a kind of "welcome home" for the executor. The executor, of course, can turn the radio off, as said radio will be, most likely, playing a song the executor has heard before. The undersigned expects that the executor is someone who, like himself, has heard it all. However, the undersigned hopes, and indeed believes, that the executor will keep on singing. The executor, he expects, will have a beautiful voice, as all voices are beautiful when singing—especially if they sing, as the undersigned thinks the executor might, slightly off-key. Perhaps, the undersigned thinks, he will hear this same voice when he descends this evening into the streets, on the way to his unmarked tomb, where his body will exhale its last breath and begin to fade.

34

Letter to a Funeral Parlor

Lydia Davis

Dear Sir,

I am writing to you to object to the word *cremains*, which was used by your representative when he met with my mother and me two days after my father's death.

We had no objection to your representative, personally, who was respectful and friendly and dealt with us in a sensitive way. He did not try to sell us an expensive urn, for instance.

What startled and disturbed us was the word *cremains*. You in the business must have invented this word and are used to it. We the public do not hear it very often. We don't lose a close friend or a family member very many times in our life, and years pass in between, if we are lucky. Even less often do we have to discuss what is to be done with a family member or a close friend after their death.

We noticed that before the death of my father you and your representative used the words *loved one* to refer to him. That was comfortable for us, even if the ways in which we loved him were complicated.

Then we were sitting there in our chairs in the living room trying not to weep in front of your representative, who was opposite us on the sofa, and we were very tired first from sitting up with my father, and then from worrying about whether he was comfortable as he was dying, and then from worrying about where he might be now that he was dead, and your representative referred to him as "the cremains."

At first we did not even know what he meant. Then, when we realized, we were frankly upset. *Cremains* sounds like something invented as a milk substitute in coffee, like Cremora, or Coffee-mate. Or it sounds like some kind of a chipped beef dish.

As one who works with words for a living, I must say that any invented word, like *Porta Potti* or *pooper-scooper*, has a cheerful or even jovial ring to it that I don't think you really intended when you invented the word cremains. In fact, my father himself, who was a professor of English and is now being called the *cremains*, would have pointed out to you the alliteration in *Porta Potti* and the rhyme in *pooper-scooper*. Then he would have told you that *cremains* falls into the same category as *brunch* and is known as a portmanteau word.

There is nothing wrong with inventing words, especially in a business. But a grieving family is not prepared for this one. We are not even used to our loved one being gone. You could very well continue to employ the term *ashes*. We are used to it from the Bible, and are even comforted by it. We would not misunderstand. We would know that these ashes are not like the ashes in a fireplace.

Yours sincerely.

35

Acknowledgments

Paul Theroux

Thanks are due to Dr. Milton Rumbellow, Chairman of the Department of Comparative Literature, Yourgrou College (Wyola Campus), for generously allowing me first a small course load and then an indefinite leave of absence from my duties; to Mrs. Edith Rumbellow for many kindnesses, not the least of which was her interceding on my behalf; to the trustees of Yourgrou College for a grant-in-aid, to the John Simon Guggenheim Memorial Foundation for extending my fellowship for two years, and to the National Endowment for the Arts, without whose help this book could not have been written; to Miss Sally-Ann Fletcher, of Wyolatours, for ably ticketing and cross-checking a varied itinerary, and to Miss Denise Humpherson, of the British Tourist Authority, who provided me with a map of the cycling paths in the areas of England lived in by Matthew Casket; to Mrs. Mabel Nittish for arranging the sublet of my Wyola apartment and providing me a folding bike.

As with many other biographers of minor West Country dialect poets, Casket's output was so small that he could feed himself only by securing remunerative employment in unrelated fields. I am grateful for the cooperation of his former employers—in particular to Bewlence & Sons (Solid Fuels), Ltd., Western Feeds, Yeovil Rubber Goods, and Raybold & Squarey (Drugs Division) Ltd., for allowing me access to their in-house files and providing me with hospitality over a period of weeks; and especially to Mrs. Ronald Bewlence for endlessly informative chats and helping me dispose of a bike, and Mrs. Margaret Squarey, F.P.S., for placing herself entirely at my disposal and sharing with me her wide knowledge of poisons and toxic weeds.

At a crucial stage in my ongoing research, I was privileged to meet Mrs. Daphne Casket Hebblewhite, who, at sixty-two, still remembered her father's run of bad luck. For three months of hospitality at "Limpet" and many hours of tirelessly answering my questions, I must express my thanks and, with them, my sorrow that the late Mrs. Hebblewhite was not alive to read this memorial to her father, which she and I both felt was scandalously overdue. It was Mrs. Hebblewhite who, by willing them to me, gave me access to what few Casket papers exist, and who graciously provided me with introductions to Casket's surviving relations—Miss Fiona Slaughter, Miss Gloria Wyngard, and Miss Tracy Champneys: I am happy to record here my debt for their warmth and openness to a stranger to their shores. Miss Slaughter acceded to all my requests, as well as taking on some extensive chauffeuring; Miss Wyngard unearthed for me a second copy of Casket's only book, but annotated in his own hand, enabling me to speculate on what he might have attempted in revised form had he had the means to do so, and allowing me the treasured memento of another warm friendship and our weeks in Swanage; Miss Champneys made herself available to me in many ways, giving me her constant attention, and it is to her efforts, as well as those of Ruck & Grutchfield, Barristers-at-Law, that I owe the speedy end of what could have been a piece of protracted litigation. To Señorita Luisa Alfardo Lizardi, who kept Mrs. Hebblewhite's house open to me after her late mistress's tragic passing and was on call twenty-four hours a day, I am more grateful than I can sufficiently express here.

Special thanks must go to the staff of Broomhill Hospital, Old Sarum, and particularly to Miss Francine Kelversedge, S.R.N., for encouraging me in my project during a needed rest from exhausting weeks of research. Colonel and Mrs. Hapgood Chalke came to my rescue at a turning point in my Broomhill sojourn; to them I owe more than I can adequately convey, and to their dear daughter, Tamsin, my keenest thanks for guiding my hand and for her resourcefulness in providing explanations when they were in short supply. To Dr. Winifred Sparrow, Director of Broomhill, I can only state my gratitude for waiving payment for my five months of convalescence; and to Stones & Sons, Tobacconists, Worsfold's Wine Merchants, and Hine's Distilleries, all of Old Sarum, my deepest thanks for understanding, prompt delivery, and good will in circumstances that would have had lesser tradesmen seeking legal redress.

I am grateful for the hospitality I received during the weeks I spent at the homes of Mr. and Mrs. Warner Ditchley, Mrs. R. B. Ollenshaw, Dr. and Mrs. F. G. Cockburn, Major and Mrs. B. P. Birdsmoor, and the late Mrs. J. R. W. Gatacre, all of Devizes, as well as for the timely intervention of Miss Helena Binchey, of Devizes, who, on short notice, placed a car at my disposal in order that I could visit the distant places Casket had known as a child. The Rev. John Punnel, of St. Alban's Primary School, Nether Wallop, provided me with safe harbor as well as a detailed record of Casket's meager education; he kindly returned Miss Binchey's car to Devizes, and it was Mrs. Dorothy Punnel who took me on a delightfully informal tour of the attic bedroom in the dorm, which cannot be very different today from what it was in 1892, when, just prior to his expulsion on an unproved charge of lewdness, Casket was a boarder.

I feel lucky in being able to record my appreciation to Pamela, Lady Grapethorpe, of Nether Wallop Manor, for admitting a footsore traveler and allowing him unlimited use of her house; for her introducing him to the Nether Wallop Flying Club and Aerodrome and to Miss Florence Fettering, who expertly piloted him to Nettlebed, in West Dorset, and accompanied him throughout his visit in the village where Casket was employed as a twister and ropeworker at the Gundry. I am obliged also to Miss Vanessa Liphook, and her indefatigable Riley, that I was able to tour the South Coast resorts where Casket, in his eighties and down on his luck, found seasonal employment as a scullion and kitchen hand; for their faith in my project and their sumptuous hospitality, I am indebted to the proprietors of The Frog and Nightgown, Bognor Regis; The Raven, Weymouth; The Kings Arms, Bridport; Sprackling House, Eype; and The Grand Hotel, Charmouth. To Miss Josephine Slape, of Charmouth, I owe the deepest of bows for the loan of a bicycle when it was desperately needed; and to the staff of the Goods Shed, Axminster, I am grateful for their speeding the bicycle back to its owner.

And to Mrs. Annabel Frampton, of the British Rail ticket office, Axminster, my sincere thanks for being so generous with a temporarily embarrassed researcher; and to Dame Marina Pensel-Cripps, casually met on the 10:24 to London, but fondly remembered, I am grateful for an introduction to the late Sir Ronald and to Lady Mary Bassetlaw, of Bassetlaw Castle, at which the greater part of this book was written over an eventful period of months as tragic as they were blissful. It is impossible for me adequately to describe the many ways in which Lady Mary aided me in the preparation of this work; she met every need, overcame every obstacle, and replied to every question, the last of which replies, and by far the hardest, was her affirmative when I asked her to be my wife. So, to my dear Mary, the profoundest of thank yous: this book should have been a sonnet.

Lastly, to Miss Ramona Slupski, Miss Heidi Lim Choo Tan, Miss Piper Vathek, and Miss Joylene Aguilar Garcia Rosario, all of the Graduate Section of British Studies, Yourgrou College, my thanks for collating material and answering swiftly my transatlantic demands; to Miss Gudrun Naismith, for immaculately typing many drafts of this work and deciphering my nearly illegible and at times tormented handwriting, my deepest thanks. And to all my former colleagues at Yourgrou (Wyola Campus), who, by urging me forward in my work, reversed my fortunes, my grateful thanks for assisting me in this undertaking.

36

Primary Sources

Rick Moody[1]

Abbe, William Parker.[2] *A Diary of Sketches*. Concord, New Hampshire: St. Paul's School, 1976.

Bangs, Lester.[3] *Psychotic Reactions and Carburetor Dung*. Edited by Greil Marcus. New York: Knopf, 1987.

Barnes, Djuna. *Interviews*. Washington, D.C.: Sun & Moon, 1985.

Barrett, Syd.[4] "Golden Hair." *On The Madcap Laughs*. EMI Cassette, C4-46607, 1990.

---

1   BORN October 18, 1961, in N.Y.C. Childhood pretty uneventful. We moved to the suburbs. I always read a lot. I did some kid stuff, but mostly I read. So this sketchy and selective bibliography—this list of some of the books I have around the house now—is really an autobiography.

2   Art instructor at St. Paul's School when I was there (1975–79). Abbe was an older, forgetful guy when I met him. He was in his late sixties, probably. He lived alone in an apartment above the infirmary at S.P.S. His studio had burned down years before, taking a lot of his paintings, and I believe this accounted for the halo of sadness around him. He could be infectiously happy, though. His house was full of jukeboxes, dolls, and electrical toys. Games of every kind. One time I showed him my *Sgt. Pepper* picture disk—remember those collector's gimmicks which revolutionized the LP for a few minutes in the seventies? The famous jacket art was printed on the vinyl. Abbe laughed for a good long time over that. He sat in the old armchair in my room, the one with the stuffing coming out of it, and laughed. He loved that kind of thing. He had a lot of Elvis on his jukeboxes.

3   Lester's last published piece, in the *Voice*, appeared in my senior year of college. I moved back to N.Y.C. a little later, after six months in California, where it was too relaxed. By the time I got to New York, the East Village galleries were already disappearing. Lester was dead. The Gap had moved in on the northwest corner of St. Mark's and Second Avenue.

4   In 1978, back at S.P.S., I took six hits of "blotter" acid and had a pretty wrenching bad trip. Eternal damnation, shame, humiliation, and an endless line of men in clown costumes chanting my name and laughing. That kind of thing. I turned myself in, confessed to a master I liked,

---

Barthes, Roland. *A Lover's Discourse*.[5] Translated by Richard Howard. New York: Hill & Wang, 1978.

Bernhard, Thomas. *The Lime Work*—. Chicago: University of Chicago Press, 1986.

Book of Common Prayer and Administration of the Sacraments and Other Rites and Ceremonies of the Church, According to the Use of the Protestant Episcopal Church[6] in the United States of America, The. New York: Harper & Brothers, 1944.

Borges, Jorge Luis. *Labyrinths*.[7] Edited by Donald A. Yates and James E. Irby. New York: New Directions, 1964.

Breton, André. *Manifestoes of Surrealism*.[8] Translated by Richard Seaver and Helen R. Lane. Ann Arbor, Michigan: University of Michigan Press (Ann Arbor Paperbacks), 1969.

Carroll, Lewis. *The Annotated Alice*. Edited, with an introduction and notes, by Martin Gardner.[9] New York: Clarkson N. Potter (Bramhall House), 1960.

Carter, Angela.[10] *The Bloody Chamber and Other Adult Tales*. New York: Harper & Row, 1979.

Cheever, John. *The Journals of John Cheever*.[11] New York Knopf, 1991.

---

the Reverend Alden B. Flanders. Somewhere in the middle of the five or six hours it took to talk me down, I asked him if he thought I would remember this moment for the rest of my life.

5 "The necessity for this book is to be found in the following consideration: that the lover's discourse is today *of an extreme solitude*. . . . Once a discourse is thus . . . exiled from all gregarity, it has no recourse but to become the site, however exiguous, of an *affirmation*."

6 I didn't get baptized until I was fifteen. The minister, who had buried my grandparents and my uncle and performed my mother's remarriage, couldn't remember my name. Right then, the church seemed like the only thing that would get me through adolescence. I was going to get confirmed later, too, but instead I started drinking.

7 Cf. "Eco, Umberto," and also n. 9, below.

8 The band I played in, in college, was called Forty-five Houses. We got our name from the first Surrealist manifesto: "Q; 'What is your name?' A. 'Forty-five houses.' (*Ganser syndrome, or beside-the-point replies*.)" Our drummer preferred women to men, but I sort of fell in love with her anyway. After we graduated, she gave me a ride on her motorcycle. It was the first time I ever rode one. I held tight around her waist.

9 See n. 20, below.

10 The first day of Angela's workshop in college, a guy asked her what her work was like. She said, "My work cuts like a steel blade at the base of a man's penis." Second semester, there was a science-fiction writer in our class who sometimes slept through the proceedings—and there were only eight or nine of us there. One day I brought a copy of *Light in August* to Angela's office hours and she said, "I wish I were reading *that*"—Faulkner—"instead of *this*" (pointing to a stack of student work).

11 As a gift for graduating from boarding school, my dad gave me a short trip to Europe. Two weeks. I was a little bit afraid of travel, though, as I still am, and in London I spent much of the time in Hyde Park, in a chair I rented for 15p a day. The sticker that served as my lease still

The Wapshot Chronicle. New York: Harper & Brothers, 1957.

Coover, Robert. *In Bed One Night & Other Brief Encounters.* Providence, Rhode Island: Burning Deck, 1983.

Daniels, Les. *Marvel: Five Fabulous Decades of the World's Greatest Comics.*[12] With an introduction by Stan Lee. New York: Abrams, 1991.

Danto, Arthur C. *Encounters & Reflections: Art in the Historical Present.* New York: Farrar, Straus & Giroux, 1990.

"Darmok."[13] *Star Trek: The Next Generation.* Paramount Television, 1991.

Davis, Lydia. *Break It Down.* New York: Farrar, Straus & Giroux, 1986.

De Montaigne, Michel. *The Complete Essays of Montaigne.* Translated by Donald M. Frame. Stanford, California: Stanford University Press, 1958.

Derrida, Jacques. *Of Grammatology.*[14] Translated by Gayatri Chakravorty Spivak. Baltimore, Maryland: Johns Hopkins Press, 1976.

Elkin, Stanley. *The Franchiser.* Boston: Godine (Nonpareil Books), 1980.

"Erospri." On *The Whole Earth 'Lectronic Link,*[15] modem; 415 332-8410, Sausalito, California, 1985.

Feelies, The. *The Good Earth.*[16] Coyote Records, TTC 8673, 1956.

---

adorns my copy of *The Stories of John Cheever*, also given to me by my dad. I haven't been back to the U.K. since.

12   We moved a lot when I was a kid. In eighth grade I had a calendar on which I marked off the days until I'd be leaving Connecticut forever. My attachments weren't too deep. I spent a lot of time with Iron Man, the Incredible Hulk, and the Avengers. I also liked self-help books and Elton John records.

13   Picard and the crew of the Enterprise attempt to make contact with a race of aliens, the Children of Tama, who speak entirely in an allegorical language. Picard doesn't figure out the language until the captain of the Tamarians is already dead. A big episode for those who realize how hard communicating really is.

14   One guy I knew in college actually threw this book out a window. Here are some excerpts from my own marginalia: "Function of art is supplementalism though devalorization of weighted side of oppositions"; "Attendance as performance: more absence creates more real presence." I'm not sure what I meant, but I loved Derrida's overheated analogies: "Writing in the common sense is the dead letter, it is the carrier of death. It exhausts life. On the other hand, on the other face of the same proposition, writing in the metaphoric sense, natural, divine, and living writing, is venerated" (page 17).

15   The WELL—as it is abbreviated—has a really good "Star Trek" conference, too. This private conference is about sex. I started messing with computers in junior high, when my grades got me out of study hall. Which was good because people used to threaten me if I didn't let them copy my homework. It was on the WELL that I learned both the address for a mail-order catalogue called Leather Toys and how to affix clothespins.

16   My drinking got really bad in graduate school. In the mid-eighties, I was in love with a

Fitzgerald, F. Scott. *The Crack-Up*. New York: New Directions, 1945.

Foucault, Michel. *Discipline and Punish: The Birth of the Prison*. Translated by Alan Sheridan. New York: Vintage, 1979.

Gaddis, William. *The Recognitions*.[17] New York: Penguin, 1986.

Genet, Jean. *The Thief's Journal*. Translated by Bernard Frechtman. New York: Bantam, 1965.

Gyatso, Tenzin, the fourteenth Dalai Lama of Tibet. *Freedom in Exile*. New York: HarperCollins, 1990.

Hawkes, John.[18] *Second Skin*. New York: New Directions, 1964.

Hawthorne, Nathaniel. *Hawthorne: Short Stories*.[19] Edited by Newton Arvin. New York: Knopf, 1946.

Hogg, James. *The Private Memoirs and Confessions of a Justified Sinner*. New York: Penguin, 1989.

Johnson, Denis. *Angels*. New York: Vintage, 1989.

Joyce, James. *Ulysses*. New York: Vintage, 1961.

Jung, C. G. "Collected Works." No. 12, Pan II. "Individual Dream Symbolism in Relation to Alchemy" (1936). Translated by R.-F. C. Hull. Princeton, New Jersey: Princeton University Press (Bollingen Series), 1968.

---

woman who was living in Paris, and I took the opportunity to get mixed up at the same time with a friend in New York. Kate, the second of these women, first played this record for me. The snap of the snare drum that begins *The Good Earth* has a real tenderness to it, for me. I was playing this record when I was really ashamed of myself and also afterward, when I was hoping for forgiveness.

17 At the end of my drinking, when I was first living in Hoboken, I started writing my first novel, *Garden State*. Later, through a chain of kindnesses, someone managed to slip a copy of it to William Gaddis, the writer I most admired, then and now. Much later, long after all this, I came to know Gaddis's son Matthew a little bit, and he said that the book had probably got covered up with papers, because that's the way his dad's desk is. But maybe there was one afternoon when it was on top of a stack.

18 The last day of class with Jack Hawkes, we were standing out on one of those Victorian porches in Providence—a bunch of us, because there was always a crowd of people trying to get into Jack's classes (and they were usually really talented)—firing corks from champagne bottles out into the street. A couple made it halfway across. Hawkes was mumbling something about how sad it was that so many writers were so afflicted by drink. In less than a week, I was going to graduate.

19 Another clergyman in New England, Mr. Joseph Moody, of York, Maine, who died about eighty years since, made himself remarkable by the same eccentricity that is here related of the Reverend Mr. Hooper. In his case, however, the symbol had a different import. In early life he had accidentally killed a beloved friend; and from that day till the hour of his own death, he hid his face from men.

Kapuscinski, Ryszard. *The Emperor*. Translated by William R. Brand and Kitarzyna Mrockowska-Brand. New York: Vintage, 1989.

Lewis, James. "Index."[20] *Chicago Review*; 35: I, 33–35 (Autumn, 1985).

Marcus, Greil. *Lipstick Traces: A Secret History of the Twentieth Century*.[21] Cambridge, Massachusetts: Harvard University Press, 1989.

Marx, Groucho. *The Groucho Letters: Letters from and to Groucho Marx*.[22] New York: Fireside, 1987.

Mitchell, Stephen. *The Gospel According to Jesus*. New York: HarperCollins, 1991.

Pagels, Elaine. *The Gnostic Gospels*.[23] New York: Vintage, 1989.

Paley, Grace. *Enormous Changes at the Last Minute*. New York: Farrar, Straus & Giroux (Noonday Press), 1991.

Pärt, Arvo. *Tabula Rasa*.[24] ECM New Series 817 764-4 (1984).

Peacock, Thomas Love. *Headlong Hall and Gryll Grange*. Oxford: Oxford University Press, 1987.

Plato. *Great Dialogues of Plato*. Translated by W. H. D. Rouse. New York: Mentor, 1956.

"Polysexuality." *Semiotext(e)*[25] 4:1 (1981).

Sacks, Oliver. *Awakenings*. New York: Summit, 1987.

Schulz, Bruno. *Sanatorium Under the Sign of the Hourglass*.[26] Translated by Celina Wieniewska. New York: Penguin, 1979.

---

20   See n. 7, above.

21   During the period when I was finishing my first novel, I had an office job in publishing, from which I was later fired. I judged everything against the books I loved when I was a teenager: *The Crying of Lot 49*, Beckett's *Murphy*, *One Hundred Years of Solitude*, etc. Besides Lester Bangs (see above), Marcus's *Lipstick Traces* was one of the few recently published books I liked. Another was *Responses: On Paul de Man's Wartime Journalism* (University of Nebraska Press).

22   In 1987, I institutionalized myself. At that moment, Thurber and Groucho Marx and anthologies of low comedy seemed like the best that literature had to offer. I thought I was going to abandon writing—something had to give—but I didn't. I felt better later.

23   "The accusation that the gnostics invented what they wrote contains some truth: certain gnostics openly acknowledged that they derived their piosis from their own experience . . . The gnostic Christians . . . assumed that they had gone far beyond the apostles' original teaching."

24   And Cage's book *Silence*; and *Music for Airports*; and La Monte Young's "The Second Dream of the High-Tension Line Stepdown Transformer from the Four Dreams of China"; and Ezra Pound after St. Elizabeth's; and *Be Here Now*; and Mark Rothko.

25   The back cover of this issue consists of a newspaper photo of a man in a wedding gown slumped over on a toilet, his skin ribbed with gigantic blisters. He's really destroyed, this guy. I'd been given to believe the photo was from the *Daily News*. And since my grandfather worked for the *News* the luridness of this horror struck close. This, I learned, was an act of *pleasure*.

26   Angela Carter assigned this book to us in sophomore year. I was taking a lot of quaaludes

Sebadoh. *Sebadoh III.*[27] Homestead Records, HMS 168-4, 1991.

Thomas à Kempis. *The Imitation of Christ.* New York: Penguin, 1952.

Williams, William Carlos. *The Collected Poems of William Carlos Williams.*[28] Volume 11; 1939–62. New York: New Directions, 1988.

Zappa, Frank. With Captain Beefheart and the Mothers of Invention. *Bongo Fury* (1975).[29] Barking Pumpkin Records, D4-74220, 1989.

that spring. One night, I stayed up all night on quaaludes and wrote a story, cribbed from Bruno Schulz, about a guy who lives in a house that is *actually his grandmother.* Later, when I told Angela that I'd written the story high, she said, cryptically, "Quaaludes, the aardvark of the drug world."

27   "All these empty urges must be satisfied."

28   "Sick as I am/confused in the head/I mean I have/endured this April/so far/visiting friends" (pages 427–8). *Garden State* was published in the spring of 1992. I was already pretty far into my second book, *The Ice Storm.* I left Hoboken for good.

29   There was a time, when I was an adolescent, when I didn't feel like I had a dad, even though he didn't live that far away, and I saw him on Sundays. This is an admission that won't please him or the rest of my family. The way I see it, though, there has never been a problem between me and my *actual* dad. But dads make the same tentative decisions we sons make. Once, my father said to me, "I wonder if you kids would have turned out differently if I had been around to kick some ass." This was during one of those long car rides full of silences. The question didn't even apply to me, I didn't think. He might have been there, he might not have. Didn't matter. I was looking elsewhere for the secrets of ethics and home.

37

Contributor's Note

Michael Martone

MICHAEL MARTONE was born in Fort Wayne, Indiana, and grew up in a small house, white with green trim, 1812 Clover Lane, in the neighborhood known as North Highlands. His neighbors across the street were the Mensings, Ed and Mildred. Mr. Mensing was a fireman, but he no longer lived and worked in a firehouse. He was an assistant chief, which meant he had a white helmet he kept on the back shelf of his fire-engine red department car he drove home at night from work. His work was fire prevention. In his dress uniform, he left each day just as Martone was leaving to walk to school (Price Elementary, Franklin Junior High School, North Side High School), got into his bright red and polished chrome car and drove to inspect factories, offices, theaters, and schools. Martone saw him inspecting his schools and would say hello as Mr. Mensing checked the panic bars on doors or the recharge records of extinguishers. Mr. Mensing also went to construction sites and ran tests on the new automatic sprinkler systems, the dry standpipes, and the emergency overrides on elevators and escalators. Martone saw him at the high school basketball tournament games at the Memorial Coliseum, counting the cheering fans sitting in the stands and standing in the aisles and hallways. Probably most exciting, however, was that every fall, Martone saw his neighbor on television during Fire Prevention week when all the schools in the city school system participated in one huge fire drill, the only fire drill that wasn't a surprise. Martone watched as Mr. Mensing (surrounded by the mayor, the school superintendent, other fire chiefs, insurance agents, radio announcers announcing and television weathermen commenting) pushed a button after all the other officials made speeches about fire safety. When Mr. Mensing, dressed up in his formal white hat and gloves, pushed the button, the fire alarms sounded all over the city, the sirens, whistles, horns, buzzers, bells. Everyone pretended the whole city was ablaze. And, each fall, no matter what school Martone was attending, he would get up from his desk and walk quickly yet orderly to the designated exit, clear the building, and assemble with his classmates at the safe specified distance away from the school, then turn and face the building and wait for further instructions. Usually on those days there was a fire truck nearby the students inspected during their lunch breaks or recesses. It was still warm, and the sun reflected off of the bright polished hardware of the fire engines or ladder trucks and blazed on the reflecting stripes taped to the helmets and coats of the bored firemen. Mr. Mensing always had extra badges and plastic fireman's hats left over from the event. The hard red plastic badges and hats were donated by the Hartford Insurance Company and featured a picture of a deer with huge antlers. He gave them out as treats for Halloween, pinning a badge on a ghost or pirate, who might also don a helmet that became part of the costume for the rest of the night. Mr. Mensing did not like to turn on his lights in his house on Halloween or on any other night of the year. He delayed turning on a light and when he did it was a single fixture, dim and dull. Martone never knew if this habit hoped to save money or demonstrated some basic mistrust of electricity or revealed some knowledge of its inherent danger. For as long as he could, Mr. Mensing read the evening newspaper, *The News-Sentinel*, while sitting in a lawn chair just inside his glass storm door, his back to the door, what little light there was falling over his shoulder to illumine the open pages he held up. He was there in the morning too, reading the morning newspaper, *The Journal-Gazette*, sitting in the webbed lawn chair inside his door. Even in winter, he sat in the doorway, collecting what little light there was through the frosted glass. When the winters were cold, Mr. Mensing would have to climb the city's water towers and make sure the elevated water in the tanks that put pressure on the system, pressure that the fire department needed at the hydrants, hadn't frozen. One particular cold spell, he spent several nights in a rubber dinghy floating inside one of the huge tanks that read on the outside FORT WAYNE, agitating the water with an oar so it wouldn't skim over with ice and then freeze solid and shut off the water. In the spring, there would be floods in Fort Wayne, and Martone, when in high school, helped fill sandbags to shore up the leaky levees. Mr. Mensing spent the floods wading beside and guiding boatloads of rescued people to dry land. He told Martone that floods were worse than fires. Manhole covers popped out of place from the pressure of the rising water, and the muddy water prevented someone walking a boat or raft from seeing the ground below. Suddenly, the solid street wasn't there, and you fell right through the hole, down under the street, impossible to see the way back up to the surface. Not like falling through ice, Mr. Mensing told Martone. With ice you swam up, escaping by ignoring the light, the solid ice illuminated by the sun. The way out was the only one above you not lit up. Against your instincts, he told Martone, swim to the spot that looks the blackest.

38

The Year's Best Fiction 2008: The Authors Speak

J. Robert Lennon

GUTMAN KLAMATH, "The Epiphany of Palmer Weiss"

The idea for "Epiphany" came to me while standing in line one morning at Starbucks. The man in front of me was typing out an e-mail on his BlackBerry, and I suddenly thought, how would this fellow react if he suddenly got a message from his mother—*who had died three years before?* And what if the message told him to leave Starbucks right now, and track down a certain vice-president of human resources for a certain investment firm, and kill him bare-handed? And what if every day, the dead mother sent this fellow a new e-mail demanding that he kill somebody, and that each of these victims was some man who had wronged the mother in her long, tragic life? And what if I then made each of these victims have some unique occupation, like candy-maker and priest? And what if, at the end, the mother *asked the fellow to kill himself*, because he himself had betrayed her herself, the mother, when he married a woman she didn't approve of? And what if, in a final assertion of his independence, the fellow smashed his BlackBerry on the ground—and then slipped on the pieces and died!

By the time I finished my soy latte and lemon-currant scone, I had my story.

JIM BURR, "Absence"

"Absence" is a reaction to the seemingly endless deluge of "reader-oriented" fiction constantly being published by the simpering, approval-seeking mass of semi-literate so-called "literary" magazines one finds one's libraries and bookstores hopelessly inundated with. One becomes horribly tired of the dreary conventions of the genre—plot, character, setting, &c.—and wishes, once and for all, to not have one's hand held by some mush-mouthed mommy-like "author" smugly leading one down the well-worn paths of storied cliché. And so one attempts to create a work unburdened by the in-name-only "rules" and "conventions" of "literature" and eschews the supposed "traditional" crutches of "punctuation" and "grammar" and the tyranny of standardized spelling.

"Absence" was rejected by 172 self-described "magazines" whose "editors" complained that they "didn't get it" before João Hooten of *Mumpsimus* finally "got" that "getting it" wasn't the point.

One is grateful to João Hooten, to the editors of this anthology, and to one's dog, Bakhtin.

JAMIE SPRINGBOTTOM, "Adrianna's Wedding"

It was while vacationing in Key West with my husband, the food photographer Merwin Fanks, and our two beautiful children, Gary (an animal rights lawyer) and Felicia (now a sophomore at Harvard), that it occurred to me that today's fiction, with its dreary glorification of death, misery, and hatred, was insufficiently expressive of the great beauty and joy that is all around us. And so, as I paddled back to shore (for at the time of this realization I was canoeing on the small lake we co-own with the architect Jeffers Paul and his wonderful family) I conceived of the most striking elements of "Adrianna's Wedding"— Adrianna's beautiful hairdo and gown; the way her bouquet, drifting through the air as though in slow motion, appears etched against the sky's pale blue; the look of deeply committed love in the eyes of Hunter, her husband-to-be; and her lovely and respectful relationship with her mother, Paulette, which has grown into more of a mutually satisfying friendship than a mere mother–daughter bond.

The story took about a week to write, as I did so using my great-grandfather's fountain pen, on pages handcrafted with a tabletop paper press by Jennifer, Gary's beautiful and thoughtful fiancée. I am grateful to the editors of the CanadAir in-flight magazine, *Drift*, for taking a chance with my story, and to the Good Earth Trading Company for their wonderful line of delicious and life-sustaining teas, which I sipped with delight as I composed.

LUPA PRZYREWSKI, "How Do You Say"

I only live in America six month, and English not so good. Therefore, I very gratitude to editor of making story in book. I very difficult try write story of emigration to America and tales of great hardship in New York and of struggle with mother and father and finding fortune and having loss of self on subway. With money of book selling soon I take English class. Thanking.

RUPERT G. B. SCHIPP, "The Assistant Lion Tamer's Wife"

Whence this shimmering urge, this shuddering desire, this longing? What makes us write? For me, it is the feeling of the revealing of truth—not the mere truth of saying what is so, but the truer truth of invention. This story was inspired by a trip to the circus, where I witnessed the profound vision of a lion tamer plying his risky art, and I imagined that he had an assistant, and that assistant was married, and the lion ate the assistant, and his wife was bereft. What, then, of the assistant's wife? Is she doomed to loneliness and grief? And what of their child, still unborn and quickening beneath the flawless creamy flesh of her belly? And of her soft, round, full breasts, yet unsuckled by the rosy lips of her incipient offspring? What of them?

It is the undeniable reality of such questions, conceived by chance, birthed by the imagination, for which I took pen in hand and scried the glittering crystals of the unseen mind.

McKENSIE KEENE, "Boomer and Hank"

Through my dedication to volunteer work and to helping others, I arrived at the idea of writing a story that addresses our collective willingness to ignore the silent and invisible nation around us: the homeless. There have been stories of the homeless before, but I decided to up the ante by wondering, what if my homeless protagonist were the second coming of Jesus—*and nobody noticed?* I went through many drafts of the story over many months, but it was my husband Phil who made the suggestion that changed everything: make the story from the point of view of the dog—and make the dog be the Holy Father Himself. After that, it was easy. The scene where Boomer–Hank/father–son stop to view the weeping statue of Mary–mother really touched me—I was crying at my desk—and it was my editor, Linda Guber, at the *Last Prairie Review* who suggested the great scene where the friendly shopkeeper gives Hank the free bag of dog food, and he and Boomer see their reflection in the shop window, and the bag reads *God Doof.* The story wouldn't have been the same without it!

ARTHUR MAURITIUS, "The Travails of Ezra £"

All I can say is, it's about time. Graphic fiction has been much in the spotlight these past few years, but scant attention has been paid to the much more difficult and far purer art form of ASCII fiction—that is, graphic storytelling using only computer keyboard symbols as visual elements. As an engineer at IBM in the seventies, I invented ASCII fiction, and when I was laid off in 1983 I began to devote myself to it full-time. This sad graphic tale of an ASCII poet and his search for meaning in a world that cares little for anything more challenging than emoticons took me more than twenty years to write, and if I say so myself fully deserves the attention it is finally getting. If for only today, I no longer feel like the "mime-in-a-box" that serves as Ezra £'s signature:

JUNE WATTS, "Thirty Below"

My goal in writing "Thirty Below" was to pull back the "testosterone curtain" of the privileged, male-dominated publishing world and address three subjects rarely seen in contemporary fiction: sexual abuse, eating disorders, and stripping. The character of Candee is inspired by my sister Kelly, who is not anorexic, abused, or a stripper, but has gone through her own issues, including the same scalp rash Candee gets from a back-alley dye job. Candee's cat Purrcival, who survives being locked in Candee's apartment for two weeks after Candee's suicide by devouring his once-beloved owner's forearms, is inspired by my own Mister Mittens, who, though he has never had to endure such an ordeal, I am sure would acquit himself wonderfully should such a thing come to pass. Candee's drug-addicted mother is not inspired by my own mother, in spite of her many emotional problems, but by her sister, my Aunt Merry; her alcoholic pedophile father comes from some suspicions I have about our former neighbor, my high school chemistry teacher, Murray Whelm. And as for Candee's three tormentors, Q-Man, Lyle, and Backdoor Joe, you know who you are.

FREDERICK PAINE PAULUS, "Three Scenes: Nova Scotia 1934"

Mr. Paulus declines to comment.

LIONEL MEEKS, "Incident at Fortieth and Vine"

This is all true, yo. It all happened just like I said. Zilch is me and Yellowman is my buddy Bo, and the times when killing got done, well, that's just how it went down, and if you don't like it, too bad. Because it's real, it's street, and it's life.

I want to give a shout-out to my homies: my agent, Blurbin'-In-Ya-Turban Amanda Urban; my #1 book critic boy from the 'hood James "Do-What'cha-Should" Wood; my main man Salman; Boom-Boom-In-Da-Room Harold Bloom; Julie Kristeva 4 Eva and Eva; the Cock-Jock of Rock, Jacques Derrida-da-da-dum, R.I.P.; my Once-A-Week-O Freak-O Critique-O Michiko Kakutani; Tommy "Tomcat" Lynchin' Pynchon; Write-Till-She-Moan Toni More-and-Morrison; Abracadabra-Gift-a-Gab Gabriel García Park-It-In-The-Fiction-Market Márquez; Donny Fill-O, Chill-O, Careful-Not-Ta-Spill-O DeLillo; and finally, the Chairman of the Boards, the Original Globe-Trotter, Sir Mike-It, Spike-It, As-You-Like-It, Mistah Bling-Bling-Play's-the-Thing, the Killa of Fear, William Shake-Bake-and-Take-A-Bow Shakespeare. Word.

M. SPACKMAN CONE, "The Frosted Glass Widower"

As always, I am reluctant to demystify my art with one of these notes, but upon this, my eleventh appearance in these pages (starting in 1958 with "Why Harold Parks Rakes Leaves"), I feel duty-bound to extend to you, dear reader, the small gift of my comments.

I do so, then, in the form of a personal anecdote. Late last year, I found myself delivering a lecture at a certain institute of higher learning (it shall remain nameless, but it is one whose reputation has been sullied, of late, by its association with a certain reluctant world leader and failed businessman), and afterward, at an exhausting wine-and-cheese affair of the sort invariably appended to such events, I was accosted by a bright-eyed young person of writerly ambitions. "Mister Cone," he said to me, "my writing teacher gave my story a C-minus, because I used dashes for dialogue instead of quotes. But Mister Cone, James Joyce used dashes instead of quotes, and he is one of the most celebrated authors in history! Why can James Joyce use dashes, but not me?"

"My dear boy," I replied with a chuckle, *"because he's James Joyce, and you're not!"*

The poor child nearly choked on his braised pork medallion!

MISTER CHIMPERS, "Black Banana Bad"

Mister Chimpers sad he not publish story. Then story appear in *Compunction 34*! Doctor Patterson show Mister Chimpers *Compunction 34*. Mister Chimpers delighted! Now Doctor Patterson say story in anthology. Mister Chimpers famous! Mister Chimpers show world chimpanzees people too! Vivisection terrible crime! It kill Mister Chimpers' friend Mango! It very bad!

Mister Chimpers prove Doctor Patterson brilliant cognitive researcher! Now maybe she get grant! Also Doctor Patterson very attractive and single! Now she find mate like Mister Chimpers did! Mister Chimpers love Luella, aka Mrs. Chimpers!

Story inspired by experience in jungle before capture. Mister Chimpers can still taste terrible banana. Mister Chimpers grateful to Doctor Patterson for translation!

Author's note interpreted by Doctor Gertrude Patterson, PhD.

JACK ROOT, "Feast of Blood"

When I found out my story was accepted into this anthology, my instinct was to tell them to go to hell. I didn't become "The Modern

Master of Terror" by falling to my knees before the literary kingmakers, that's for sure—I did it by writing my hairy working-class behind off. But my wife told me it would be stingy not to accept, and that the sales of this anthology were probably crap and why not be generous and let them put my name on the cover, so I said okay.

I don't have anything to say about "Feast of Blood," because any idiot can understand it, unless they have an Ivy League education and start looking for allegories and metaphors and what have you. Hey Harvard, guess what: there aren't any. It's a *story*, not a dissertation. Symbolism is for pussies, you read it here first.

I do want to say something about fear, though, which is my stock in trade. Let me make it clear, this isn't a scary story. Here's a scary story: a soccer mom drops her kids off at violin practice, then goes home and cleans the kitchen so her dentist husband won't be mad. Or how about this: a guy wakes up, puts on a suit and tie, drives to work, has some meetings, makes a bunch of cell phone calls, then goes back to his suburban house and watches the Home and Garden Channel. That's terror, America: your fat lazy selves, being controlled by the Princeton-educated mass media. Compared to that, my stuff is a walk in the park.

Anyway, don't be embarrassed if my story is the only one in this book that you read. Be proud! And tonight . . . sleep tight, my pretties.

ADAM STEIN FOWLER, "Man Espies Reflection In Falling Glass"

Striding down a Park Slope ave., about to step into the crosswalk, a glassmaker's truck passes before me, and loose comes the cargo, the plate glass tipping, tipping then falling toward the pavement, and in that moment a vision, the brimming efficacy of impending destruction, the deadly potentiality of the mirrored surface, myself framed in the twisting, straining trapezoid, like the bad guys in the Superman movie, there I stand, my tousled hair, my secondhand suit pants and tennis sneakers, my T-shirt bearing the name of an industrial lubricant, my eyeglasses twin trapezoids of their own, themselves reflecting the reflection of myself, and in this moment the story gushes from between the thighs of Eupheme: the inviolability of the instant, the repugnant weight of reflected selfhood, to be American in the twenty-first century, to stand upon the terminal moraine that is Brooklyn, oh Brooklyn, Brooklyn, my Brooklyn, the ludicrousness of terror, the terror of existence, the existence of the self, the selfishness of mankind: this is America, this is New York, this is Park Slope, my home, my enemy, my lover, my mother, and through the splash of shattered windowglass I dash, back to my walkup, through the door with its peephole in reverse, concentrating the (w)holeness of my apartment in its infinitesimal dot, past the teetering coatrack of Burberry castoffs, over the threshold to the study, where beneath the Flaming Lips poster, beside the Charlie Tuna lamp, astride the paint-splattered swivelchair, I fling open my Macbook Pro and out it flows, this refulgence of language, this vomited echolalia, my salivary testimony, my man-struation, the jizz of ages pours through me, and I come, I come.

39

About the Typefaces
Not Used in This Edition

Jonathan Safran Foer

ELENA, 10 POINT: This typeface—conceived of by independent typographer Leopold Shunt, as the moon set on the final night of his wife's life—disintegrates over time. The more a word is used, the more it crumbles and fades—the harder it becomes to see. By the end of this book, utilitarian words like *the*, *a* and *was* would have been lost on the white page. Henry's recurrent joys and tortures—*bathwater, collarbone, vulnerability, pillowcase, bridge*—would have been ruins, unintentional monuments to bathwater, collarbone, vulnerability, pillowcase, and bridge. And when the life of the book dwindled to a single page, as it now does, when you held your palm against the inside of the back cover, as if it were her damp forehead, as if you could will it to persevere past its end, *God* would have been nearly illegible, and I completely invisible. Had Elena been used, Henry's last words would have read

TACTIL, VARIABLE POINT: "A text should reveal the heart's emotional condition, as an EKG readout reveals its physical one." This idea was the inspiration for Basque typographer Clara Seville to create Tactil, a good example of the early interface types. The size of a letter corresponds to how hard the key is pressed. Air-conditioning blows its story over the keys, as does the breath of a bird on the sill, as does the moonlight, whose infinitesimally small exertion also tells a tale. Even when there is nothing applying pressure to the keys, a text is still being generated—an invisible transcript of the world without witnesses. And if one were to hammer the keyboard with infinite force, an infinitely large nonsense word would be produced.

If this book had been typeset in Tactil, Henry's various *I love you*s could have been distinguished—between narcissistic love ("**I** love you."), love of love rather than love of another ("I **love** you"), and traditional, romantic love ("I love **you**"). We could have learned where Henry's heart leaned when on the unsafe wooden bridge he confessed himself to Sophy. And we could have learned if it is true that one can love only one thing at a time, making **I love you** definitionally impossible.

Tactil was not used because preliminary calculations suggested that the author was striving—intentionally or not—to recreate the physical world. That is, *tree* was typed with the force to make the word as large as a tree. *Pear*, *cumulus* and *Band-Aid* typed to make the words to the scale of a pear, a cloud and a Band-Aid. To print the book in this way would have required bringing another world into existence, a twin world composed entirely of words. We finally would have known the sizes of those abstract ideas whose immeasurability makes us, time and time again, lose our bearings. How does existentialism compare to a tree? Orgasm to a pear? A good conversation to a cumulus cloud? The mending of a gnarled heart to a Band-Aid?

But even if logistics had permitted, this typeface still would have been rejected, because as a quantitative, rather than qualitative, measure, it could have been quite misleading. That is, Henry's **love** for Sophy may have been the size that it was because of hate, sympathy, jealousy, neediness or, however unlikely, love. We would never have known, only that there was much of it, which is to know very little.

TRANS-1, 10 POINT: This typeface refreshes itself continuously on the screen, words being replaced by their synonyms. *Now autumn begins* exists only for long enough to bring *present fall commences* into existence, which instantly disappears to make room for *gift descend embarks*, which dies so that *talent alight boards ship* can live. Trans-1's creator, I. S. Bely (1972–), said that he hoped the typeface would illuminate the richness of language, the interconnectedness, the nuance of the web. But instead, Trans-1 reveals language's poverty, its inadequate approximations, how a web is made of holes, how the river of words flows always away from us.

TRANS-2, 10 POINT: This typeface also refreshes continuously, but unlike Trans-1, words are replaced by their antonyms. *Now autumn begins* exists only for long enough to bring *later spring ceases* into existence, which instantly disappears to make room for *presently dry riverbed persists*, which dies so that *never flowing water perishes* can live. It was Bely's intention, with Trans-2, to illuminate the poverty of language, its inadequate approximations, how a web is made of holes. But instead, we see the string connecting those holes, and caught in the net is the shadow of meaning. This typeface frequently freezes in place, fixed on words that cannot be refreshed. What, after all, is the opposite of God? The meaning is liberated from the words by the typeface's inability to translate them. These nonexistent antonyms are the reflections of the words we are looking for, the non-approximations, like watching a solar eclipse in a puddle. The antonym of God's nonexistent antonym is closer to God than *God* will ever be. Which, then, brings us closer to what we want to communicate: saying what we intend, or trying to say the opposite?

TRANS-3, 10 POINT: This typeface also refreshes continuously, but unlike Trans-1 and -2, words are replaced by themselves. *Now autumn begins* exists for only long enough to bring *now autumn begins* into existence, which instantly disappears to make room for *now autumn begins* which dies so that *now autumn begins* can live. A word, like a person, exists for exactly one moment in time. After that moment, only the letters—cells—are shared. What *autumn* meant when uttered by Stephen Wren in Cincinnati at 10:32:34 on April 14, 2000, was quite different from what it meant one second later when he said it again, and was entirely unlike what it meant one hundred years before, or one thousand years before, or at the same moment, when cried by a palsied schoolgirl in Wales. This typeface tries to keep pace with language, to change as the world changes, but like chasing the long black cape of a fleeing dream, it will never catch up. *Now autumn begins* will never mean what it does, but what it did.

AVIARY, VARIABLE POINT: One of the more unorthodox typefaces of the end of the twentieth century, Aviary relies on the migration of birds. The typesetter, who is preferably an ornithologist, tattoos each word onto the underside of a different bird's wing, according to its place in the flock. (The first word of this book, *Elena*, would have been tattooed onto the wing of the natural leader. The last word, *free*, onto the wing of the bird who carries the rear.) Alexander Dubovich, Aviary's creator, said his inspiration was a copy of *Anna Karenina* that fell from the shelf and landed spread, text-down, on the floor.

Among many other reasons, this typeface was not used because the order of birds in a flock shifts regularly. The natural leader never remains the leader, and the bird in the rear always moves forward. Also, Aviary is only coherent when the birds are in flight. When perched in trees, or collecting the thrown scraps from some kind park-goer, or sleeping on the sills of high apartment windows, the birds are in disarray, and so would be the book. It could exist only in flight, only between places, only as a way to get from here to there. Or there to here.

ICELAND, 22:13:36, APRIL 11, 2006, VARIABLE POINT: There are 237,983 words in this book. The same number of people were alive in Iceland at 22:13:36, April 11, 2006. The designer of this typeface, Bjorn Jaagern, devised it to give each person a word to memorize, according to age. (The youngest citizen would be given *Elena*, the oldest *free*.) In an annual festival the people of Iceland would line up, youngest to oldest, and recite the story of Henry's tragic love and loss from beginning to end. As citizens died, their roles in the recitation would be given to the youngest Icelander without a word, although the reading would still proceed from youngest to oldest. It was the hope of the citizens of Iceland that the book would cycle smoothly: from order to disorder, and back to order again. That is: *Let our fathers and mothers die before their children, the old before the young.*

Iceland, 22:13:36, April 11, 2006, was not used because life is full of early death, and fathers and mothers sometimes outlive their children. The editor's concern was not that the book would become a salad of meaning, but that hearing it once a year would be too painful a reminder that we are twigs alighted on a fence, that each of us is capable of experiencing not only Henry's great love, but also his loss. Should a child recite a word from the middle—from the scene in which Henry's brother stuffs up the cracks with wet towels, and loses his ashes in the oven—we would know that he or she replaced someone who died in middle-age, too soon, before making it to the end of the story.

REAL TIME, REAL WORLD, TO SCALE: This typeface began organically with the popularization of e-mail. Such symbols as :) came to stand for those things that words couldn't quite get at. Over time, every idea had a corresponding symbol, not unlike the drawings from the dark caves of early man. These symbols approximated what a word described better than a word ever could. (A picture of a flower is closer to the flower it describes than *flower* is.) Here, for example, is how the final conversation between Henry and his brother would have read in such symbols:

And here is the scene on the unsafe wooden bridge, when Henry confesses himself to Sophy:

→|←

The evolution continued. The typographical symbol for flower (❀) became a sketch of a flower, then an oil painting of a flower, then a photograph of a flower, then a sculpted flower, then a video of a flower, and is, now, a real-time real-world flower. Henry exists: he blinks, he inhales, he tells his older brother, *I love you more now than I did before*, he stammers, he sways, he begs, *Sophy, believe in me, always.*

This typeface was not used because of the fear that it would be popularized, that all books would be printed in real-time real-world, making it impossible to know whether we were living as autonomous beings, or characters in a story. When you read these words, for example, you would have to wonder whether you were the real-time real-world incarnation of someone in a story who was reading these words. You would wonder if you were not the you that you thought you were if you were about to finish this book only because you were written to do so, because you had to. Or perhaps, you think, it's otherwise. You approach this final sentence because you are you, your own you, living a life of your own creation. If you are a character, then you are the author. If you are a slave to your own weaknesses then you are unconstrained. Perhaps you are completely free.

40

The Index

J. G. Ballard

EDITOR'S NOTE. From abundant internal evidence it seems clear that the text printed below is the index to the unpublished and perhaps suppressed autobiography of a man who may well have been one of the most remarkable figures of the twentieth century. Yet of his existence nothing is publicly known, although his life and work appear to have exerted a profound influence on the events of the past fifty years. Physician and philosopher, man of action and patron of the arts, sometime claimant to the English throne and founder of a new religion, Henry Rhodes Hamilton was evidently the intimate of the greatest men and women of our age. After World War II he founded a new movement of spiritual regeneration, but private scandal and public concern at his growing megalomania, culminating in his proclamation of himself as a new divinity, seem to have led to his downfall. Incarcerated within an unspecified government institution, he presumably spent his last years writing his autobiography of which this index is the only surviving fragment.

A substantial mystery still remains. Is it conceivable that all traces of his activities could be erased from our records of the period? Is the suppressed autobiography itself a disguised *roman à clef*, in which the fictional hero exposes the secret identities of his historical contemporaries? And what is the true role of the indexer himself, clearly a close friend of the writer, who first suggested that he embark on his autobiography? This ambiguous and shadowy figure has taken the unusual step of indexing himself into his own index. Perhaps the entire compilation is nothing more than a figment of the overwrought imagination of some deranged lexicographer. Alternatively, the index may be wholly genuine, and the only glimpse we have into a world hidden from us by a gigantic conspiracy, of which Henry Rhodes Hamilton is the greatest victim.

F

Fairbanks, Douglas, 281

Faulkner, William, 375

Fermi, Enrico, reveals first controlled fission reaction to HRH,
299; terminal cancer diagnosed
by HRH, 388; funeral eulogy
read by HRH, 401

Fleming, Sir Alexander, credits
HRH, 211

Ford, Henry, 198

Fortune (magazine), 349

Freud, Sigmund, receives HRH in
London, 198; conducts
analysis of HRH, 205; begins
Civilization and its Discontents,
230; admits despair to HRH,
279

G

Gandhi, Mahatma, visited in
prison by HRH, 251; discusses
Bhagavad-gita with HRH, 253;
has dhoti washed by HRH,
254; denounces HRH, 256

Garbo, Greta, 381

George V, secret visits to
Chatsworth, 3, 4–6; rumored
liaison with Mrs. Alexander
Hamilton, 7; suppresses court
circular, 9; denies existence of
collateral Battenburg line to
Lloyd George, 45

Goldwyn, Samuel, 397

Grenadier Guards, 215–18

Gstaad, 359

H

Hadrian IV, Pope, 28, 57, 84, 119,
345–76, 411, 598

Hamilton, Alexander, British
Consul, Marseilles, 1, 3, 7;
interest in topiary, 2; unexpected marriage, 3; depression
after birth of HRH, 6; surprise
recall to London, 12; first
nervous breakdown, 16;
transfer to Tsingtao, 43

Hamilton, Alice Rosalind (later
Lady Underwood), private
education, 2; natural gaiety, 3;
first marriage annulled, 4;
enters London society, 5; beats
George V at billiards, 5, 7, 9, 23;
second marriage to Alexander
Hamilton, 3; dislike of Marseilles, 7; premature birth of
HRH, 8; divorce, 47; third
marriage to Sir Richard
Underwood, 48

Hamilton, Henry Rhodes, accident-proneness, 118; age, sensitiveness about, 476; belief in telepathy, 399; childhood memories, 501; common man, identification with, 211; courage: moral, 308; physical, 201; generosity, 99; Goethe, alleged resemblance to, 322; hobbies, dislike of, 87; illnesses: concussion, 196; hypertension, 346; prostate inflammation, 522; venereal disease, 77; integrity, 89; languages, mastery of, 176; Orient, love of, 188; patriotism, renunciation of, 276; public speaking, aptitude for, 345; self-analysis, 234–67; underdog, compassion for, 176; will-power, 87

Hamilton, Indira, meets HRH in Calcutta, 239; translates at Gandhi interviews, 253; imprisoned with HRH by British, 276; marries HRH, 287; on abortive Everest expedition, 299; divorces HRH, 301

Hamilton, Marcelline (formerly Marcelline Renault), abandons industrialist husband, 177; accompanies HRH to Angkor, 189; marries HRH, 191; amuses Ho Chi Minh, 195; divorces HRH, 201

Hamilton, Ursula (later Mrs. Mickey Rooney), 302–7; divorces HRH, 308

Hamilton, Zelda, rescued from orphanage by HRH, 325; visit to Cape Kennedy with HRH, 327; declines astronaut training, 328; leads International Virgin Bride campaign, 331; arrested with HRH by Miami police, 344; Frankfurt police, 359; divorces HRH, 371; wins Miss Alabama contest, 382; go-go dancer, 511; applies for writ of habeas corpus, 728

Harriman, Averell, 432

Harry's Bar, Venice, 256

Hayworth, Rita, 311

Hemingway, Ernest, first African safari with HRH, 234; at Battle of the Ebro with HRH, 244; introduces HRH to James Joyce, 256; portrays HRH in *The Old Man and the Sea*, 453

Further Reading:
An Incomprehensive List of
Additional Fraudulent Artifacts

INSTRUCTIONS

Eric D. Anderson, "The Instructions"
Rick DeMarinis, "Rudderless Fiction: Lesson One"
Junot Díaz, "How to Date a Brown Girl (blackgirl, whitegirl, or halfie)"
Becky Hagenston, "How to Keep Busy While Your Fiancé Climbs Mt. Everest"
Shelley Jackson, "The Putti"
Lucy A. Snyder, "Installing Linux in a Dead Badger"
Teddy Wayne, "Rules and Regulations for Benehmen!, the German Board Game of
    Discipline"
Laura Madeline Wiseman, "How to Measure Your Breast Size"

INTERVIEWS AND INTERROGATIONS

Charles Baxter, "The Lawrence Quint Interview"
Wendy Brenner, "Questions for the Lawyer" (written on cocktail napkin for *Esquire*)
Ben Marcus, "On Not Growing Up"
Julie Schumacher, "An Explanation for Chaos"
David Foster Wallace, *Brief Interviews with Hideous Men* (excerpt)

GUIDES

Jonathan Safran Foer, "A Primer for Punctuation of Heart Disease"
Amelia Gray, "Trip Advisory: The Boyhood Home of Former President Ronald
    Reagan"

Thomas Hopkins, "*An American Casanova in New York*, by Balthus Poindexter: A Reading Group Guide"

INTRODUCTIONS

R. M. Berry, "History"
Marsha Koretzky, "Kurt Vonnegut Didn't Know Doodly-Squat about Writing"

INQUIRIES, ASSIGNMENTS, AND STORY PROBLEMS

Peter Cherches, "Reading Comprehension"
Ian Frazier, "Have You Ever?"
Myla Goldberg, "Comprehension Test"
A. B. Paulson, "The Minnesota Multiphasic Personality: A Diagnostic Test in Two Parts"
Padgett Powell, *The Interrogative Mood: A Novel?* (excerpt)

ASSESSMENTS

Chris Bachelder, "On a Difficult Sentence in *Gatsby*"
R. M. Berry, "Second Story"
Brian Evenson, "Moran's Mexico: A Refutation, by C. Stelzmann"
Ralph Gamelli, "The Stick, Recently Inducted into the Toy Hall of Fame, Is Now Available at Amazon.com"
Alix Ohlin, "An Analysis of Some Troublesome Recent Behavior"
Naomi J. Williams, "The Report"

DESCRIPTIONS & EXPLANATIONS

Ron Carlson, "The Disclaimer"
Amelia Gray, "Code of Operation: Snake Farm"
Shelley Jackson, "Dildo"
Ben Marcus, "The New Female Head"

Stephen Millhauser, "A Game of Clue"
V. S. Naipaul, "The Night Watchman's Occurrence Book"
Daniel Orozco, "Orientation"
J. David Stevens, "What We Sell in the Room Today"

TRANSCRIPTS

Chris Bachelder, "Deep Wells, USA"
Arthur C. Clarke, "The Shining Ones"
Don DeLillo, "Videotape"
John Griswold, "Transcript of a World War I Veteran's Narrative: Nickelton,
    Kentucky"
Matthew Vollmer, "Man-O'-War"

HIGH SCHOOL ESSAYS

Caitlin Horrocks, "It Looks Like This"
Eric Puchner, "Essay #3: Leda and the Swan"

NOTES

Rick Moody, "The Preliminary Notes"
Keith Lee Morris, "Notes for an Aborted Story Called 'The Cyclist' That Turned Out
    to Be Too Much Like 'The Swimmer'"
Robert Anthony Siegel, "The Memoirs of Edwin Chester, Who Would Have Discov-
    ered the Origin of Species Had His Place on *HMS Beagle* Not Been Taken by
    Charles Darwin"

LISTS

Donald Barthelme, "The Glass Mountain"
Roxane Gay, "You Never Knew How the Waters Ran So Cruel So Deep"
Wendy Rawlings, "The Fleischer/Giaccondo Online Gift Registry"

ADDRESSES

Sean Adams, "I Remember When I Was Your Age, Twin Brother"

Ron Carlson, "Gold Lunch"

Jason Grunebaum, "Major Nixon"

Pat Kewley, "A Hot Air Balloon Captain Addresses His Crew on the Eve of a Very Important Hot Air Balloon Race"

Colin Nissan, "It's Decorative Gourd Season, Motherfuckers"

Joyce Carol Oates, "Ladies and Gentlemen"

Teddy Wayne, "Okay, America: We're Turning Everything into Vampires"

OFFICIAL DOCUMENTS

Amie Barrodale, "Prospectus"

Janet Burroway, "Report on Professional Activities"

Doug Dorst, "Splitters: H. A. Quilcock's Profiles in Botany: A Lost Manuscript Restored"

Ian Frazier, "Coyote v. Acme"

Heidi Julavits, "Marry the One Who Gets There First: Outtakes from the Sheidegger–Krupnik Wedding Album"

Stewart O'Nan, "Report on the Traffic Fatality Involving Lady Diana Spencer"

Alexi Zentner, "The Adjuster"

SYLLABUS

Ron Carlson, "Syllabus"

CORRESPONDENCE

Rosellen Brown, "Inter-Office"

Tessa Brown, "In Reference to Your Recent Communications"

Ron Carlson, "Recommendation for Gordon Lee Bunsen"

Raymond Carver, "Why, Honey?"

Dave Eggers, "Letters from Steven, a Dog, to Captains of Industry"

Nell Freudenberger, "Letter to the Last Bastion"

Amelia Gray, "This Quiet Complex"
Gabe Hudson, "Dear Mr. President"
Michael Kimball, "Excerpts from the Suicide Letters of Jonathon Bender (b.1967–d.2000)"
Alyce Miller, "Aftershock"
Alice Munro, "A Wilderness Station"
George Saunders, "Ask the Optimist!"
David Shields, "Comp Lit 101: Walt Grows Up"
David Shields, "Possible Postcards from Rachel, Abroad"
Joe Wenderoth, "Letter of Recommendation"

WEBSITE

Rob Wittig, "The Fall of the Site of Marsha," http://www.robwit.net/MARSHA/

NEWSLETTERS

Meg Favreau, "The San Diego Snake Company's September Newsletter"
Allan Gurganus, "Preservation News"

STYLE GUIDE

Ron Carlson, "My True Style Guide"

COMPENDIUM

Michael Parrish Lee, "The People Catalogue"
Joanna Ruocco, *A Compendium of Domestic Incidents* (excerpt)

FAQS

Ben Doller (previously Doyle), "FAQ"

EBAY LISTING

Patrick Madden, "Writer Michael Martone's Leftover Water"

HOLY SCRIPTURES

Kevin Brockmeier, "The Jesus Stories"
A. J. Packman, "First Drafts of the Parables of Jesus"
J. M. Tyree, "The First Book of the Chronicles of the Cola Wars"

SCREENPLAY

Amelia Gray, "The Pit"

CASE STUDY

Steven Millhauser, "Phantoms"

ENCYCLOPEDIA ENTRY

China Miéville, "Entry Taken from a Medical Encyclopedia"

DIARIES

Amelia Gray, "Diary of the Blockage"
China Miéville, "Details"

SUBMISSIONS

Oyl Miller, "A Cover Letter from an Art Major Seeking a Job that Literally Requires
    Him to Apply the Skills He Learned in School"
Jack Pendarvis, "Sex Devil"

PERSONALS

Frank Ferri, "Selected Personals from the American Psychiatric Association's Dating Website"

ANNOTATIONS

Jonathan Lethem, "Liner Note"
Rick Moody, "Wilkie Fahnstock, The Boxed Set"

INDEXES/TABLE OF CONTENTS

Matt Bell, "An Index of How Our Family Was Killed"
Christopher Hellwig, *An Archive from the Lives of Retired Gunslingers* (excerpt)
Lance Olsen, "Table of Contents"

ACKNOWLEDGMENTS

Michael Martone, "Acknowledgment"

BOOK-LENGTH WORKS

Kate Bernheimer, *The Complete Tales of Ketzia Gold*; *The Complete Tales of Merry Gold*
Roberto Bolano, *The Savage Detectives*; *Nazi Literature in the Americas*
Jorge Luis Borges, *The Book of Imaginary Beings*
Christopher Boucher, *How to Keep Your Volkswagen Alive*
Robert Olen Butler, *Had a Good Time*
A. S. Byatt, *Possession*
Italo Calvino, *The Castle of Crossed Destinies*
Mary Caponegro, *The Complexities of Intimacy*
Jerome Charyn, *The Tar Baby*
Stanley Crawford, *The Log of the S. S. the Mrs. Unguentine*
Stanley Crawford, *Petroleum Man*
Stanley Crawford, *Some Instructions to My Wife Concerning the Upkeep of the House and Marriage, and to My Son and Daughter Concerning the Conduct of Their Childhood*

Mark Z. Danielewski, *House of Leaves*; *The Whalestoe Letters*

Charles Duff, *A Handbook on Hanging*

Max Ernst, *The Hundred-Headed Woman*; *A Week of Kindness*

Richard Flanagan, *Gould's Book of Fish: A Novel in 12 Fish*

Matthew Geller, *Difficulty Swallowing: A Medical Chronicle*

Lauren Groff, *The Monsters of Templeton*

Steven Hall, *The Raw Shark Texts*

B. S. Johnson, *The Unfortunates*

Michael Kimball, *Dear Everybody*

Sam Lipsyte, *Home Land*

Alison Lurie, *The Truth About Lorin Jones*

Kuzhali Manickavel, *Insects Are Just Like You and Me Except Some of Them Have Wings*

Stephen Marche, *Shining at the Bottom of the Sea*

Michael Martone, *The Blue Guide to Indiana*

Carole Maso, *The Art Lover*

Kevin McIlvoy, *The Complete History of New Mexico*

McSweeney's, issue 17

Steven Millhauser, *Edwin Mullhouse: The Life and Death of an American Writer 1943–1954 by Jeffrey Cartwright*

David Mitchell, *Cloud Atlas*

Vladimir Nabokov, *Pale Fire*

Georges Perec, *Life: A User's Manual*

W. G. Sebald, *The Emigrants*; *The Rings of Saturn*

Leanne Shapton, *Important Artifacts and Personal Property from the Collection of Lenore Doolan and Harold Morris, Including Books, Street Fashion, and Jewelry . . .*

Gilbert Sorrentino, *Aberration of Starlight*; *Lunar Follies*; *Mulligan Stew*

Bram Stoker, *Dracula*

Mark Twain, *Diaries of Adam and Eve*

Colson Whitehead, *John Henry Days*

Permissions Acknowledgments

"Disclaimer" by David Means. Used by permission of the Wylie Agency LLC. Originally published in the *Paris Review*. Copyright © 1997 by David Means.

"I CAN SPEAK!" by George Saunders. From *In Persuasion Nation: Stories* by George Saunders. Copyright © 2006 by George Saunders. Used by permission of Riverhead Books, an imprint of Penguin Group (USA) Inc.

Some Instructions to My Wife Concerning the Upkeep of the House and Marriage, and to My Son and Daughter Concerning the Conduct of Their Childhood by Stanley Crawford. Reprinted by permission of Dalkey Archive Press.

"One Thousand Words on Why You Should Not Talk During a Fire Drill" by Mark Halliday. Reprinted by permission of the author. Originally published in the *North American Review*.

"Problems for Self-Study" by Charles Yu. From *Third Class Superhero* by Charles Yu. Reprinted by permission of Harcourt, Inc. Copyright © 2006 by Charles Yu. Originally published in the *Harvard Review*.

"Permission Slip" by Caron A. Levis. Reprinted by permission of the author. Originally published in *Fence* magazine.

"How to Become a Writer" by Lorrie Moore. From *Self-Help* by Lorrie Moore. Copyright © 1985 by M. L. Moore. Used by permission of Alfred A. Knopf, a division of Random House, Inc.

"The Dead Sister Handbook: A Guide for Sensitive Boys" by Kevin Wilson. From *Tunneling to the Center of the Earth* by Kevin Wilson. Copyright © 2009 by Kevin Wilson. Reprinted by permission of HarperCollins Publishers.

"Interview with a Moron" by Elizabeth Stuckey-French. Reprinted by permission of the author. Originally published in *Narrative Magazine*.

"Reference #388475848-5" by Amy Hempel. Reprinted with the permission of Scribner, a division of Simon & Schuster, Inc., from *The Dog of the Marriage* by Amy Hempel. Copyright © 2005 by Amy Hempel. All rights reserved. Originally published by *The Ontario Review*.

"The Explanation" from *Forty Stories* by Donald Barthelme. Reprinted by permission of the Wylie Agency LLC. Copyright © 1987 by Donald Barthelme.

Excerpt from *Letters to Wendy's* by Joe Wenderoth. Published by Verse Press. Reprinted by permission of Wave Books and the author. Copyright © 2000.

"This Is Just to Say That I'm Tired of Sharing an Apartment with William Carlos Williams" by Laura Jayne Martin. Reprinted by permission of the author. Originally published in *McSweeney's Internet Tendency*.

"Single Woman for Long Walks on the Beach" by Ron Carlson. From *At the Jim Bridger* by Ron Carlson. Reprinted by permission of St. Martin's Press, LLC. Copyright © 2002 by Ron Carlson.

"My Beard, Reviewed" by Chris Bachelder. Reprinted by permission of the author. Originally published in *McSweeney's Internet Tendency*.

"The Varieties of Romantic Experience: An Introduction" by Rob Cohen. Reprinted with the permission of Scribner, a division of Simon & Schuster, Inc., from *The Varieties of Romantic Experience* by Rob Cohen. Copyright © 2002 by Rob Cohen. All rights reserved.

"Vis à Vis Love" by Mieke Eerkens. Reprinted by permission of the author.

"Practice Problem" by Joseph Salvatore. Reprinted with the permission of The Permissions Company, Inc. on behalf of BOA Editions Ltd., www.boaeditions .org, from *To Assume a Pleasing Shape*. Copyright © 2011 by Joseph Salvatore.

"Officers Weep" by Daniel Orozco. From *Orientation: And Other Stories* by Daniel Orozco. Copyright © 2011 by Daniel Orozco. Reprinted by permission of Faber and Faber, Inc., an affiliate of Farrar, Straus, and Giroux, LLC.

"Subtotals" by Greg Burnham. Reprinted by permission of the author. Originally published in *Harper's*.

"Our Spring Catalog" by Jack Pendarvis. Originally appeared in *Mysterious Secret of the Valuable Treasure: Curious Stories* by Jack Pendarvis, MacAdam Cage.

"Reply All" by Robin Hemley. Copyright © 2004 Robin Hemley. Reprinted by permission of Indiana University Press.

"Chaucer Tweets the South by Southwest Festival" by Kari Anne Roy. Reprinted by permission of the author. Originally published in *McSweeney's Internet Tendency*.

"Iconographic Conventions of Pre- and Early Renaissance: Italian Representations of the Flagellation of Christ" by Rachel B. Glaser. Reprinted by permission of the author. Originally appeared in *Pee on Water*.

"The Human Side of Instrumental Transcommunication" by Wendy Brenner. Reprinted by permission of Algonquin Books of Chapel Hill, from *Phone Calls from the Dead* by Wendy Brenner. Copyright © 2001 by Wendy Brenner. All rights reserved.

"Class Notes" by Lucas Cooper. First published in *Sudden Fiction* by Gibbs Smith, copyright © 1986.

"Dear Stephen Hawking" by Samantha Hunt. Reprinted by permission of the author. Originally published in *Manual, or, The Lives of Famous Men*.

"National Treasures" by Charles McLeod. From *National Treasures* by Charles McLeod, published by Vintage Books. Reprinted by permission of The Random House Group Ltd.

"Discarded Notions" by Matthew Williamson. Reprinted by permission of the author. Originally appeared in *Gulf Coast: A Journal of Literature and Fine Arts*.

"Star Lake Letters" by Arda Collins. Reprinted by permission of the author. Originally published in *Ghost Town*.

"Life Story" by David Shields. Reprinted by permission of the author. Originally published in *Remote*, Knopf.

"Instructions for Extinction" by Melanie Rae Thon. Reprinted by permission of Houghton Mifflin Harcourt Publishing company, from *Sweet Hearts* by Melanie Rae Thon. Copyright © 2000 by Melanie Rae Thon. All rights reserved.

"Will & Testament" by Matthew Vollmer. Reprinted by permission of the author. Originally appeared in *Future Missionaries of America: Stories*, Salt Publishing.

"Letter to a Funeral Parlor" by Lydia Davis. From *The Collected Stories of Lydia Davis* by Lydia Davis. Copyright © 2009 by Lydia Davis. Reprinted by permission of Faber and Faber, Inc., an affiliate of Farrar, Straus, and Giroux, LLC.

"Acknowledgments" by Paul Theroux. Copyright © 1979, 1980 by Paul Theroux. Used by permission of the Wylie Agency LLC.

"Primary Sources" by Rick Moody. From *The Ring of Brightest Angels Around Heaven* by Rick Moody. Copyright © 1992, 1993 by Rick Moody. Reprinted by permission of Little, Brown and Company and Melanie Jackson Agency, LLC. All rights reserved.

"Contributor's Note" by Michael Martone. Reprinted by the permission of the author. Originally published in *Harper's*.

"The Year's Best Fiction 2008: The Authors Speak" by J. Robert Lennon. Reprinted by permission of the author. Originally published in *Epoch*, May 2009.

"About the Typefaces Not Used in This Edition" by Jonathan Safran Foer. Reprinted by permission of the author. Originally published in *The Paris Review*.

"The Index" by J. G. Ballard. From *The Complete Short Stories of J. G. Ballard* by J. G. Ballard. Copyright © 2001. Reprinted by permission of HarperCollins Publishers Ltd.